Theory of Mind and Language
in Developmental Contexts

Springer Series on Human Exceptionality

Series Editors:
Donald H. Saklofske, *University of Calgary, Alberta, Canada*
Moshe Zeidner, *University of Haifa, Mount Carmel, Israel*
Vicki L. Schwean, *University of Saskatchewan, Saskatoon, Canada*

THEORY OF MIND AND LANGUAGE IN DEVELOPMENTAL CONTEXTS
Edited by Alessandro Antonietti, Olga Liverta-Sempio, Antonella Marchetti

NEUROBIOLOGY OF EXCEPTIONALITY
Edited by Con Stough

DYNAMIC ASSESSMENT OF YOUNG CHILDREN
By David Tzuriel

STUDENT MOTIVATION
Edited by Farideh Salili, Chi-yue Chiu, Ying-yi Hong

HANDBOOK OF PSYCHOSOCIAL CHARACTERISTICS OF YOUNG CHILDREN
Edited by Vicki L. Schwean, Donald H. Saklofske

A Continuation Order Plan is available for this series. A continuation order will bring delivery of each new volume immediately upon publication. Volumes are billed only upon actual shipment. For further information please contact the publisher.

Theory of Mind and Language in Developmental Contexts

Edited by

Alessandro Antonietti
Catholic University of the Sacred Heart, Milan, Italy

Olga Liverta-Sempio
Catholic University of the Sacred Heart, Milan, Italy

Antonella Marchetti
Catholic University of the Sacred Heart, Milan, Italy

 Springer

Alessandro Antonietti
Department of Psychology
Catholic University of Sacred Heart
Milan, Italy 20123

Olga Liverta-Sempio
Department of Psychology
Catholic University of Sacred Heart
Milan, Italy 20123

Antonella Marchetti
Department of Psychology
Catholic University of Sacred Heart
Milan, Italy 20123

Library of Congress Control Number: 2005923472

ISBN-10: 0-387-24994-X   e-ISBN 0-387-24997-4   Printed on acid-free paper.
ISBN-13: 978-0387-24994-0

Printed in the United States of America. (SB)

9 8 7 6 5 4 3 2 1

springeronline.com

Contents

PREFACE

Alessandro Antonietti,[1] Olga Liverta-Sempio,[2] Antonella Marchetti.[2]
[1]Catholic University of the Sacred Heart, Milan; [2]The Theory of Mind Research Unit, Department of Psychology, Catholic University of the Sacred Heart, Milan.

Contextual perspectives on cognitive development have recently declared the importance of the socio-cultural dimension in theory of mind (ToM) development, so for this reason that it is now crucial to study the relation between ToM and language. In this book it is discussed from a developmental perspective (early infancy to adulthood), and attention is paid both to typical and atypical situations, focusing in particular on socio-cultural factors. On the one hand, studies on typical development describe a chronological path that helps to find "prototypical" ways of understanding, as well as delays and deviances, on the other, studies on atypical development help to highlight aspects of normal development. A more detailed analysis of the theme is given below.

The chapters by Antonietti, Liverta-Sempio, Marchetti and Astington ("Mental language and understanding of epistemic and emotional mental states: contextual aspects") and Olson, Antonietti, Liverta-Sempio and Marchetti ("Mental verbs in different conceptual domains and different cultures") examine the relationship between ToM and language by studying the comprehension of mental verbs. The first study analyses the developmental trend of such understanding, in the first years of school, and its relation to standard linguistic tests and theory of mind. The second examines the later phase in the development of mental verb understanding, as such, up to the university years, in order to show how it may be linked to conceptual domains (folk psychology, history, mathematics) and countries (Canada, Italy, Serbia, Tanzania). Two main finding emerge from these studies: the first shows that mental verb understanding is a lengthy process that may still not be entirely consolidated even during university years; the cultural plausibility of standard theory of mind tasks should be questioned. In fact, performances showed interpretable trends in Euro-American cultural contexts, whereas they were more or less random in African contexts.

Thanks to the chapters by Pelletier ("Theory of mind and story comprehension in first and second language learners") and by Shatz, Marchetti, Dyer and Massaro ("Culture and mental states: a comparison of English and Italian versions of children's books"), we move from a consideration of the relationships between ToM and language to the analysis of the link between ToM and "languages". Pelletier examines the connection between ToM, meta-cognitive language, reading skills, and higher order story comprehension in L1 and L2 learners. In such a case the "languages" are seen to be co-present and active in ToM in each individual: in fact, especially for lower achieving L2 children, metacognitive language and theory of mind are influential on understanding and on the ability to make inferences. The chapter by Shatz, Marchetti, Dyer and Massaro, analyses the socio-linguistic communalities and variability in mental language in the translation of storybooks for children. Both studies have some educational implications. Pelletier emphasises how important it is for educators to take into account the diverse needs of first and second language learners and those of low and high achieving children. In their chapter, Shatz and her colleagues argue that children's books are an important environmental source of information about mental states, so translations offers an excellent opportunity for children to meet the similarities and differences in ToM in various cultures.

In their chapters Lucariello, Le Donne, Durand and Yarnell ("Social and intrapersonal theories of mind: I interact therefore I am") and Lillard ("The socialization of theory of mind: cultural and social class differences in behavior explanation") discuss the relationships between socialisation and ToM development. Lucariello and co-workers analyse the role that linguistic socialisation has in building two kinds of ToM - the social and the intrapersonal ToM - at the core of each of which there are verbal interaction models which children make use of at an early age. Thus, the linguistic socialisation model on the one hand leads to language learning models, and on the other it structures different types of ToM. The language learning models are also closely connected to the socio-demographic levels of the individual's background. The specific meaning of the latter can also be found in Lillard's chapter which analyses the link between growth and socio-economic status (SES) with regard to external (e.g., actor's physical circumstances), rather than internal (e.g. character traits or mental states) behaviour explanations. There is space for ToM here, as explanations referring to the constructs of mental states play a crucial role within internal explanations. The sources of internal behaviour explanations vary according to the SES and age of the individuals: family and early for high SES individuals; extra-family (school and the media) and late in low SES individuals.

The chapter entitled "Discursive practices and mentalization ability in adults at work" by Gilardi, Bruno and Pezzotta shows that, from a life span perspective, examining the "mind at work" means looking at social and interpersonal functions of ToM in the workplace. The theoretical coordinates on which the authors base their considerations link psychoanalytical thought with some areas of the recent cognitive research on ToM and on epistemological beliefs, placing individual and reflexive organisations at the centre of their analyses. Clarifications about the epistemological premises to their argument have also facilitated the authors in opening new paths to empirical research and training. The studies reported in the chapters by Siegal, Varley and Want ("Mind over grammar: reasoning in aphasia and development") and by Marchetti, Liverta-Sempio and Lecciso ("The silent understanding of the mind: the deaf child") deal with the relations between language and ToM in atypical situations: aphasia in adults and deafness in developmental age. Both studies embrace the conversational hypothesis for ToM development, according to which it is made possible by precocious conversational experience about mental states. As far as aphasic individuals are concerned, the hypothesis is substantiated by the fact that these patients are capable of propositional reasoning involving ToM understanding in the absence of explicit grammatical knowledge. In the deaf, the lack of early conversational experience delays ToM development, but the delay ceases to exist when the educational processes in school environment are strongly oriented towards increasing verbal communication.

Since the chapters in this book describe different methodologies and focus on different issues, we think that they offer an excellent overview of this field of investigation. It will undoubtedly enhance the discussion of the topics mentioned in similar volumes, since this book includes new, as yet unpublished, papers with which to update the state of the art. The volume also contains additional empirical data and gives an insight into the link between typical and atypical development and the connections between ToM and language across the life span.

We are very much grateful to Barbara Lucchini who edited carefully all the chapters included in this book.

Chapter 1

MENTAL LANGUAGE AND UNDERSTANDING OF EPISTEMIC AND EMOTIONAL MENTAL STATES
Contextual Aspects

Alessandro Antonietti,[1] Olga Liverta-Sempio,[2] Antonella Marchetti,[2] Janet W. Astington.[3]
[1]Department of Psychology, Catholic University of the Sacred Heart, Milan; [2]The Theory of Mind Research Unit, Department of Psychology, Catholic University of the Sacred Heart, Milan;[3]Institute of Child Study, OISE, University of Toronto

The cognitive psychologist Steven Pinker (1994) maintained that man can speak more or less in the same sense as a spider can weave its web. It is unlikely that spiders are able to represent to themselves the webs they produce, but human beings can represent the meaning of the words they use. It is not surprising that humans can represent to themselves a hammer when they say or listen to the word "hammer" or that they can represent to themselves abstract concepts when words concern, for instance, a mathematical theorem. But, what do they represent to themselves when they are faced with verbs such as *to remind* or *to hope*? These so-called *mental verbs* are considered to be metarepresentational expressions since it is assumed that in order to understand them (as well to use them correctly) individuals must represent the representational attitude that such verbs involve (that is, *remembering, hoping*, and so on) and the content of the representational state (that is, what is *remembered* or *hoped*). For example, a person, who understands the difference existing between two sentences such as "I *remember* that you did so-and-so" and "I *hope* that you did so-and-so", must be aware that two different mental states underlie these sentences. In other words, metarepresentational competencies seem to be involved in linguistic expressions which include mental verbs. If we listen to someone who is saying that he/she is *remembering* or *hoping* something, we have to take into account the "status" that what he/she is saying has in his/her mind, namely, the particular mental perspective he/she assumes when he/she is saying that thing. Thus, we are induced to hypothesise a link between competences for mental verb understanding and metarepresentational competences (Olson, 1994).

The connection between the mastery of mental language - that is, the language used, either explicitly or implicitly, to talk about the mind - and metarepresentation falls within the wider, much discussed question of the connection between language and thought. On a general theoretical level, the most representative perspectives about this question are two: the Piagetian conception, in which language depends on thought (Piaget, 1945; Piaget & Inhelder, 1966), and the Vygotskian conception, according to which language is one of the principal tools involved in the construction of thought (Vygotsky, 1934). To adopt the Piagetian perspective means to accept the idea that verbal expressions of mental states reflect the level of understanding that an individual has of the mind. Typical of the first perspective are the works of Wellman & Bartsch (1994; Bartsch & Wellman, 1995) who supported the hypothesis of a specific developmental pattern of the understanding of mind, proposing as evidence just the mental language spontaneously produced by children from 2 to 5 years of age. By contrast, to choose the Vygotskian point of view leads us to believe that children, through taking part in cultural activities, come to share the concept of mind used by their culture as it is expressed in language. As an example of the Vygotskian perspective, we can mention the Brunerian view, after which the theory of mind inherent in the folk psychology of a certain culture is present in the child at first as social practice, as proto-linguistic representation, to be fully acquired as a tool of interaction together with the mastery of language (Bruner, 1990).

If we adopt the Vygotskian perspective, the empirical research of the latest years gains importance as it is specifically centred on the connection between mental language and mind understanding (Astington, 1996). This research considers mainly two interesting themes. On one side there are studies that enquire directly the relationships between talking about the mind and mind comprehension within specific, actual interactive contexts. On the other side, there are studies on the connections between mental language competence and understanding of the mind.

As regards the connection among children's daily interactive contexts, mental state language use, and theory of mind, we can refer to research done in the family, since the studies on other interactive contexts relevant to the growing of the child - such as school (Astington & Pelletier, 1996) or friendly relationships among children (Hughes & Dunn, 1998) - are more rare.

Firstly, the mother's use of mental state language when children are 2 years old predicted the use of mental terms by children at 3:6 years of age (Furrow, Moore, Davidge & Chiasson, 1992). Mother's use of state mental language also predicted children's later theory of mind understanding (Ruffman, Slade & Crowe, 2002). Mother-child interaction characterised by the use of mental state language was positively connected with the child's theory of mind (Youngblade & Dunn, 1995; Hughes & Dunn, 1998).

Relationships between maternal use of elaborative discourse about mental states and children's comprehension of mental states are supported by other studies (Ontai & Thompson, 2002; Peterson & Slaughter, 2003). Moreover, the child's use of mental language in conversations with siblings and friends at 47 months of age was correlated with performance in false-belief tasks (Brown, Donelan-McCall & Dunn, 1996). Children who had better performance at 47 months of age in false-belief, deception, and emotion understanding tasks, gave more satisfactory and differentiated reports of the emotions of mother and siblings 7 months later (Dunn & Hughes, 1998). Individual differences in the frequency of mental discourse in fraternal game dyads, observed in children of 3:11 years, correlated with performances assessed 13 months later in false-belief tasks and tasks concerning the understanding of emotions (Hughes & Dunn, 1998). Dunn's research about individual differences in child social competence revealed that at 40 months of age individual differences in social comprehension - which include the capacity to explain and predict behaviour in terms of beliefs -were associated with family variables, such as participation in talk about feelings and behavioural causality, and cooperative games with siblings, as measured 7 months earlier (Dunn, Brown, Slomkowski, Tesla & Youngblade, 1991).

Other investigations about pretend play among siblings (Youngblade & Dunn, 1995; Hove, Petrakos & Rinaldi, 1998) gave value to the hypothesis - supported by studies on the relationships between family size and theory of mind development (Perner, Ruffman & Leekam, 1994; Jenkins & Astington, 1996; Lewis, Freeman, Kyriakidou, Maridaki-Kassotaki & Berridge, 1996; Ruffman, Perner, Naito, Parkin & Clements, 1998) - that children understand the mind through the intensive interaction with caregivers and siblings. These findings indirectly suggest the importance of the linguistic interaction between child and family for theory of mind development or, in any case, pushing us towards examining in detail the relationship between mental talk in the family and the development of the understanding of the mind.

As regards the kind of linguistic competence implied in theory of mind development, the studies at our disposal investigated different aspects of usage, revealing a more or less powerful relationship with the performances in false-belief tasks (Astington, 2000; 2001). A close association between general linguistic ability and understanding of false-beliefs was reported, as it seems that children need a certain linguistic ability to pass the false-belief tasks (Jenkins & Astington, 1996).

Conversational competence after Grice's (1975) criteria appears to be necessary to allow children to face the experimental standard tests of false-belief understanding. In such tasks the experimenter often uses a level of conversation higher than that commonly used by pre-school children (Siegal, 1997). Besides, Harris (1996) assumed that the shifting from desire psychology to the notion of beliefs is possible in the third year of the child, thanks to the growing commitment of the child to conversation, in the sense of a use of language to exchange information even when the discourse does not include explicit talk about *knowing* and *thinking* or psychological states in general.

The relationships between the child's syntactic and semantic competences and his/her performances in false-belief tasks were investigated by Astington & Jenkins (1999). These authors showed that there is a relationship between language and theory of mind that points to the dependence of the understanding of the mind on language, in particular on syntactic competence. According to de Villiers (de Villiers & de Villiers, 2000; de Villiers & Pyers, 2002), syntactic competence needed for embedding utterances in language is analogous to competence needed for embedding utterances to comprehend mental states. But Astington (2000) affirmed that the acquisition of the syntactic structure suitable to represent the beliefs - namely, object complementation (*x thinks that y ...*) - is not sufficient to explain the correct performance of the child in false-belief tasks, since children who failed in the false-belief tasks produced linguistic expressions that are examples of object complementation in pretend play at the same time. Consistently with this claim, Charman & Shmueli-Goetz (1998) found no relationships between performance in a second-order false belief task, belief-desire reasoning task, and syntactic complexity of children narratives elicited by a story picture book. More recently Ruffman, Slade, Rowlandson, Rumsey & Garnham (2003) reported that syntax poorly predicts false-belief task performance, as well as emotion and desire, understanding. Perner, Sprung, Zauner & Haider (2003) demonstrated that the syntactic competence is not sufficient for development of false belief. In fact, in a linguistic community (Germany) in which desire (for something to happen) can be expressed with the same finite *that*-complement as belief, children between 2.5 and 4.5 years still are more competent in comprehending talk about desire than about belief, that is their performances are according to the well-established developmental belief-desire gap. This finding complements Tardiff & Wellman's (2000) data recorded from Chinese-speaking children. The Chinese language provides the same simple syntax to talk about belief and desire, however the children talk about desire earlier than about belief (Lee, Olson & Torrance, 1999).

If syntax plays a minor role in theory of mind, we could look at the role of the specific competence in dealing with the meaning of mental terms. In fact, such a competence should allow children to think explicitly about the mental states underlying expressions like *to pretend, to remember, to learn,* and so forth, and to make fine distinctions among them. Consistently with this claim, Moore, Pure & Furrow (1990), as well as Astington (2000) and Pelletier (2003), found associations between theory of mind tasks and comprehension of the semantics of mental terms such as *to know* and *to think.* However, Charman & Shmueli-Goetz (1998) failed to find relationships between performance in a theory of mind task and references to mental states - such as emotions, physiological states, and cognitive processes - in children's narratives elicited by stories. Thus, as yet no convincing conclusions can be drawn from studies carried out about the link between mental language competence and mental state understanding. Further research about such a topic seems to be needed.

In the present chapter three studies are reported whose first goal was to explore in detail the relationships between the mastery of mental language, receptive vocabulary, and the understanding of both epistemic and emotional mental states. The developmental period chosen for our investigation came from the preschool years to the beginning of literacy promoted by school. Even if there are a lot of studies about the two kinds of tasks employed to assess mental state understanding (respectively, the false-belief tasks and the belief-desire reasoning tasks), the present research considers different versions of such tasks (for instance, first-order jointly with second-order false-belief tasks, articulating each of them in two different tasks). This should allow us to obtain a fine description of how different forms of comprehension of the mind develop and how they are related with each other.

The second goal was to identify possible influences of contextual factors on mental language competence, receptive vocabulary, and understanding of the mind. Contextual factors considered here concern both the content of the tasks and social variables, such as the position of the child within his/her family, the cultural environment in which the child lives, and the level of competence showed by the child in interpersonal relationships.

1.1 MENTAL VOCABULARY AND UNDERSTANDING OF EPISTEMIC MENTAL STATES: CONTEXT AS TASK CONTENT

Four different false-belief tasks were chosen to test metarepresentational competencies involved in understanding epistemic mental states. We employed two first-order false-belief tasks: a standard Change-in-location task (Wimmer & Perner, 1983) and a standard Unexpected-content task (Perner, Leekam & Wimmer, 1987; Gopnik & Astington, 1988). In the first task children were presented a short puppet story. The story said that John put a ball in a box. Then John went away. While he was gone, Bob took the ball and put it in a basket. John came back. At this point the child was asked: (1) "Where will John look for the ball?" (first-order false-belief question). Then two control questions were presented: "Where did John put the ball?" (Control question for memory); "Where is the ball really?" (Control question for reality). During story-telling the experimenter performed actions described either by moving puppets or by moving the real objects mentioned (ball, box, basket).

The second task was as follows: the child was shown a closed crayon box and was asked: "What is in it?" (Control question about box appearance); the child was expected to answer "Crayons" (right answer). Then the box was opened and the child could see that it contained a doll; the child was asked "What is in it?" (Control question about the content); the expected (right) answer was "A doll". Then the box was closed and child was asked "What is in it?" (Control question about the content); the expected (right) answer was again "A doll". Afterwards the child was asked: "What will a child who has not seen inside the box think is inside it before s/he opens it?" (first-order other's belief question). And finally: "What did you think was inside the box before opening it?" (first-order one's own belief question). Also in this case the experimenter accompanied the task script with actions performed on the real objects (box, doll) mentioned.

We employed also two second-order false-belief tasks. In the Look-prediction task (adapted from Perner & Wimmer, 1985, see Astington, Pelletier & Homer, 2002) it was told that John and Mary were in John's room. John put his pack of cards into the desk and then he went away. John knew that Mary liked to play tricks on him, and so he peeked back around the door at Mary. When Mary saw that John had left, she moved the pack of cards from the desk to the basket. John saw Mary do this but Mary could not see John. The following questions were asked: "Can John see Mary?" (Control question); "Where does John think the pack of cards is?" (Control question); "Does Mary think John can see her?" (first-order false-belief question); "Where does Mary think John will look for the pack of cards?" (second-order false-belief question); "Why does Mary think this?" (Justification).

In the Say-prediction task (adapted from Sullivan, Zaitchik & Tager-Flusberg, 1994, see Astington et al., 2002) it was told that Mom had got a surprise birthday present (a puppy) for Jenny and had hidden it in the basement. Jenny hoped Mom would get her a puppy for her birthday. Mom, who wanted to surprise Jenny with the puppy, told Jenny she had got a great toy instead. When Mom was away, Jenny saw the birthday puppy. The child was asked these questions: "Did Jenny see the puppy?" (Control question); "What does Jenny think she will get for her birthday?" (Control question); "Does Mom think Jenny saw the puppy?" (first-order false-belief question); "What does Mom think Jenny will tell her friends she's getting for her birthday?" (second-order false-belief task); "Why does Mom think this?" (Justification). In this task, as well as in the previous one, children were presented coloured pictures illustrating the situations described.

Competences regarding mental verbs were measured through the Metacognitive Vocabulary Test devised by Astington & Pelletier (1998). The test consists of a set of 12 short stories accompanied by pictures. In each story children were asked to choose which of two verbs can express the mental state of a character. This is an example of the items of the test: "Dad comes into the room and says: "Time for bed. If it's sunny tomorrow, we'll go to the park". In the morning John gets out of the bed and looks out the window. He sees the rain pouring down. "Oh no" says John, "Look at that! We won't be going to the park today": Does John *know* it is raining or does John *remember* it is raining?". Five different versions of the test had been devised by rotating the order of presentation of the stories and by varying the wrong verb which was paired to the right answer. Each version of the test was presented the same number of times both in the total sample and within each age level. The target verbs were: to deny, to explain, to figure out, to forget, to guess, to know, to learn, to predict, to remember, to teach, to understand, to wonder.

Twenty 4-yr-olds (ranging in age from 4:1 to 4:10, mean age = 4:4), 20 6-yr-olds (from 6:2 to 6:11, mean age = 6:5), and 20 8-yr-olds (from 8:0 to 8:10, mean age = 8:5) took part in the first study. They were randomly selected in a kindergarten school and in a primary school in Milan (Italy). The two schools, situated in the same neighborhood, were attended by children of the same socio-cultural status. Males and females were equally distributed within each age level.

The tasks were presented within the school in two days separated by a week. In the first day the two first-order false-belief tasks and the first 6 items of the Metacognitive Vocabulary Test were presented; the other materials in the second day. The tasks were presented individually to each child.

Participants who did not correctly answer the first-order false-belief question were not asked the second-order question. Children who failed to answer correctly one or two control questions devised for the false-belief task were excluded from analyses carried out on false-belief answers in that task. Responses to the justification questions were considered only when children had given the correct answers to the corresponding false-belief questions.

1.1.1   False-Belief Tasks

In the false-belief tasks score "1" was assigned if the child gave the correct answer, score "0" if he/she gave a wrong response or did not answer. This scoring system allows one easily to convert mean scores into percentages by multiplying the first by 100: for example, a mean score equal to 0.90 means that 90% of participants gave the right answer. Table 1 reports mean scores under each age level in the false-belief tasks. In this study, as well as in the following ones, no significant gender effect emerged; so we considered together males' and females' performances.

In the Change-in-location task all 6- and 8-yr-olds and 95% of the 4-yr-olds answered correctly the control questions: thus, they had no problems in understanding and remembering information presented in the story. A clear developmental trend emerged in rates of false-belief answers: whereas only 25% of 4-yr-olds correctly identified the mental state involved, almost all 6- and all 8-yr-olds succeeded (in Table 1, as well as in the similar following ones, the last column synthesises the results of the application of the Newman-Keuls test by reporting the levels of the independent variable according to the increasing order of their mean values and by separating levels which were significantly different with a blank space: for instance, "4 68" means that 4-yr-olds had significantly poorer performances than 6- and 8-yr-olds, who were not significantly different between themselves).

In the Unexpected-content case all children gave the correct answers to the control questions. In the false-belief questions response trends were similar as in the Change-in location task: 6- and 8-yr-olds, whose mean scores were not significantly different, were significantly better than 4-yr-olds. Differences between the 4-yr-olds and the older children were higher in the other's belief question (which was similar to the question of the previous task) than in the one's own belief question. A 3 X 2 ANOVA was carried out by assuming responses to the false-belief questions as dependent variable and age level and the one's own-other distinction as independent variables (respectively, between and within subjects): significant main effects of age, $F(2,57) = 14.30$, $P < .001$, and of the one's own-other distinction, $F(1,57) = 9.22$, $P < .005$, and an interaction effect, $F(2,57) = 4.44$, $P < .05$) emerged. Four-yr-olds had better performance in the one's own than in the other's belief questions, whereas no significant differences between the two questions occurred in 6-and 8-yr-olds. This result seems to support simulation theory (Harris, 1989). When the understanding of false belief emerges (at age four) the comprehension of one's own earlier belief is easier than the comprehension of the mistaken belief of another person, since the latter is based on the former and involves the further request to imagine the mental state of the other as he/she was in one's own previous situation.

In the Look-prediction task no significant differences in rates of correct answers in the control questions were found among age levels,

$F(2,57) = 2.27$ in the first and $F(2,57) = 1.07$ in the second control question. Even though performance in the false-belief questions increased through age levels, a significant effect due to age was found only in the second-order false-belief question, where 6- and 8-yr-olds, not significantly different between themselves, significantly outperformed 4-yr-olds.

Also in the Say-prediction task control questions revealed a good comprehension and memory of the story at all age levels (comparisons among rates of correct answers: $F(2,57) = 2.66$, n.s. in the first and $F(2,57) = 0.07$, n.s. in the second control question). In this case no significant improvement in false-belief performance across ages was found: all children had poor performance. As far as responses to the justification questions were concerned, no significant effects due to the age level were found both in the Look-, $F(2,37) = 2.68$, and in the Say-prediction task, $F(2,16) = 0.72$.

We focused attention on the 47 children who gave the correct response to the second-order false-belief question in at least one of the two prediction tasks. A 3X2 ANOVA was carried out by assuming responses to the second order false-belief questions as dependent variable and age level and the Look-Say distinction as independent variables (respectively, between and within subjects): significant principal effects due to age, $F(2,44) = 4.20$, $P < .05$, and to the Look-Say distinction, $F(1,44) = 17.31$, $P < .001$, emerged; the interaction was not significant, $F(2,44) = 2.05$. The Look prediction task was easier than the Say prediction task, presumably since the choice to perform an action to achieve a concrete goal in the physical environment (getting the cards) is potentially influenced by a smaller and more predictable number of factors than the choice to say something to somebody so producing a representational effect on his/her mind (For instance, in the Say prediction task, Jenny might tell her friends that she's getting a great toy for her birthday, even though she knows that her mummy has bought a puppet in order to surprise her friends)

If we collapse performances in the Look and Say prediction tasks, an increase of correct answers through ages emerged (4-yr-olds' performance was significantly poorer than 6-yr-olds' performance that was, in turn, significantly poorer than 8-yr-olds' performance). Furthermore, at each age level the Say prediction task is significantly more difficult than the Look prediction task. The same analysis was carried out on justification scores. No significant age difference was found, $F(2,44) = 2.62$; the Look prediction task resulted to be significantly easier than the Say prediction task, $F(1,44) = 12.48$, $P < .001$; the interaction was not significant, $F(2,44) = 0.29$. We also carried out a similar analysis on scores in the first-order question by considering the same 47 children: we found no significant effect (age: $F(2,44) = 1.82$; Look-Say distinction: $F(1,44) = 0.23$; age X Look-Say distinction: $F(2,44) = 0.18$).

Table 1. Performances in the False-Belief Tasks under each Age Level (First Study)

Tasks	Age							Post-hoc
	4 years		6 years		8 years		F(2,57)	Newman-Keuls test
	M	SD	M	SD	M	SD		
Change in location	0.25	0.44	0.90	0.31	1.00	0.00	34.06 ***	4 68
Unexpected content								
- Own belief	0.75	0.44	0.95	0.22	1.00	0.00	4.24 *	4 68
- Other's belief	0.40	0.50	0.85	0.37	1.00	0.00	15.12 ***	4 68
Look prediction								
-1st order question	0.78	0.44	0.89	0.32	0.90	0.31	0.43 n.s.	
-2° order question	0.44	0.53	0.89	0.32	0.95	0.22	7.50 ***	4 68
- Justification	0.44	0.53	0.72	0.46	0.85	0.37	2.68 n.s.	
Say prediction								
-1st order question	0.67	0.50	0.89	0.32	0.90	0.31	1.50 n.s.	
-2° order question	0.33	0.50	0.28	0.46	0.50	0.51	1.03 n.s.	
- Justification	0.22	0.44	0.33	0.49	0.45	0.51	0.72 n.s.	

* P < .05 ** P < .01   *** P < .001

1.1.2   Metacognitive Vocabulary Test

As far as the Metacognitive Vocabulary Test was concerned, no significant differences among the five versions in mean total scores and in scores for each verb were found (also in this case score "1" was attributed to right answers and score "0" to wrong answers): it seems that neither the order of the stories nor the kind of alternative verb paired to the correct verb influenced performance. Table 2 shows that in only 3 out of 12 verbs girls significantly outperformed boys, even though the mean total score of the former was significantly higher than that of the latter. It is worth noticing that *to learn* and *to forget* were the most recognisable verbs; *to figure out, to deny*, and *to predict* the most difficult; *to remember* and *to know* - that literature suggests to be among the first mental cognitive verbs produced by children (Bretherton & Beegly, 1982; Shatz, Wellman & Silber, 1983; Shatz, 1994) - did not have the highest scores.

Table 2. Metacognitive Language Task: Mean Scores and Standard Deviations for each Verb According to Gender (First Study)

Verb	Gender				
	Female		Male		t_{58}
	M	SD	M	SD	
Females > Males					
to forget	0.97	0.18	0.87	0.35	8.93 **
to know	0.77	0.43	0.60	0.50	7.16 **
to predict	0.70	0.47	0.60	0.50	2.42 n.s.
to teach	0.97	0.16	0.77	0.43	31.61 ***
to wonder	0.80	0.41	0.73	0.45	1.46 n.s.
Males > Females					
to deny	0.63	0.50	0.67	0.48	0.28 n.s.
to figure out	0.60	0.50	0.73	0.45	4.40 n.s.
to guess	0.83	0.38	0.90	0.31	2.32 n.s.
to understand	0.87	0.35	0.90	0.31	0.63 n.s.
Females = Males					
to explain	0.83	0.38	0.83	0.38	0.00 n.s.
to learn	0.93	0.25	0.93	0.25	0.00 n.s.
to remember	0.73	0.45	0.73	0.45	0.00 n.s.
Total	9.63	1.45	9.26	1.83	9.87 ***

** $P < .01$ *** $P < .001$

If we look at Table 3 we realise that only in 4 out of 12 verbs performances increased significantly across age. A quasi-linear improvement from 4 to 8 years emerged. When significant differences occurred, post-hoc tests indicated that two sets of subsamples can be identified: 4-yr-olds on one hand and 6- and 8-yr-olds on the other hand. Thus, also in this case, as in the first-order but not in the second-order false-belief questions, a remarkable improvement occurs between 4 and 6 years. The total score of the Metacognitive Vocabulary Test - obtained by summing up scores in each verb - indicated that each age level was significantly different from the others.

Table 3. Metacognitive Vocabulary Test: Mean Scores for each Verb under each Age Level (First Study)

Verb	Age level						F(2,57)	Post-hoc Newman-Keuls test
	4 years		6 years		8 years			
	M	SD	M	SD	M	SD		
No significant differences:								
to deny	0.50	0.51	0.65	0.49	0.80	0.41	2.01 n.s.	
to explain	0.70	0.47	0.90	0.31	0.90	0.31	1.95 n.s.	
to figure out	0.55	0.51	0.60	0.50	0.85	0.37	2.39 n.s.	
to forget	0.80	0.41	0.95	0.22	1.00	0.00	2.98 n.s.	
to guess	0.75	0.44	0.85	0.37	1.00	0.00	2.86 n.s.	
to know	0.60	0.50	0.55	0.51	0.90	0.31	3.54 n.s.	
to learn	0.85	0.37	1.00	0.00	0.95	0.22	1.90 n.s.	
to predict	0.50	0.51	0.60	0.50	0.85	0.37	3.00 n.s.	
Significant differences:								
to remember	0.50	0.51	0.75	0.44	0.95	0.22	5.97 **	4 6 6 8
to teach	0.65	0.49	0.95	0.22	1.00	0.00	7.43 ***	4 6 8
to understand	0.65	0.49	1.00	0.00	1.00	0.00	10.23 ***	4 6 8
to wonder	0.50	0.51	0.80	0.41	1.00	0.00	8.80 ***	4 6 8
Total	7.55	2.35	9.60	1.10	11.20	0.83	27.07***	4 6 8

** P < .01   *** P < .001

1.1.3   Relationships between False-Belief Tasks and Metacognitive Vocabulary Test

Table 4(a) and (b) report coefficients concerning correlations between performance on each verb and on each false-belief question. In these tables, the last three columns refer to some global measures of false-belief ability: 1) a score resulting by summing up scores in the three false-belief questions (spontaneous responses) of first-order, first (ball) and second (doll: one's own and the other's) tasks; 2) a score resulting by summing up the five false-belief questions of first-order among the four tasks (first- and second-order tasks); 3) a score resulting by summing up scores in the two second-order questions of the two (Look and Say) second-order tasks. The ability to identify the correct metacognitive verb tended to be associated with correct responses in the first-order false-belief tasks but not in the other false-belief tasks. In fact the highest correlation coefficients concerned relations between mental verbs and first-order false-belief questions; significant coefficients concerned mostly first-order questions (36 out of 91 cases) rather than second-order questions (5 out of 65 cases).

The results of the first study showed that the developmental trend of false-belief understanding depends on the metarepresentational level involved in the task. In fact, children reached a quite full comprehension of first-order false-belief at 6 years of age, whereas at that stage they did not yet master second-order false-belief, which is achieved (in the Look prediction task) at 8 years of age. As regards first-order false-belief understanding, children are sensitive to the specific features of the tasks (Change-in-location versus unexpected content; one's own versus the other's belief) only at the first age level here considered and then they acquire the comprehension of the first metarepresentational level fully and homogeneously through the tasks, whereas the characteristics of the tasks (Look versus Say prediction) involving the second metarepresentational level – whose acquisition is not completed also at the higher age here considered - continue to affect children's performances still at 8 years of age.

Metacognitive vocabulary competence showed a developmental trend which was more similar to the trend of the first-order than that of the second-order false-belief tasks yet had characteristics of both. In fact the overall score increased both from 4 to 6 and from 6 to 8 years of age; furthermore, the performance continued to differ in function of the specific verb considered at 8 years of age.

Table 4 (a). Correlations (Spearman's ρ) between Metacognitive Vocabulary Task and False-Belief Tasks (First Study)

Verb	False Belief Questions					
	Change-in-location	Unexpected Content Own belief	Unexpected content Other's belief	Look prediction 1st order question	Look prediction 2nd order question	Look prediction justification
to deny	.08	.22	.14	.15	- .07	- .02
to explain	.21	.15	.15	- .16	.29	.14
to figure out	.03	.00	.00	-. 14	.03	.16
to forget	.48 **	.50 **	.38 **	.39 **	- .07	- .09
to guess	.30 *	.52 **	.23	-.12	.06	.15
to know	.05	.01	.10	.01	.18	- .01
to learn	.28 *	.36 **	.31 *	- .06	- .07	.24
to predict	.16	.10	.22	.03	.08	.12
to remember	.46 **	.18	.44 **	.17	.25	- .03
to teach	.30 *	.52 **	.45 **	-.10	.11	.03
to understand	.58 **	.05	.27 *	.16	.34 *	.23
to wonder	.35 **	.47 **	.32 **	- .01	.10	.09
Total	.55 **	.51 **	.52 **	.03	.28 *	.20

* P < .05   ** P < .01

Table 4 (b). Correlations (Spearman's ρ) between Metacognitive Vocabulary Task and False-Belief Tasks (First Study)

Verb	False Belief Questions					
	Say prediction 1st order question	Say prediction 2nd order question	Say prediction justificatior	Total 1st order questions (change-in-location + unexpected content)	Total 1st order questions (all tasks)	Total 2nd order questions (look + say prediction)
to deny	.10	.26	.23	.16	.19	.16
to explain	- .01	.08	.19	.21	.09	.24
to figure out	.20	.20	.17	.02	.15	.18
to forget	- .06	.12	.11	.53 **	.36 **	.05
to guess	.09	- .23	- .25	.39 **	.15	- .14
to know	- .03	.07	.04	.07	.11	.16
to learn	.35 *	- .19	.11	.37 **	.13	- .19
to predict	- .01	.03	.10	.20	.01	.07
to remember	.13	.12	.11	.45 **	.32 *	.25 *
to teach	.38 **	.2	.20	.49 **	.23	.23
to understand	- .11	- .15	.02	.39 **	.37 **	.09
to wonder	- .03	.12	.22	.44 **	.23	.16
Total	.18	.20	.28 *	.62 **	.44 **	.32 *

* P < .05   ** P < .01

1.2   POSSIBLE VARIABLES AFFECTING MENTAL VOCABULARY AND FALSE-BELIEF UNDERSTANDING: CONTEXT AS SOCIO-CULTURAL DIMENSIONS

The first study showed that mental vocabulary tends to be connected with the first rather than with the second metarepresentational level. The first goal of the second study was to replicate this finding by considering a larger sample of children and by also measuring their general linguistic competence. The first study also proved that task content - assumed as a context dimension - is influential in determining the rate of success in false-belief tasks. A further aim of the second study was to assess whether other contextual variables, concerning individual differences linked with social and cultural factors, may modulate children's performance both in the false-belief and in the metacognitive vocabulary tasks. Among a variety of possible candidates, we chose the following: cultural environment (children living in Northern versus Southern Italy), family size (only-children versus children with siblings), and social competence (with cognitive competence recorded as a control measure).

In the second study, the same false-belief tasks employed in the first study, as well the Metacognitive Vocabulary Test, were administered to a new sample consisting of one-hundred and eighty children: half of them were recruited in a city of Northern Italy and the other half in a city in the South of Italy. Children were selected so that two equal-size subgroups were formed: only-children and children with one or more siblings. Approximately the same percentage of males and females were included in each condition of the experimental design. For each child, his/her teacher had to fill out a short questionnaire asking the teacher to rate both social and cognitive skills on a 5-point scale (ratings were requested from the teacher who, within the teacher team, spent the highest number of hours with that child). Finally, all children completed the Peabody Picture Vocabulary Test (PPVT) (Dunn & Dunn, 1981), as a measure of general receptive linguistic competence. Since there were missing data in some protocols, the sizes of the sample involved in statistical analyses vary, as indicated by the degree of freedom values.

In the first study we reported a thorough analysis of performances in the false-belief tasks and in the metacognitive vocabulary test since these materials were translated (with some little adaptations) from English into Italian and were applied in Italy for the first time. For this reason we wanted to have a detailed picture of the response patterns of Italian children. In the second and third study such kind of analysis were not carried out.

1.2.1 False-Belief Tasks

In this study no significant gender differences emerged, $F(1,224) = 1.03$. Only-child participants' performance was not significantly different from performance by children with siblings, $F(1,232) = 0.79$. In the second-order false-belief tasks Southern children outperformed Northern children in the first-order questions, $F(2,162) = 9.56$, $P < .01$, and in the second-order questions, $F(2,162) = 4.61$, $P < .05$; similar significant differences emerged by comparing Northern and Southern children with respect to the total scores in the second-order tasks (first-order questions + second-order questions), $F(2,218) = 10.13$, $P < .01$, and in the total false-belief tasks (scores obtained by summing up scores in each of the four tasks), $F(2,162) = 7.87$, $P < .01$.

As far as performances in the Change-in-location and in the Unexpected-content task were concerned, mean values of correct responses were similar to those recorded in the first study, as well as the developmental trend: if we combine data from the first and the second task, we obtain a significant age effect, $F(2,162) = 113.75$, $P < .001$; the Newman-Keuls test showed that 4-yrs-olds performed significantly worst than 6- and 8-yr-olds, who did not differ from each other.

As far as the performances in the Look- and Say-prediction tasks were concerned, by combining responses given to the second-order false-belief questions, significant differences among each age level group emerged, $F(2,162) = 25.94$, P < .001.

As far as relationships between false-belief tasks were concerned, we observed that responses in the first-order task were associated both to responses to the first-order questions of the second-order tasks ($r = .62$, P < .001) and to the second-order questions of the second-order tasks ($r = .52$, P < .001); in the second-order tasks scores in the first-order questions were associated to scores in the second-order questions ($r = .56$, P < .01).

Participants were classified as low or high according to their performances in the false-belief tasks by assuming the medians of the combined scores (for the first-order and for the second-order questions) as cut-off points; they were also classified as low and high in social and cognitive competence by assuming the medians of the corresponding distributions of the teachers' ratings as cut-off points. Significant associations between cognitive competence and performance level in the first-order, χ^2 (N = 1) = 5.41, P < .05, and second-order, χ^2 (N = 1) = 5.06, P < .05, questions emerged; social competence was not related to false-belief understanding.

1.2.2 Metacognitive Vocabulary Test

In the total scores of the Metacognitive Vocabulary Test no significant differences emerged by comparing male and female participants, $F(1,228 = 1.87$, and by comparing only-children and children with siblings, $F(1,230) = 2.12$. If we consider total scores, age effects appeared, $F(2,162) = 52.91$, P < .001: 4-year-olds (M = 8.10, SD = 1.87) were significantly different from 6-year-olds (M = 9.75, SD = 1.98), who in turn were significantly different from 8-year-olds (M = 10.97, SD = 0.98).

Children were classified as low, medium or high according to the total scores. This classification was related to teachers' evaluation of children's competence. A significant positive association between performance in the Metacognitive Vocabulary Test and cognitive competence emerged, χ^2 (N = 2) = 9.93, P < .01, whereas no significant association with social competence was found, χ^2 (N = 2) = 1.34.

1.2.3   Relationships between False-Belief Tasks and Metacognitive Vocabulary Test

Correlations between responses both in the first- and in the second-order questions on the false-belief tasks and the total score in the Metacognitive Vocabulary Test are reported in Table 5. Significant coefficients emerged in all cases. However, metacognitive vocabulary ability was more strictly connected with first-order than with second-order tasks.

Table 5. Correlations (Spearman's ρ) between the Metacognitive Vocabulary Test and the False-Belief Tasks (Second and Third Study)

Metacognitive Vocabulary Test (Total score)	False-Belief questions						
	Change-in-location	Unexpected Content Own belief	Other's belief	Look prediction 1st order question	Look prediction 2nd order question	Buy prediction 1st order question	Buy prediction 2nd order question
Second study	.50 **	.47 **	.51 **	.40 **	.32 **	.49 **	.39 **
Third study	.32 **	.51 **	.43 **	.58 **	.38 **	.40 **	.33 **

** P < .01

1.2.4   Peabody Picture Vocabulary Test

Total PPVT scores were not affected by gender, $F(1160) = 3.56$, family size, $F(1,178) = 1.28$, or by cultural context (Northern versus Southern Italy: $F(1,158) = 2.76$). Significant differences in PPVT total scores depending on age were found, $F(2,162) = 187.22$, P < .001: 4-yr-olds' performances (M = 44.57, SD = 2.61) were significantly worse than 6-yr-olds' performances (M = 72.03, SD = 3.03), which were significantly lower than 8-yr-olds' performances (M = 115.70, SD = 2.88).

Children were classified as low, medium and high according to the Peabody Picture Vocabulary Test total scores. Cross tabulation between such a classification and the level of cognitive competence (low – high) showed a significant association between the two variables, χ^2 (N = 2) = 11.02, P < .01. No association between Peabody Picture Vocabulary Test performance and social competence emerged.

1.2.5   Relationships between False-Belief Tasks and Peabody Picture Vocabulary Test

Table 6 reports correlation coefficients concerning relationships between false-belief tasks and PPVT: in all cases significant values were found.

Table 6. Correlations (Spearman's ρ) between the PPVT and the False-Belief Tasks (Second and Third Study)

PPVT		False-Belief questions					
	Change-in-location	Unexpected Content Own belief	Unexpected content Other's belief	Look prediction 1st order question	Look prediction 2nd order question	Say prediction 1st order question	Say prediction 2nd order question
Study 2	.59 **	.69 **	.64 **	.60 **	.54 **	.65 **	.48 **
Study 3	.44 **	.37 **	.29 *	.41 **	.27 *	.33 *	.23 *

* P < .05   ** P < .01

1.2.6   Relationships between Metacognitive Vocabulary Test and Peabody Picture Vocabulary Test

A significant positive correlation between total Metacognitive Vocabulary Test and PPVT scores was found, r = .62, P < .001.

1.3   FALSE-BELIEF UNDERSTANDING, BELIEF-DESIRE UNDERSTANDING AND METACOGNITIVE VOCABULARY

The third study had two aims. The first one was to replicate the results obtained in the first and second studies about the relationships between mental vocabulary and the comprehension of epistemic mental states; the second one was to examine the developmental trend of a different kind of mental state understanding, i.e. emotional mental state understanding, and its relationship with the comprehension of false belief. We present only the new tasks introduced in this study. The other measures used were the false-belief tasks and Metacognitive Vocabulary Task already described above.

The belief-desire reasoning task, consisting of four stories, was presented to children to test their understanding of the impact of beliefs and desires on emotion (Harris, Johnson, Hutton, Andrews & Cooke, 1989). Children were told stories and were asked to predict the emotional reactions of animal characters who were offered various types of container. Children were introduced to four animals and to their preference for a particular food or drink. The experimenter then proceeded to introduce the monkey, who played tricks on each of the other four animals by replacing the contents of a container the animal wanted with other contents that he/she did not like (or vice versa by replacing unwanted contents with ones that were liked). The children were asked to make two predictions (questions 3 and 5) about the duped character's emotion and to justify these predictions (questions 4 and 6); in addition, their memory for the actual contents of the container was checked (questions 1 and 2).

Sixty children (27 males and 33 females) – equally distributed among the three age levels considered (4, 6 and 8 years) - participated in the study. They attended kindergartens and primary schools in Northern Italy. 33.3% of the sample was comprised of only-children and 66.6% were children with siblings: percentages were approximately the same at each age level. Cognitive and social competence was assessed as in the second study.

1.3.1   False-Belief Tasks

In this study, by collapsing responses given, respectively, to the first-order and to the second-order tasks, neither gender (first-order: $F(2,58) = 2.34$; second-order: $F(2,58) = 1.17$) nor family size (first order: $F(2,58) = 0.78$; second-order: $F(2,58) = 2.00$) differences emerged. Developmental trends were analogous to those observed both in the first and second study. In the first-order false-belief tasks (collapsed responses), 4-yr-olds performed significantly worse than 6- and 8-yr-olds, who did not differ from each other, $F(2,57) = 14.52$, $P < .001$. In the second-order false-belief tasks (collapsed responses) significant differences among each age level group emerged, $F(2,57) = 8.37$, $P < .001$.

As regards social and cognitive competences, we observed a significant effect of the former on second-order false-belief question in the Look prediction task and on justification answers to second-order false-belief question in the Say prediction task (respectively, $t_{58} = -2.07$, $P < .005$; $t_{58} = -2,11$, $P < .005$) and of the latter on the answers to second-order false-belief in Say prediction task, $t_{58} = -2,02$, $P < .005$.

As far as the relationship between false-belief tasks was concerned, we observed that responses in the first-order task were significantly associated with responses to the first-order questions of the second-order tasks, r = .30, P < .005, but not with the second-order questions of the second-order tasks, r = . 22; in the second-order tasks, scores on the first-order questions were associated with scores in the second-order questions, r = .40, P < .001).

1.3.2   Metacognitive Vocabulary Test

As regards total scores, significant differences emerged, $F(2,57) =$ 44.29, P < .001: 4-yr-olds (M = 8.30, SD = 1.38) significantly differed from 6-yr-olds (M = 10-25, SD = 0.97), who were significantly different from 8-yr-olds (M = 11.50, SD = 0.83). Results did not show significant differences either between male and female in total scores, $t_{58} = -0.10$) or between only-children and children with siblings, $t_{58} = -0.53$.

Children with high cognitive competence obtained higher mean total scores than children with lower cognitive competence, even though this difference does not reach significance, $t_{58} = -1.17$. No significant differences between children with high or low social competence appeared, $t_{58} = -1.51$.

1.3.3   Relationships between False-Belief Tasks and Metacognitive Vocabulary Test

In the third study significant correlations between first- and second-order questions and MVT emerged (Table 5) and also in this case, as in the previous studies, coefficients were higher when first-order tasks, instead of second-order tasks, were involved.

1.3.4   Peabody Picture Vocabulary Test

Neither gender nor family size influenced total scores. Children showing high cognitive and social competence obtained scores significantly higher than children showing low cognitive and social competence (respectively, $t_{58} = -2.02$, P < .05; $t_{58} = -2.34$, P < .05). Age influenced total scores, $F(2,57) = 48.88$, P < .001: 4-yr-olds (M = 59.40, SD = 16.10) significantly differed from 6-yr-olds (M = 86.8, SD = 21.95), who were significantly different from 8-yr-olds (M = 129.25, SD = 27.92).

1.3.5   Relationships between False-Belief Tasks and Peabody Picture Vocabulary Test

Table 6 reports correlation coefficients concerning relationships between performance in the false-belief tasks and in PPVT. In all cases significant values were recorded.

1.3.6   Relationships between Metacognitive Vocabulary Test and Peabody Picture Vocabulary Test

Total scores in MVT and PPVT were significantly correlated, r – .66, P < .01.

1.3.7   Belief-Desire task

Neither gender not family size influenced responses to each question in Harris's task (F values varied from 0.89 to 2.03). As Table 7 shows, ceiling effects occurred in control questions (questions 1 and 2) and this can explain the lack of significant age effects. In some prediction and justification questions significant age differences were found. However, it is worth noticing that no remarkable and recurrent increase between age 4 and age 6 and between age 6 and age 8 took place.

In 8 out of 24 questions significant differences depending on cognitive competence emerged: high level children scored higher than low level children. This occurred when participants were requested to predict the emotions (happiness or sadness) experienced by a story character in front of a closed box apparently containing, respectively, an object he/she desired but really containing an object he/she disliked or vice versa (question 3), t_{58} = - 2.06, -2.06, -2.37, P < .01, and when they were requested to justify their answers (question 4), t_{58} = -2.72, -3.02, -3.24, P < .01, in 3 out of 4 stories; when they were requested to predict the emotion experienced by the story character when he/she discovered the real content of the box (question 5: t_{58} = -2.37, P < .05) and to justify their responses (question 6: t_{58} = -2.69, P < .01) in 1 out of 4 stories. Social competence did not affect responses in Harris's task.

Table 7. Performances in the Harris' Tasks under each Age Level (Third Study)

Questions			Age Level				F (2,57)	Post-hoc Newman-Keuls test
	4 years		6 years		8 years			
	M	SD	M	SD	M	SD		
Story 1								
Question 1	0.95	0.22	0.95	0.22	1.00	0.00	0.50	
Question 2	0.80	0.41	0.65	0.49	1.00	0.00	4.53 *	64 48
Question 3	0.60	0.50	0.70	0.47	0.95	0.22	3.72 *	46 68
Question 4	0.55	0.51	0.80	0.41	1.00	0.00	7.11 **	4 68
Question 5	0.65	0.49	0.65	0.49	0.90	0.31	2.18	
Question 6	0.65	0.49	0.65	0.49	0.95	0.22	3.40 *	46 8

Tab. 7 cont.

Questions		Age Level				F (2,57)	Post-hoc Newman-Keuls test
	4 years		6 years		8 years		
	M	SD	M	SD	M	SD	
Story 2							
Question 1	0.95	0.22	1.00	0.00	1.00	0.00	1.00	
Question 2	0.80	0.41	0.85	0.37	1.00	0.00	2.15	
Question 3	0.70	0.48	0.65	0.49	0.90	0.31	1.89	
Question 4	0.45	0.51	0.65	0.49	0.90	0.31	5.13 **	46 68
Question 5	0.75	0.44	0.85	0.37	1.00	0.00	2.86	
Question 6	0.70	0.47	0.85	0.38	1.00	0.00	3.80 *	46 68
Story 3							
Question 1	0.95	0.22	1.00	0.00	1.00	0.00	1.00	
Question 2	0.90	0.31	0.80	0.41	0.95	0.22	1.18	
Question 3	0.40	0.50	0.65	0.49	0.85	0.37	4.87 *	46 68
Question 4	0.35	0.49	0.65	0.49	0.85	0.37	6.20 **	4 68
Question 5	0.75	0.44	0.85	0.37	0.90	0.31	0.82	
Question 6	0.75	0.44	0.85	0.37	0.90	0.31	0.82	
Story 4							
Question 1	1.00	0.00	1.00	0.00	1.00	0.00	0.00	
Question 2	0.85	0.37	0.90	0.31	1.00	0.00	1.53	
Question 3	0.65	0.49	0.70	0.47	0.85	0.37	1.09	
Question 4	0.50	0.51	0.70	0.47	0.85	0.37	2.99	
Question 5	0.75	0.44	0.90	0.31	1.00	0.00	3.25 *	46 68
Question 6	0.70	0.39	0.85	0.37	1.00	0.00	3.80 *	46 68

* $P < .05$ ** $P < .01$

1.3.8   Relationships between False-Belief Tasks and Belief-Desire Task

Significant correlations were recorded between responses to question 5 of all the 4 stories and first-order question of the Look-prediction task (respectively, $r = .26, .34, .36$, and $.39$, $P < .05$ in the first case, $P < .01$ in the other three cases) and the second-order question of the same task ($r = .27$, $.33, .33$, and $.39$; $P < .05$ in the first three cases, $P < .01$ in the fourth case). Responses to question 5 were also significantly correlated to the Change-in-location - the other's belief question, $r = .30$, $P < .05$, Unexpected content – one's own belief, $r = .27$, $P < .05$, and Say-prediction – first-order, $r = .25$, $P < .05$.

1.3.9 Relationships between Metacognitive Vocabulary Test and Belief-Desire Task

The total Metacognitive Vocabulary Test score was significantly correlated with question 3 in 2 stories (r = .35, P < .01; r = .31, P < .05) and with question 5 in 3 stories (r = .38, .35, and .37, P < .01).

1.3.10 Relationships between Peabody Picture Vocabulary Test and Belief-Desire Task

The total Peabody Picture Vocabulary Test score was significantly correlated with question 3 in 2 stories (r = .35, P < .01; r = .30, P < .05) and with question 5 in 2 stories (r = .26 and .30, P < .05).

1.4 CONCLUSIONS

In this chapter we presented three studies on theory of mind development in 4-,6-, and 8-year-old normal children. Objects of investigation were the comprehension of both epistemic mental states (first- and second-order false-belief understanding) and of desires and emotions, and mental language, as well as the relationships among the above mentioned skills. The studies considered contextual aspects both at the cognitive level (i.e., the task content) and at the social level (i.e., the geographical district of residence, the family size, the teacher-assessed social competences); the participants' linguistic receptive ability was controlled for. This gave us an analytic description of the development of different forms of mind understanding and of their relationships.

We used a theory of mind test battery that includes the standard measures of the first-and second-order false-belief tasks, the belief-desire reasoning task, and a recent measure of mental language, the Metacognitive Vocabulary Test devised by Astington & Pelletier (1998). As a way to control for linguistic understanding, we used the Peabody Picture Vocabulary Test (Dunn & Dunn, 1981) as a measure of general receptive linguistic competence.

Results showed that the understanding of mental states significantly increased from 4 to 6 years of age in the following tasks: Change-in-location, unexpected content (first-order false-belief), Look prediction (second-order false-belief), belief-desire reasoning task. As far as the Say-prediction task is concerned, we noticed that children's performances were very poor until 8 years of age. These results are in accord with other reports in the literature (e.g., Wimmer & Perner, 1983; Perner & Wimmer, 1985; Wellman, 1985; Gopnik & Astington, 1988; Harris et al., 1989; Wellman et al., 2001). In this developmental trend we can see some analogies between first-order and second-order false-belief understanding. In fact in both developmental paths the acquisition is "step by step" instead of "all or nothing": children start from a false-belief understanding based on the kind of task which they face to a full understanding, independent of task factors.

The observed difficulty in perfectly mastering second-order false belief cannot be explained with reference to the difficulty in understanding and retaining the information relevant to the comprehension of the story which was tested by control questions (where participants succeeded in very high proportions at all ages). A possible explanation could be found in the syntactic complexity of the sentence expressing false-belief questions, particularly sophisticated because a complementation is embedded into another one ("What does Mom think Jenny will tell her friends she's getting for the birthday?"). The possible influence of this syntactic construction on responses to the second-order false-belief tasks is not yet investigated, since the available studies (Astington & Jenkins, 1999; de Villiers & de Villiers, 2000; Tardiff & Wellman, 2000; de Villiers & Pyers, 2002, Perner et al., 2003) were focused on the complement object present in the sentences expressing first-order false-belief questions (e.g., "Does Mom think Jenny saw the puppy?"). The explanation based on the complexity of the linguistic medium can be articulated with a further hypothesis referring to the task content, previously mentioned, which clarifies the bigger difficulty of the Say with respect to the Look prediction task. Predicting behaviour in the Look prediction task regards the choice of performing an action to achieve a concrete goal in the physical environment ("Where does Mary think John will Look for the pack of cards?"), whereas in the Say prediction task the prediction regards an action which influences another person's representational world, and the aim of this action is not explicit.

Also the mastery of metacognitive vocabulary significantly improved from 4 to 6 and from 6 to 8 years of age in the whole sample. In particular, the verbs dealing with school activities seem to be better understood than the other verbs: *to learn* and *to forget* were the most recognisable verbs and there was a significant increase of performance from 4 to 6 years of age in the case of the verbs *to teach* and *to understand*. Thus, we can hypothesize that the mastery of metacognitive vocabulary constitutes an ability which is strongly connected with literacy processes. Literacy in fact seems to promote this kind of metarepresentational competence needed to enhance thought on cognitive and linguistic activities (Olson & Astington, 1993). Specifically, the formal language of schooling promotes the language of epistemology, that is the language for talking about how we think and why we believe and, so, to scrutinizing and revising our own and others' thoughts (Olson, 2003).

The overall picture that emerged suggests that mental verb competence and metarepresentational abilities are only partially overlapping. Only first-order, but not second-order false-belief tasks, were strictly related to metacognitive vocabulary. Furthermore, the developmental trend of correct responses in the mental verb test tended to be similar to that of first-order false-belief tasks and different from that of second-order tasks. This can be explained by the fact that metacognitive vocabulary considers only first-order mental states ("Does John *know* it is raining or does John *remember* it is raining?") and not recursive mental states (e.g., "Does John *know* that Mary *thinks…*") and, as regards syntactic complexity, it uses the kind of complemention which is present in the first-order false-belief task. Moreover, the low correlations between mental verbs and second-order false-belief tasks can be understood considering a further aspect of the representational content implied by false-belief task questions. In the first-order false-belief questions children were asked to represent a mental state, that is, the product or the content of a mental act, whereas in the second-order questions they were asked to represent a mind's activity, a mind which is thinking, namely, a mental process. The mental verbs included in the Metacognitive Vocabulary Test are more likely concerned with mental states than with mental acts. Furthermore, it seems that second-order tasks involve higher level thinking abilities – a kind of recursive thought ("I think that he thinks that she thinks") – in which linguistic or metalinguistic components may play a minor role. In conclusion, the relationships between metarepresentational competence – as measured by false-belief tasks – and the mastery of mental verbs is not so obvious and some distinctions and caveats seem to be needed. More precisely, it appears that at a basic level the two kinds of competences are linked, but then they become relatively independent.

Total PPVT scores were not affected by gender, family size, and cultural context, whereas they were affected by age: 4-year-olds performed significantly worse than 6-year-olds, whose performances were significantly worse than 8-year-olds'. As far as theory of mind is concerned, significant correlations between first-order as well as second-order questions emerged; in particular, coefficients were higher when first-order tasks, instead of second-order tasks, were involved. A significant positive correlation between total Metacognitive Vocabulary Test scores and PPVT scores was also found. The overall picture suggests that, at these age levels, theory of mind is connected with language in a general way, with mental language not playing a specific role. The results suggest that the link between theory of mind and semantic competence, which has already been demonstrated as uninfluential on first-order false-belief understanding (Astington & Jenkins, 1999), becomes still weaker in the case of second-order false-belief understanding.

Now we are going to consider the relationships between theory of mind development and the following contextual conditions: family size, cultural environment (children living in Northern *vs.* Southern Italy), and social competence as assessed by teachers. We found no significant results as regards the relationships between the development of false-belief understanding and family size (only children *vs.* children with siblings). Neither did family size influence the performances in the Metacognitive Vocabulary Test. This finding is inconsistent with the studies mentioned in the Introduction (Perner et al., 1994; Jenkins & Astington, 1996; Lewis et al., 1996; Ruffman et al., 1998), but not with other studies (Cole & Mitchell, 1998; Carlson & Moses, 2001; Arranz, Artamedi, Olabarrieta & Martìn, 2002; Pears & Moses, 2003). The "sibling effect" is not clear, perhaps because until now it has been investigated as a structural variable (sibling number, sibling status), but not as a developmental context characterized by the quality of the interaction among siblings (Arranz at al., 2002). In this perspective, Foote & Holmens-Lonergan (2003) examined the relationship between specific features of sibling conflicts and the development of false-belief understanding, showing the link existing between the latter and the types of arguments occurring during sibling conflicts. We can reasonably hypothesize that structurally similar aspects, like number of siblings, older or younger siblings, the hierarchical status within the sibling group, the difference in age between siblings, constitute interactive contexts which differ according to personal (e.g., temperamental factors) as well as interpersonal (e.g., affective dimensions) variables. Considering the sibling effect in this way is coherent with the Vygotskian approach mentioned in the Introduction. In fact, we see that the relational approach to theory of mind development, centred on the quality of mother-child interaction, has produced new insights on theory of mind development: Fonagy, Redfern & Charman (1997) and Meins (1997; Meins, Fernyough, Russell & Clark-Carter, 1998; Meins et al., 2002; 2003) showed a positive link emerging between secure attachment and the development of mentalization.

As far as the relationship between false-belief understanding and cultural environment was concerned (children living in Northern *vs.* Southern Italy), in the first-and second-order false-belief tasks Southern children outperformed Northern children. Southern people's higher tendency to extroversion and sociability is likely to enhance the ability to cope with and to reflect on their own and the other's mental states.

Performances in mental tasks (first- and second-order false-belief tasks and Metacognitive Vocabulary Test) were mainly associated with cognitive and less with social competences as judged by classroom teachers. In other words, the child who is able to understand false-beliefs and mental language is likely to be judged more able from a cognitive than from a social point of view by his/her teacher. This can appear paradoxical, since theory of mind is considered to be the core of human social functioning: we interact with other persons on the basis of our "normal" and "usual" representation of them, but not on the basis of their "real" way of being. Furthermore the studies on the link between false-belief understanding and social abilities as evaluated by the teachers showed the positive relationship between the two abilities (Lalonde & Chandler, 1995, Watson, Nixon, Wilson & Capage, 1999; Astington, 2003). The discrepancy between our results and those emerging from the quoted studies on one side is connected with the kind of evaluation requested of the teachers, on the other side it could be only apparent. In fact, in the present study teachers were asked for an evaluation concerning the whole social behaviour of the children within the classroom context, which is usually linked by the teachers to the child's ability to follow the discipline, whereas in the above mentioned researches the evaluation concerned the social behaviour divided into different aspects. Lalonde & Chandler's (1995) study, as well as the first part of Astington's (2003) longitudinal study, distinguished between conventional social skills (ability to follow social conventions and to control impulses) and intentional social skills (ability to take into account other people's mental states); in the second part of Astington's (2003) study, teachers evaluated children's social skills on the basis of four behavioural dimensions: prosocial, aggressive, disruptive, and withdrawn; finally in Watson at al.'s (1999) study, social skill has been evaluated by the teachers using an adaptation of Harter's Perceived Competence Scale for Children (Harter, 1982), measuring peer relationships skill and popularity. So, our data regard a social ability similar to the conventional social skills as described by Lalonde & Chandler (1995); from this point of view, our results are coherent with their data, showing the relationship between false-belief understanding and intentional but not conventional social skills.

Finally, we found a relationship between false-belief understanding, metacognitive vocabulary and cognitive abilities as assessed by teachers. This can be explained as the teachers' tendency to see mainly the cognitive dimension of the representational activity and of its products, neglecting the social or affective or relational part of this activity.

REFERENCES

Arranz E., Artamedi J., Olabarrieta F., Martin J. Family context and theory of mind development. Early Child Development and Care 2002; 172: 9-22.

Astington, J.W. "What is theoretical about the child's theory of mind? A Vygotskian view of its development." In *Theories of theories of mind*, P. Carruthers, P.K. Smith (Eds.), Cambridge: Cambridge University Press, 1996.

Astington, J.W. "Language and metalanguage in children's understanding of mind." In *Minds in the making*, J.W. Astington (Ed.), New York: Blackwell, 2000.

Astington J.W. The future of theory-of-mind research: Understanding motivational states, the role of language, and real-world consequences. Child Development 2001; 72: 685-687.

Astington, J.W. "Sometimes necessary, never sufficient. False-belief understanding and social competence." In *Individual differences in theory of mind. Implications for typical and atypical development*, B. Repacholi, V. Slaughter (Eds.), New York: Psychology Press, 2003.

Astington J.W., Jenkins J.M. A longitudinal study of the relation between language and theory of mind development. Developmental Psychology 1999; 35: 1311-1320.

Astington, J.W., Pelletier, J. "The language of mind: Its role in teaching and learning." In *The handbook of education and human development*, D.R. Olson, N. Torrance (Eds.), Oxford: Blackwell, 1996.

Astington, J.W. Pelletier, J. *Metacognitive Vocabulary Test*. Institute of Child Study, University of Toronto, Unpublished, 1998.

Astington J.W., Pelletier J., Homer B. Theory of mind and epistemological development: The relation between children's second-order false-belief understanding and their ability to reason about evidence. New Ideas in Psychology, 2002; 20: 131-144.

Bartsch K., Wellman H. M., *Children talk about the mind*. New York: Oxford University Press, 1995.

Bretherton I., Beegly M. Talking about internal states: The acquisition of an explicit theory of mind. Developmental Psychology 1982;18: 906-921.

Brown J.R., Donelan-Mccall N., Dunn J. Why talk about mental states? The significance of children's conversations with friends, siblings, and mothers. Child Development 1996; 67: 836-849.

Bruner, J. *Acts of meaning*. Cambridge, MA: Harvard University Press, 1990.

Camaioni, L., Ercolani, A.P. , *Peabody Picture Vocabulary Test-revised*, Italian version under validation, Roma: Università "la Sapienza", 1998.

Carlson S.M., Moses L.J. Individual differences in inhibitory control and children's theory of mind. Child Development 2001; 72: 1032-1053.

Charman T., Shmueli-Goetz Y. The relationship between theory of mind, language, and narrative discourse: An experimental study. Cahiers de Psychologie Cogntive/Current Psychology of Cognition 1998; 17: 2, 245-271.

Cole K., Mitchell P. Family background in relation to deceptive ability and understanding of the mind. Social Development 1998; 7, 2: 181-197.

de Villiers, J.G., de Villiers, P.A. "Linguistic determinism and the understanding of false belief." In *Children's reasoning and the mind*, P. Mitchell, Riggs (Eds.), Hove: Psychology Press, 2000.

de Villiers J.G., Pyers, J.E. Complements to cognition: A longitudinal study of the relationship between complex syntax and false-belief-understanding. Cognitive Development 2002; 17: 1037-1060.

Dunn J., Brown J., Slomkowski C., Tesla C., Youngblade L. Young children's understanding of other people's feelings and beliefs: Individual differences and their antecedents. Child Development 1991; 62: 1352-1366.

Dunn, L.M., Dunn, J. *Peabody Picture Vocabulary Test – Revised*. Circle Pines: American Guidance Service, 1981.

Dunn J., Hughes C. Young children's understanding of emotions within close relationship. Cognition and Emotion 1998; 12: 171-190.

Fonagy P., Redfern S., Charman T. The Relationship between belief-desire reasoning and a projective measure of attachment security (SAT). British Journal of Developmental Psychology 1997; 15: 51-61.

Foote R.C., Holmes-Lonergan H.A. Sibling conflict and theory of mind. British Journal of Developmental Psychology 2003; 21: 45-58.

Furrow, D., Moore, C., Davdige, J., Chiasson, L. Mental terms in mothers and children speech: Similarities and relationships. Journal of Child Language 1992; 19: 617-631.

Gopnik A., Astington J.W. Children's understanding of representational change and its relation to understanding of false belief and the appearance-reality distinction. Child Development 1988; 59: 26-37.

Grice, P.H. "Logic and conversation." In *Syntax and semantics, 3 Speech acts*, P. Cole, J.L. Morgan (Eds.), New York: Academic Press, 1975.

Harris, P.L. *Children and emotion. The development of psychological understanding.* Oxford: Basic Blackwell, 1989.

Harris, P.L. "Desires, beliefs, and language." In *Theories of theories of mind*, P. Carruthers, P.K. Smith (Eds.), Cambridge: Cambridge University Press, 1996.

Harris P.L., Johnson C.N., Hutton D., Andrews G., Cooke T. Young children's theory of mind and emotion. Cognition & Emotion 1989; 3, 4: 379-400.

Harter S. The perceived competence scale for children. Child Development 1982; 53: 87-97.

Hove N., Petrakos H., Rinaldi C.M. All the sheep are dead. He murdered them: Sibling pretence, negotiation, internal state language, and relationship quality. Child Development 1998; 69: 82-191.

Hughes C., Dunn J. Understanding mind and emotion: Longitudinal associations with mental-state talk between young friends. Developmental Psychology 1998; 34(5): 1026-1037.

Jenkins J.M., Astington J.W. (1996). Cognitive factors and family structure associated with theory of mind development in young children. Developmental Psychology 1996; 32, 1: 70-78.

Lalonde C.E., Chandler M. False belief understanding goes to school: On the social-emotional consequences of coming early or late to a first theory of mind. Cognition and Emotion 1995; 9: 167-185.

Lee K., Olson D.R., Torrance N. Chinese children's understanding of false beliefs: The role of language. Journal of Child Language 1999; 26: 1-21.

Lewis C., Freeman N.H., Kyriakidou C., Maridaki-Kassotaki K., Berridge D.M. Social influences of false belief access: Specific sibling influences or general apprenticeship? Child Development 1996; 67: 2930-2947.

Meins E. *Security of attachment and the social development of cognition.* Hove: Psychology Press, 1997.

Meins E., Fernyough C., Russell J., Clark-Carter D. Security of attachment as a predictor of symbolic and mentalising abilities: A longitudinal study. Social Development 1998; 7: 1-24.

Meins E., Fernyough C., Wainwright R., Das Gupta M., Fradley E., Tuckey M. Maternal mind-mindedness and attachment security as predictors of theory of mind understanding. Child Development 2002; 73: 1715-1726.

Meins E., Fernyough C., Wainwright R., Clark-Carter D., Das Gupta M., Fradley E., Tuckey M. Pathways to understanding mind: Construct validity and predictive validity of maternal mind-mindedness. Child Development 2003; 74: 1194-1211.

Moore C., Pure K., Furrow D. Children's understanding of the modal expression of speaker certainty and uncertainty and its relation to the development of a representational theory of mind. Child Development 1990; 61: 722-730.

Olson, D.R., *Psychological theory and educational reform. How school remakes mind and society.* Cambridge: Cambridge University Press, 2003.

Olson, D.R., *The world on paper.* Cambridge: Cambridge University Press, 1994.

Olson D.R., Astington J.W. Thinking about thinking: Learning how take statements and hold beliefs. Educational Psychologist 1993; 28, 1: 7-23.

Ontai L.L., Thompson R.A. Patterns of attachment and maternal discourse effects on children's emotion understanding from 3 to 5 years of age. Social Development 2002; 11: 4, 433-450.

Pears K.C., Moses L.J. Demographics, parenting, and theory of mind in preschool children. Social Development 2003; 12, 1-20.

Pelletier J., Relations among theory of mind, metacognitive language, reading skills, and higher order story comprehension in L1 and L2 learners. XIth European Conference on Developmental Psychology, August 27-31; Milan, Italy: 2003.

Perner J., Leekam S.R., Wimmer H. Three-year-olds difficulty with false-belief: The case for a conceptual deficit. British Journal of Developmental Psychology 1987; 5: 125-137.

Perner J., Ruffman T., Leekam S.R. Theory of mind is contagious: You catch it from your sibs. Child Development 1994; 65: 1228-1238.

Perner J., Sprung M., Zauner P., Haider H. Want that is understood well before say that, think that, and false belief: A test of de Villiers's linguistic determinism on German-speaking children. Child Development 2003; 74: 179-188.

Perner J., Wimmer H. "John thinks that Mary thinks ...": Attribution of second-order beliefs by 5-to 10-year-old children. Journal of Experimental Child Psychology 1985; 5: 125-137.

Peterson C., Slaughter V. Opening windows into the mind: Mothers' preference for mental state explanations and children's theory of mind. Cognitive Development 2003; 18: 399-429.

Piaget, J., *La formation du symbole chez l'enfant*. Neuchatel: Delachaux & Niestlé, 1945.

Piaget, J., Inhelder, B., *La psychologie de l'enfant*. Paris: Presses Universitaires de France, 1966.

Pinker, S, *The language instinct*. New York: William Morrow and Company, 1994.

Ruffman T., Slade L., Crowe E. The relation between children's and mothers' mental state language and theory of mind understanding. Child Development 2002; 73: 3, 734-751.

Ruffman T., Slade L., Rowlandson K., Rumsey C., Gamham A. How language relates to belief, desire, and emotion understanding. Cognitive Development 2003; 18, 2: 139-158.

Ruffman T., Perner J., Naito M., Parkin L., Clements W.A. Older (but not younger) siblings facilitate false belief understanding. Developmental Psychology 1998; 34: 161-174.

Shatz, M. "Theory of mind and the development of social-linguistic intelligence in early childhood." In *Children's early understanding of mind: Origins and development,* C. Lewis, P. Mitchell (Eds.), Hillsdale: LEA, 1994.

Shatz M., Wellman H.M., Silber S. The acquisition of mental verbs: A systematic investigation of the first reference to mental state. Cognition 1983; 14: 301-321.

Siegal, M. *Knowing children: Experiments in conversation and cognition.* Washington: Psychology Press, 1997.

Sullivan K., Zaitchik D., Tager-Flusberg H., Preschoolers can attribute second-order beliefs. Developmental Psychology 1994; 30: 395-402.

Tardiff T., Wellman H.M. Acquisition of mental state language in Mandarin-and Cantonese-speaking children. Developmental Psychology 2000; 36: 25-43.

Vygotsky, L.S. (1934). *Thought and language*. Cambridge: MIT Press, 1962.

Watson A.C., Nixon C.L., Wilson A., Capage L. Social interaction skills and theory of mind in young children. Developmental Psychology 1999; 35, 386-391.

Wellman, H.M. "The origins of metacognition." In *Metacognition, cognition and human performance,* D.L. Forrest-Pressley, G.E. MacKinnon, T.G. Waller (Eds.), New York: Academic Press, 1985.

Wellman, H.M., Bartsch, K "Before belief: Children's early psychological theory." In *Children's early understanding of mind: Origins and development,* C. Lewis, P. Mitchell (Eds.), Hillsdale: LEA, 1994.

Wellman H.M., Cross D., Watson J. Meta-analysis of theory-of-mind development: The truth about false belief. Child Development 2001; 72: 655-684.

Wimmer H., Perner J Beliefs about beliefs: representation and constraining of wrong beliefs in young children understanding of deception. Cognition 1983; 13: 103-128.

Youngblade L.M., Dunn J. Individual differences in young children's pretend play with mother and sibling: Links to relationship and understanding of other people's feelings and beliefs. Child Development 1995; 66, 5: 1472-1492.

Chapter 2

THE MENTAL VERBS IN DIFFERENT CONCEPTUAL DOMAINS AND IN DIFFERENT CULTURES

David R. Olson,[1] Alessandro Antonietti,[2] Olga Liverta-Sempio,[3] Antonella Marchetti.[3]

[1]*HDAP, Ontario Institute for Studies in Education (OISE), University of Toronto;* [2]*Department of Psychology, Catholic University of the Sacred Heart, Milan.* [3]*The Theory of Mind Research Unit, Department of Psychology, Catholic University of the Sacred Heart, Milan.*

2.1   CULTURE, LITERACY, SCHOOL AND METAREPRESENTATION

This chapter focuses on relationships between the development of mental language comprehension and culture. In a wide sense, culture refers to the general system of values, beliefs, practices, as well as institutions, shared within a country. All these aspects of culture reach individuals through the semiotic mediation constituted by language. Such a mediating role of language acts both by means of the common syntactic, semantic and pragmatic grounds of language itself and by means of the specific communicative sub-systems developed by the different contexts of experience. Among a variety of educational agencies, in most countries it is specially and formally the school which has the task of introducing pupils into the mastery of the general linguistic competence as well as into the mastery of the domain-specific linguistic abilities.

In school settings the acquisition of both general and domain-specific linguistic capacities requires children to reflect about language itself, so prompting and enhancing metalinguistic competence. Such a kind of competence includes the awareness of the mental activity involved in language. This suggests a close relationship between metalinguistic and metacognitive skills. To give an example, metalinguistic competence allows children to separate the propositional content of an expression (what is said) from its illocutionary force (depending on the mental state of the speaker), so helping to consider statements independently on the agreement or the disagreement with the speaker. This separation, or lack of separation, can also affect adulthood. As Olson & Astington (1993) pointed out, the results of Luria's (1976) investigations about illiterate adults' reasoning showed that these persons focused onto the statements of the syllogisms that they were asked to solve, by considering them merely as expressions of the interviewer's beliefs (illocutionary) instead of considering their propositional content. Furthermore, to discover the tacit inferences implied in talk and in written texts people must often identify the mental states underlying words. Finally, the language of schooling is also the language of epistemology: it allows us to talk about beliefs and reasons for believing (Astington, Pelletier & Homer, 2002; Burr & Hofer, 2002; Olson, 2003).

Literacy, starting from the already existing abilities, promotes the mastery of metalinguistic and metacognitive competencies needed to understand other's mind expressed by formal texts by which disciplines transmit different kinds of knowledge (Olson & Astington, 1993; Olson & Homer, 1996; Olson & Torrance, 1996; Groppo, Antonietti, Liverta-Sempio & Marchetti, 1999). School should favour (at least in the higher degrees of instruction) the capacity to connect the contents of the disciplines taught with the aims and intentions of those who first worked them out. This should have a double effect. First, it could avoid the pupil to build up a misleading concept of knowledge, viewed as uniquely objective, not dependent on the perspectives and motives of its proposes. Second, it would help to understand the ways by which knowledge is acquired, thus favouring the identification of the tools necessary to construct knowledge itself.

Olson & Astington (1993) stressed how mental verbs are central to the process of education and the role that schooling may play in their acquisition (Astington, 1998). Literacy, they argued, enhances metalinguistic and metacognitive skills through the discussion in school of what texts say, mean, claim, prove, and so forth, namely, some concepts central to disciplined knowledge. The Vygotskyan derivation of the approach (see also Astington, 1996) appears in the idea that literacy is not simply built on the acquired level of cognitive development but contributes to re-structure cognition itself (Olson, 1996). In fact, literacy activities lead one to listen to and to think about language in a new way. They do not only promote the capacity to "write" the speech; they provide children with a scriptic model to be used in thinking about language. The script-as-model (Olson, 1994; Olson & Homer, 1996; Homer & Olson, 1999) predicts that in learning the script of their culture, children are also acquiring a model to think about language.

Consequently, Olson & Astington (1993) claimed that teachers should talk more about what they themselves think, know, expect, remember, wonder about, guess, assume, infer, conclude and so on, and need to encourage students to do the same. By consciously introducing and using such language about thinking in the classroom, teachers will lead students to reflect on and articulate their thinking and its expression. Texts are not to be learned: they are to be interpreted. And interpretation is, in part, a matter of assigning the appropriate attitude or force to the utterance. Learning is deciding how a statement is to be taken.

In this perspective, metalinguistic and metacognitive terms provide both language for thinking and language about thinking, allowing the speaker to communicate his/her stance towards a proposition. One of the ways in which preschoolers' development of a theory of mind first becomes evident is in their use of simple metacognitive and metalinguistic vocabulary (Bretherton & Beeghly, 1982; Shatz et al., 1983). While children are acquiring this vocabulary, they are coming to understand more about minds and thoughts (Astington & Gopnik, 1991).

Research on children's understanding of mental verbs has grown in importance during the last fifteen years, dealing mainly with the following topics: the chronology of acquisition of such terms (Misciones et al., 1978; Wellman & Johnson, 1979; Breterthon & Beeghly, 1982; Shatz et al., 1983; Shatz, 1994; Astington & Olson, 1990; Wellman & Bartsch, 1994; Bartsch & Wellman, 1995; Camaioni & Longobardi, 1997); the psychological use of mental lexicon (Breterthon & Beeghly, 1982; Shatz et al., 1983; Olson & Torrance, 1987; Shatz, 1994; Siegal & Peterson, 1995; Olson, 1997; Camaioni, Longogardi & Bellagamba, 1998; Zanobini, Scopesi & Cattani, 1998); the referents of mental lexicon (Breterthon & Beeghly, 1982; Shatz et al., 1983); the relationship between mother's use and child's development of mental state language (Furrow, Moore, Davidge & Chiasson, 1992; Jenkins et al. 2003); the understanding of the polysemic nature of cognitive verbs as "to know" (Booth & Hall, 1995).

As regards this last topic, a hierarchical six-levels model has been proposed, which organizes the meaning of cognitive verbs from the less to the most abstract and difficult from a conceptual point of view (respectively, "to know" as act of perception and "to know" as belief or attitude towards the truth of a statement) (Booth & Hall, 1995).

Finally, the topic which has elicited and continues to elicit the biggest amount of studies is the relationship between theory of mind development and the use of mental language.

From this perspective, the object of investigation is mothers' or children's mental language in daily interaction within the family and children's theory of mind development (see Dunn, Bretheton & Munn, 1987; Dunn et al, 1991; Dunn, 1994; Antonietti, Liverta-Sempio, Marchetti &

Astington in this volume). It is worth noticing that in these studies the mental language is examined in everyday life, while cognitive and in general epistemic mental verbs are especially used in the formal contexts of disciplines, where they can assume particular meanings deriving from the specific discipline considered. Or example, "to think" can be use in mathematics to mean "to evaluate" (e.g. "What do you "think" is the result of 31x5?" "I think - that is "I evaluate" - it is about 150") and in natural sciences to mean "to predict" (e.g., "What do you "think" will happen if a glass falls down?". "I think" – that is "I predict" - it will be broken"). The polysemic nature of mental verbs depends also on the context of use or discursive practice within which the verb is mentioned.

Following these considerations it seems important to determine if metalinguistic/metacognitive competencies we are dealing with represent a general acquisition, crossing the specific domains of knowledge, or if their developmental patterns vary depending on the particular domain they are applied to. Metalinguistic/metacognitive awareness might be a system consisting in a series of separately acquired subsystems which can be responsible for the observed décalages. That is, performance may depend on the specific kind of metalinguistic/metacognitive ability under investigation and on the more or less explicit understanding required by the task. Furthermore, since culture gives children the model to be used to think about language, there will be relevant cross-cultural differences as far as metalinguistic/metacognitive awareness is concerned.

The present chapter moves from these general considerations to investigate the relationships between the cultural activity of literacy and the development of the language to think and talk about the mind. An important assumption of this work is that metalinguistic/metacognitive abilities are adequately represented by children's understanding of metalinguistic and metacognitive verbs. The first purpose of this research is to investigate the development of these abilities as a function of cultural and literacy demands of different school levels.

Secondly, do these metarepresentational competencies represent a general acquisition, crossing the specific domains of knowledge, or do their developmental patterns vary depending on the particular domain they are applied to? The question is relevant since, as we have said, school represents the institutional context aimed at promoting the capacities here considered. For this reason, the second purpose of this research is to investigate the relation between appearance of metalinguistic and metacognitive abilities across domains of knowledge. Three different domains have been considered: folk psychology, history, and mathematics. Specifically, the first (folk psychology) represents a "control" domain because it is not an object of formalised teaching (at least in the general school curriculum), whereas the other two are taught beginning in Primary School. Considering Brunerian distinction between "narrative" and "paradigmatic" thought (Bruner, 1986), we can say that mathematics relies on a more formal or paradigmatic way of thinking whereas history relies on a narrative way of thinking. This justifies the choice of these two disciplines.

Thirdly, are there cross-cultural differences in children's acquisition of metarepresentational concepts? Although the difficulties of developing tests which are comparable across cultures is well known, an attempt was made to compare children's knowledge of these concepts across different countries: Italy, Canada, Serbia, and Tanzania. Differences, if found, may reflect the curriculum of study or the structure of language itself.

Thus, to summarise, the following variables should be manipulated in the three studies here reported:
- school level;
- domain of knowledge (history vs. mathematics vs. folk psychology);
- cultural-linguistic context (Italy vs. Canada vs. Serbia vs. Tanzania).

2.2   A TEST TO ASSESS THE UNDERSTANDING OF METAREPRESENTATIONAL VERBS

The investigation is based on a series of trials whose goal is to assess the ability to understand metacognitive and metalinguistic verbs. These trials are grounded on a task devised by Astington & Olson (1990). Three different versions have been constructed; each version concerns a specific domain of knowledge (folk psychology, history, and mathematics). Trials are arranged as follows. For each target verb a short story is presented. In such story a general metacognitive or metalinguistic verb (to think or to say) occurs. Subject's task is to select the correct response among four possible answers. The correct response corresponds to the specific metarepresentational verb (for instance, to hypothesise or to conclude) which can be used instead of the general verb. Students must substitute the general verb to think or to say with the appropriate metacognitive or metalinguistic verb.

An example of item is reported above:

Jim learned from his history teacher that Napoleon won battles because he was an experienced general. Jim is now reading the story of a battle where a small army led by an old experienced general was fighting against a large army led by a young general. Jim *thinks* that the battle would be won by the old general. However, when he goes on reading, he realises that the battle was won by the young general.

A. Jim predicts
B. Jim knows
C. Jim interprets
D. Jim implies

The complete sets of items are reported in the Appendix.

Appropriateness of the correct response was tested by asking 5 adults with a high level of education to find out a good, specific synonymous for the verb to say or to think within each story. In all cases they agreed selecting the more precise term corresponding to the target verb for that story. In each story, in addition to the correct target verb, three incorrect verbs served as distractors. Distractors were set up as follows: one incorrect answer was another (incorrect for that story) target verb randomly selected among the eight remaining target verbs so that each target verb occurred as incorrect answer the same number of times; the other two incorrect answers were two filler verbs selected randomly among a list of metarepresentational verbs used by Astington & Olson (1990) that differed from those which have been chosen as target (e.g., to understand, to believe, to demonstrate, to explain). The order of the correct and of the wrong answers was varied systematically in each story.

The nine considered verbs are, by following the Astington & Olson's (1990) distinction:

- *metacognitive verbs*: to assume, to doubt, to hypothesise, to infer, to remember;

- *metalinguistic verbs*: to admit, to conclude, to confirm, to predict.

These verbs were selected from the twelve utilised by Astington & Olson (1990); three verbs - namely, to assert, to interpret, and to imply - have been excluded because a direct counterpart was not available in Italian.

In the present study the original structure of the task has been changed to avoid some methodological flaws. More precisely, the order of presentation of the items and the order of the four possible responses in each item have been counterbalanced. Furthermore, in each item the three wrong responses are varied systematically so that their meaning is neither too close nor too far from the meaning of the correct response.

For each target verb three different versions of the story - each corresponding to one of the three specific domain of knowledge considered here (folk psychology, history, and mathematics) - have been provided. The task pertaining each domain was articulated in 9 different versions so that each story could be presented to participants in each of the 9 possible positions the same number of trials. We attempted to write stories of almost the same length and whose protagonist was a male in about half the number of times and a female in the other half. Furthermore, the verb to say or to think was always used at the present tense.

2.3 MENTAL VERBS IN DIFFERENT DOMAINS

The task was presented to two-hundred and seven Italian students, divided in the following school levels:

- Grade 3 (eight years of age) and 5 (ten years of age) of Primary School (respectively: 20 males plus 14 females and 20 males plus 24 females);

- Grade 2 (twelve years of age) of Junior High School (19 males plus 17 females);

- Grade 2 (fourteen years of age) of Senior High School (20 males plus 22 females);

- undergraduates attending different faculties (25 males plus 26 females, ranging in age from twenty to twenty-five years of age).

All students lived in a Lombardia, a region of northern Italy.

The first two subsamples (Grade 3 and 5) were constituted in order to study the development of metarepresentational competencies in children younger than ones considered in Astington & Olson's (1990) study, in which the youngest subsample was drawn from Grade 6 children; we can presume that in earlier ages children should have acquired adequate metarepresentational abilities and basic literacy skills needed to perform in the task. The first four subsamples were separated by 2 years of age in order to evaluate very precisely possible developmental changes. Undergraduates were included as the alleged endpoint in the development of the competence under investigation; their performances should be used to evaluate possible gaps observed in the preceding school levels.

Items presented to half primary school pupils were conjugated in the grammatically correct way (using the subjunctive mood of the verb where needed); items presented to the remaining primary school pupils were conjugated using the same verbal mood appearing in the story. We devised this procedure believing that younger subjects could be affected by the grammatical "surface" of the verb in choosing their answer among the four proposed verbs[1].

The researcher explained to students that an anonymous, non-evaluative task will be presented to them. Students were asked to give only one answer for each item. The task was individually administered without temporal limitations.

The whole set of trials was submitted to students over two days: the first day the task concerned one domain of knowledge; the following day the other two domains. The order of the presentation of three domains has been counterbalanced across participants.

---

[1] In Italian the form of the subjunctive mood of verbs is different from the form of the indicative mood.

Score "1" was assigned to each correct answer and score "0" to each wrong answer. For each participant a total score (minimum = 0; maximum = 9) was computed for each domain by counting the number of correct responses he or she answered in that domain. For instance, if a student identified the correct verb in three stories out of the nine provided, the score "3" was assigned to that student.

As far as the possible effects of verbal mood are concerned, we found that neither verbs' conjugation nor interaction between this factor and school level have been shown to be significant.[2] We did not obtain significant gender effects except in three cases: *to admit* in folk psychology and in history and *to doubt* in mathematics: in all these cases females outperformed males. Analyses of total scores in each domain showed that in folk psychology and mathematics females were significant more correct than males.

Comparing students from humanistic faculties with students from scientific faculties, a significant difference emerges only in the case of the verb *to assume* in the domain of mathematics, where students from humanistic faculties were significantly more correct than students attending scientific courses. Furthermore, humanities students performed significantly better than scientific students also as regards total scores.

By considering the developmental trend, we notice that the acquisition of metarepresentational verbs is a complex process, lasting till advanced school grades. In fact, even undergraduates did not reach perfect performance (only the verb *to admit* in folk psychology domain obtained the maximum of correct answers). Undergraduates succeeded within wide ranges of variation (especially for metacognitive verbs), reaching higher levels of performance as far as metalinguistic verbs are concerned (Table 1). The developmental trend varies both within the same verb in different domains and between different verbs in the same domain. Post hoc analyses showed a variety of patterns of homogeneous subgroups of school levels. For instance, significant differences occurred between primary students (Grade 3 and 5) and the older ones (*to remember* in history); only Grade 3 primary children performed significantly worse than other participants (*to hypothesise* in history); undergraduates outperformed significantly all the other levels (*to predict* in mathematics); Primary School pupils (Grade 3 and 5) gave a significant lower number of correct responses than Junior School students who, in turn, gave a lower number of right responses than High School students and undergraduates (*to conclude* in folk psychology) (Table 1). The overall picture suggests that metalinguistic verbs are mastered before metacognitive verbs and that the former ones are in general easier to identify than the latter ones as proved by the overall mean of correct responses (0.62

---

[2] Detailed statistical analyses are reported in Antonietti, Liverta-Sempio & Marchetti (1998a; 1998b).

vs. 0.50) and by the ranges of the means which is from 0.49 to 0.77 in the first case and from 0.33 to 0.61 in the second case.

Table 1– Mean Numbers of Correct Answers under each School Level for each Verb in each Domain (First Study)

Verb	Primary School Grade 3	Primary School Grade 5	Junior High School Grade 2	Senior High School Grade 2	University
To admit					
psychology	0.61	0.87	0.81	0.94	1.00
history	0.71	0.66	0.72	0.93	0.86
mathematics	0.43	0.57	0.69	0.81	0.89
To assume					
psychology	0.32	0.49	0.61	0.61	0.62
history	0.68	0.70	0.81	0.69	0.67
mathematics	0.27	0.45	0.44	0.33	0.36
To conclude					
psychology	0.20	0.28	0.50	0.83	0.94
history	0.27	0.55	0.78	0.88	0.76
mathematics	0.11	0.32	0.39	0.72	0.91
To confirm					
psychology	0.61	0.57	0.81	0.89	0.96
History	0.47	0.57	0.61	0.76	0.65
mathematics	0.36	0.49	0.58	0.86	0.72
To doubt					
psychology	0.23	0.47	0.42	0.78	0.81
History	0.26	0.45	0.47	0.64	0.65
mathematics	0.16	0.51	0.58	0.64	0.81
To hypothesise					
psychology	0.14	0.30	0.47	0.44	0.62
History	0.18	0.45	0.57	0.69	0.69
mathematics	0.05	0.06	0.06	0.14	0.04
To infer					
psychology	0.07	0.36	0.36	0.69	0.53
History	0.29	0.39	0.50	0.69	0.86
mathematics	0.16	0.51	0.58	0.64	0.81
To predict					
psychology	0.25	0.64	0.64	0.75	0.79
History	0.36	0.52	0.67	0.64	0.61
mathematics	0.20	0.13	0.19	0.28	0.60

Tab. 1 cont.

Verb	Primary School Grade 3	Primary School Grade 5	Junior High School Grade 2	Senior High School Grade 2	University
To remember					
psychology	0.59	0.60	0.56	0.75	0.66
History	0.30	0.27	0.56	0.69	0.76
mathematics	0.57	0.72	0.67	0.72	0.72
Total					
psychology	3.02	4.57	5.17	6.69	6.91
History	3.51	4.57	5.81	6.62	6.39
mathematics	2.41	3.70	4.03	5.08	5.96

If we consider the total scores obtained in each domain (Table 1), we realise that in mathematics the highest number of significant increases among school levels emerged (Grade 3 of Primary School vs. Grade 5 Primary and Junior School vs. High School vs. University); at the opposite, only a significant increase occurred (from Primary School to the subsequent grades) in history. The three domains shared the presence of a significant change at the primary school level: from Grade 3 to 5 in folk psychology and mathematics; from Grade 5 and junior school in history.

As regards the three domains of knowledge, in some verbs the metarepresentational ability under investigation was modulated by the domain. For instance, as far as the verb *to hypothesise* was concerned, we noticed that the rates of correct identifications were markedly lower in mathematics (0.07) as compared to folk psychology (0.39) and history (0.53) and that such a trend was present at each school level. The same trend can be observed in the verb *to assume*, even though marked differences between mathematics and the other domains have recorded from junior school to university but not in primary school.

Some verbs are more difficult overall such as *to assume*, *to doubt*, and *to conclude*, but there is considerable variability across items and domains. The wide range of variation in the acquisition of the metarepresentational verbs shows that we dealing with "families" of verbs inherently heterogeneous. The meaning of these verbs appears to be strongly situated and depending on the specific context of occurrence. We suggest that it can depend on the higher "concreteness" of thinking about of speech acts compared with thinking about thinking: the former are more instantiated in social relationships and exchanges, whereas the latter, though originating from communication, ends in internalisation and abstraction.

Table 2 - Mean Numbers of Correct Answers to each Verb Ordered in Term of Difficulty According to the Total Scores (Second Study)

	Canada	Italy	Total
Metacognitive verbs			
to assume	.59	.57	.58
to remember	.43	.58	.52
to doubt	.35	.39	.37
to infer	.39	.36	.37
to hypothesize	.21	.28	.25
Metalinguistic verbs			
to confirm	.41	.55	.49
to admit	.22	.65	.47
to conclude	.28	.35	.38
to predict	.38	.38	.38

2.4 A CROSS-CULTURAL COMPARISON BETWEEN TWO WESTERN COUNTRIES

The first study suggested that the period between Primary and Junior School is critical in the development of mental verb comprehension. Thus, we were induced to deepen the analysis of such a period through by administering the same test to a new sample of children. A further aim of our second study was to acquire information about the response patterns to the test in different cultural contexts, by choosing an environment like Italy which is considered belonging to the Western culture, but in another continent.

Sixty Canadian and sixty Italian students volunteered for the study. In each country three school levels were chosen: Primary School Grade 3 (8 years of age), Primary School Grade 5 (10 years of age), and Junior High School Grade 7[3] (12 years of age). Twenty students were selected at each grade level in each country according to the following procedure. Two schools judged to be typical of their regions (respectively, the provinces of Ontario and Lombardia) were selected for each country. In each school, for each level, two classes, again judged as typical of the school, were picked. In each class 10 students were selected randomly among a group of volunteers.[4] Because of some omissions in the protocols, some participants have been

---

[3] In this cross-national study we adopt the labels of the North American school system: Junior High School Grade 7 corresponded to the Junior High School Grade 2 in the Italian school system where the number of grades begins again from 1 by passing from the Primary School to the Junior High School.

[4] We thank Dr. Vittoria Ardino for contacting the schools participating in the study, for test administering, and for collaboration in data analyses.

excluded; this accounts for the differences in the number of participants considered in each analysis.

The study was carried out within the school environment during the school day. The researcher explained to students that an anonymous, non-evaluative task would be presented to them. The materials and the procedure were the same as in the first study. The stories constituting the test were translated into English by applying the backward translation procedure (Hambleton, 1994; Sperber, Devellis & Boehlecke, 1994).

Table 2 shows the mean total scores recorded under each school level by each country.[5] As far as the folk psychology domain is concerned, significant effects due to the country and to school level emerged; the interaction between these two factors was not significant. At each school level Italian students performed better than Canadian ones. The ability to identify the correct target verb increased across school level in both countries: Primary School Grade 3 children obtained a mean total score significantly lower than the other grades, which were not significantly different each other. In the history domain school level significantly affected responses, whereas no significant differences between Canada and Italy occurred; the interaction between these two variables was not significant. In mathematics, Italian students obtained scores higher than Canadian participants in all school levels. The higher the school level, the higher was the metarepresentational ability; also in this case Primary School Grade 5 and Junior High School students outperformed Primary School Grade 3 students. The two factors did not interact. It is worth noticing that under each school level mean scores in the domain of folk psychology and history were higher than in mathematics.

On the whole, by looking at mean scores, we observed the following patterns:

1. A regular growth of metalinguistic and metacognitive abilities emerges with regards to school level. This result is applicable for both Canada and Italy. To a greater or a lesser degree Grade 3 students performed more poorly compared to Grade 5 and Junior High students as post hoc tests showed in all domains.

2. Folk psychology had the highest number of correct answers.

3. Italian students performed better than Canadian: total scores showed that in mathematics and folk psychology Italian students may have a more shaped metarepresentational knowledge than Canadian students at all school levels considered here.

Figure 1 reports proportions of correct answers for each verb by collapsing all students (across age level and country of origin. The most recognisable verbs were two metacognitive verbs (*to remember* and *to*

---

[5] Detailed statistical analyses are reported in Groppo, Antonietti, Ardino, Liverta-Sempio, Marchetti & Olson (2000).

assume). It is worth noticing that, whereas the first verb is quite used both in Canada and Italy, the second is seldom employed. Thus, it seems that the ability to recognise the proper meaning of metarepresentational verbs is relatively independent from the frequency with which such verbs occur in everyday language but it may be learned in school. Difficulty of a verb might also depend on the distinctiveness of the distractors. For instance, the verb *to remember* might be easy to identify because none of the other target verbs and none of the filler verbs has a meaning close to that of *to remember*; conversely, *to hypothesise* might be difficult to identify because it is partially overlapping with *to believe*. However, this claim can not be maintained with respect to verbs such as *to assume* - which is well-recognised even though it might be confused with *to hypothesise*, *to believe* or *to doubt* whose meaning can not be confused with other target and filler verbs.

Italy

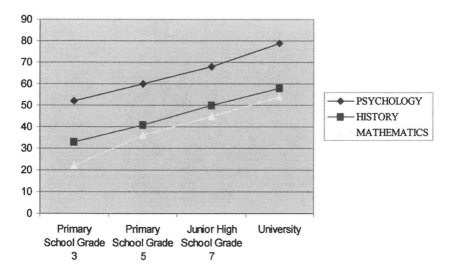

Serbia

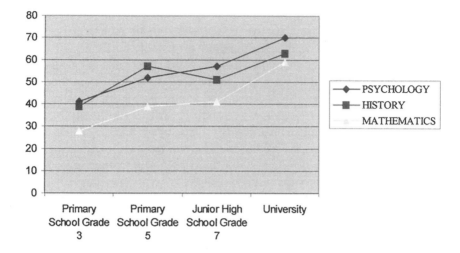

Tanzania

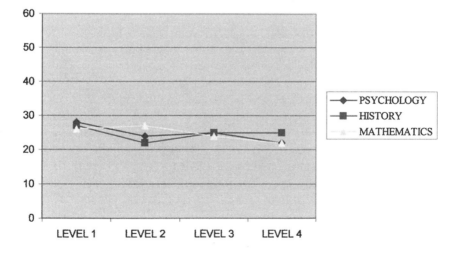

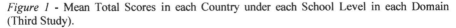

Figure 1 - Mean Total Scores in each Country under each School Level in each Domain (Third Study).

Table 3 gives a detailed report of proportions of correct responses for each verb in each domain under each school level both for Canadian and Italian students. This table allows one to figure out the effects on performance produced by the independent variables. For example we could focus attention on the verb *to remember*: on the whole, this verb was less recognised in folk psychology than in the other two domains; furthermore

Italians showed an improvement across school level while Canadian students showed a decreasing proportion of correct, perhaps because they preferred a more technical term.

In order to have an overview of the effects observed in the set of the 9 verbs here studied, we can underline the following issues. As regard to the developmental trend, we can notice that an increase of the proportion of correct answers across school level occurred in 10 out of 27 cases (these 27 cases resulted by multiplying the 9 verbs by the 3 domains) in the Canadian subsample and in 16 out of 27 cases the Italian subsample. Thus, it seems that Italian students increased their metarepresentational competencies across school levels to a larger extent than Canadian ones. Moreover, this kind of improvement appeared in 9 out of 18 cases (these 18 cases resulted by multiplying the 9 verbs by the 2 countries) in the folk psychology domain, in 10 out of 18 cases in history, and in 6 out of 18 cases in mathematics. This suggests that items were more discriminating in the Italian form than in English.

To consider the influence of the domains on the verbs, we collapsed responses given under the three school levels and in the two countries and found out that in 6 verbs (*to admit, to assume, to confirm, to doubt, to hypothesise* and *to predict*) rates of correct answers in mathematics were lower than in the other domains; students recognised the verb *to admit* and *to hypothesise* in history better than in the other domains; in folk psychology participants obtained rates higher than in the other domain with the verbs *to conclude, to doubt* and *to assume* and lower rates with the verb *to infer* and *to remember*. In conclusion, there was evidence that at all school levels participants had the greatest difficulty in identifying the correct verb in mathematics, whereas the easiest domain was folk psychology for the younger children, history for the middle school level, and both history and folk psychology for the oldest subjects.

As far as the effects due to the country were concerned, if we examine global performances (by combining responses given under each school level), we can observe that Italians outperformed Canadians in all the 9 verbs in folk psychology and in 6 out of 9 verbs both in history and mathematics. Also this analysis showed that differences between the two countries are larger in folk psychology than in the other domains. If we collapse responses given in each school level in the three domains, we notice that in Primary School Grade 3 Canadian outperformed Italian students in 12 cases, whereas Italians outperformed Canadians in 14 cases (in 1 cases they obtained the same response rate); in Primary School Grade 5 Canadian outperformed Italian students in 8 cases whereas Italians outperformed Canadians in 19 cases; in Junior High Grade 7 Canadian outperformed Italian students in 7 cases whereas Italians outperformed Canadians in 20 cases. In sum, differences between the two countries increased along with grade level.

A first finding of the study was that metarepresentational abilities show some development with age but are quite limited even in Junior High School students. Furthermore they vary in a widely across verbs. Total scores give an overall picture of the ability to recognise the meaning of metalinguistic and metacognitive verbs but hide interesting differences among verbs which the present study has allowed us to highlight. Variations in correctly identifying the mental verbs are likely to depend more on a strong variability among the meanings of the mental terms employed in the study than on the variability among the steps followed in the acquisition of a mental lexicon. A possible explanation stresses the influence of the context of the stories and of the alternative verbs offered in each case on the identification of the correct synonyms for the general mental verbs. Whichever explanation we adopt, variability might be connected with the discursive practices appropriate to specific situations.

Variability in performance allowed us to rank metacognitive verbs from the easiest to the most difficult to be identified as follows (see Table 2, total scores): to assume, to doubt, to hypothesise, to infer, to remember. This ranking could be explained by referring to the different use frequencies of metarepresentational verbs in, respectively, everyday speech and school speech. However, this seems not to be the case because, for example, to infer - which is seldom used in everyday language but sometimes occurs in school language - is recognised at the same extent as to doubt - which is often used also in common language. A possible alternative explanation is that talking about the already available knowledge (e.g., memories) is easier than talking about the construction of knowledge itself (e.g., inferences). In other words, considering the particular set of the verbs analysed in this study, we can say that mental verbs like "to infer" elicit the idea of a mind which is building knowledge (that is a process), whereas verbs like to remember mainly refer to the existing products of cognition. As far as the patterns of responses to each verb within each domain (Table 3) was concerned, we can observe that the relative degree of difficulty varies according to the domain. For instance, the verbs *to doubt* and *to hypothesise* are the most poorly recognised verbs within mathematics at all school levels, presumably because this subject is perceived by students as the domain of certainty and not of conjectural knowledge. Conversely, regards history *to infer* and *to hypothesise* are the best recognised verbs at all school levels because it is likely that in this domain argumentation is prevalently conjectural. An interesting finding concerns the verb *to remember*. Even though such a verb is one of the best recognised verb in general (Table 2), at each school level it is the worst within the folk psychology domain and the best within mathematics: this suggests that *to remember* is conceived by pupils as the typical "school" verb, connected with the traditional instructional activities (to study and to remember).

A further evidence regarding the development of metarepresentational awareness concerns the different trend shown by Canadian versus Italian students: it seems that Italian students improved in performance across school levels to a larger extent than Canadian ones. This difference might derive from: (1) linguistic factors, (2) test factors, (3) use-frequency factors, and (4) instructional factors.

1. The different structures of the English and Italian language might affect performance in the task; for instance, the items did not contain phrasal verbs which are typical for English but not for Italian.

2. Italian students might get an advantage from the fact that the test material was originally written in Italian and then translated into English (even though the accuracy of the English version was controlled through the back-translation procedure).

3. A crucial factor could be the different use frequency of the mental verbs used in the test within each country; for example, in some cases in English, but not in Italian, a more colloquial verb is available to replace a technical verb which was employed (e.g., "to figure out" or "to guess" instead of "to infer").

4. The specific frequency can interact with instructional variables which are cultural in nature, such as the different educational practices of the two countries, curricula, organisational characteristics of the school systems, teachers' course of study, evaluation criteria.

Table 3 - Mean Numbers of Correct Answers for each Verb under each Domain in each School Level (Second Study)

Verb	Domain											
	Folk Psychology				History				Mathematics			
	Primary School Grade 3	Primary School Grade 5	Junior High School Grade 7	Tot	Primary School Grade 3	Primary School Grade 5	Junior High School Grade 7	Tot	Primary School Grade 3	Primary School Grade 5	Junior High School Grade 7	Tot
Metacognitive Verbs												
to doubt												
Canada	0.64	0.40	0.25	0.42	0.47	0.50	0.47	0.48	0.09	0.24	0.16	0.17
Italy	0.40	0.60	0.40	0.47	0.21	0.30	0.42	0.31	0.05	0.55	0.55	0.38
Total	0.52	0.50	0.32	0.44	0.34	0.40	0.44	0.39	0.07	0.39	0.35	0.27
to hypothesise												
Canada	0.07	0.13	0.06	0.09	0.40	0.50	0.40	0.43	0.09	0.18	0.11	0.13
Italy	0.20	0.55	0.70	0.48	0.11	0.20	0.53	0.28	0.05	0.05	0.10	0.07
Total	0.13	0.24	0.38	0.28	0.25	0.35	0.46	0.35	0.07	0.11	0.10	0.10

table 3 cont.

Verb	Domain											
	Folk Psychology				History				Mathematics			
	Primary School Grade 3	Primary School Grade 5	Junior High School Grade 7	Tot	Primary School Grade 3	Primary School Grade 5	Junior High School Grade 7	Tot	Primary School Grade 3	Primary School Grade 5	Junior High School Grade 7	Tot
to infer												
Canada	0.21	0.20	0.56	0.33	0.47	0.58	0.40	0.48	0.27	0.41	0.37	0.36
Italy	0.15	0.55	0.50	0.40	0.11	0.30	0.42	0.28	0.30	0.45	0.45	0.40
Total	0.18	0.37	0.53	0.36	0.29	0.44	0.21	0.38	0.28	0.43	0.41	0.38
to predict												
Canada	0.21	0.20	0.56	0.33	0.20	0.42	0.67	0.43	0.27	0.41	0.42	0.38
Italy	0.35	0.50	0.60	0.48	0.21	0.70	0.58	0.50	0.20	0.15	0.15	0.17
Total	0.28	0.35	0.58	0.40	0.20	0.56	0.62	0.46	0.23	0.28	0.28	0.27
to remember												
Canada	0.36	0.47	0.31	0.38	0.60	0.42	0.40	0.48	0.64	0.41	0.32	0.43
Italy	0.30	0.40	0.55	0.42	0.47	0.75	0.58	0.60	0.60	0.75	0.85	0.73
Total	0.33	0.43	0.43	0.40	0.53	0.58	0.49	0.54	0.62	0.58	0.58	0.58
Metalinguistic Verbs												
to admit												
Canada	.07	.20	.13	.13	.07	.42	.47	.31	.18	.24	.26	.23
Italy	.80	.75	.65	.73	.58	.75	.79	.71	.40	.50	.65	.52
Total	.43	.47	.39	.43	.32	.58	.63	.51	.29	.37	.45	.37
to assume												
Canada	.43	.53	.81	.60	.47	.50	.67	.55	.36	.53	.84	.62
Italy	.80	.70	.70	.73	.47	.55	.68	.57	.40	.30	.50	.40
Total	.61	.61	.75	.56	.47	.52	.67	.56	.38	.41	.67	.51
to conclude												
Canada	.21	.27	.56	.36	.20	.00	.47	.24	.27	.18	.32	.26
Italy	.25	.50	.70	.48	.21	.15	.53	.29	.00	.30	.55	.28
Total	.23	.48	.63	.42	.20	.07	.50	.26	.13	.24	.43	.27
to confirm												
Canada	.43	.43	.63	.50	.33	.67	.40	.45	.18	.24	.37	.28
Italy	.45	.50	.65	.53	.47	.55	.79	.60	.40	.45	.70	.52
Total	.44	.42	.64	.51	.40	.61	.54	.52	.29	.34	.53	.40

2.5 A CROSS-CULTURAL COMPARISON BETWEEN THREE COUNTRIES: ITALY, SERBIA, TANZANIA

A third study was carried out to compare country which differ in a larger extent than the two previously considered. The variables taken into account in this investigation were, as in the previous studies, different grades of schooling (from primary school to the university) and different domains of knowledge (folk psychology, history, mathematics). Participants belonged to the following countries:
- Italy (students living in Milan and in neighbourhood);
- Serbian Republic (students attending schools in Beograd)[6];
- Tanzania (participants come from three schools in the villages of Did^a and Bug^si, near the city Shinyànga, in the north-western part of the country.[7]

The same test used in the previous studies was employed. It was translated both in Serbo-Croatian and in Swahili by following the same procedure (backward translation) adopted for the translation form Italian to English.

After the experimenters has been training, the test has been administered to the selected groups. The data which allowed us to compare Italy and Serbia were obtained from the following subgroups of participants:

	Primary School Grade 3	Primary School Grade 5	High Junior High School Grade 7	University	Whole sample
ITALY	41	52	31	53	177
SERBIAN REPUBLIC	26	18	25	47	116

In Tanzania the subgroups of participants were differently structured than in Italy and in Serbia depending on the particular aspects of schooling in that country. In Tanzania the formal educational system consists of: a 7-year primary stage, beginning when pupils are seven-year-old; a 6-year secondary stage, which starts passing a selection mainly based on

---

[6] We thank Dr. Luca Valtorta for contacting the schools participating in the study and for test administration.
[7] We thank Dr. Eleonora Riva for finding the schools participating in the research and for test administration.

evaluations achieved in primary stage; and vocational education and university studies of varying length. Even though the general structure of the school system is not very different from Italy and Tanzania, the congruence between students' age and class attended is very weak. In fact in Tanzania pupils can start attending school one or two years after the due time of seven years of age for different reasons: the school building is too far away from home and parents prefer to wait their son/daughter growing up to send him/her to school; a school is built nearby the house and the child, who did not go to school when he/she was seven-eight –year-old because of the distance, starts now in the new school. Entering secondary school can be delayed for the same reasons, or to get the opportunity given to pupils to repeat primary school's courses to achieve better evaluations so passing the selection. Furthermore private secondary schools often offer students one year of preparation to the school itself. Finally it is worth noticing that the Tanzanian education suffers of various difficulties, among them: teacher absenteeism, large classes, high student dropout rate, gender inequality, poor academic achievement (Malmberg, Wanner, Sura & Little, 2001).

In consideration of these characteristics of the Tanzanian students, the test was administered in primary stage starting from Grade 3 (since the two preceding grades are devoted to early literacy) and in every class of the secondary stage. In Tanzania 518 subjects took part in the study, divided between primary and secondary schools as follows:

TANZANIA	SCHOOL LEVEL. 1 Primary 3-4-5	SCHOOL LEVEL 2 Primary 6-7	SCHOOL LEVEL 3 Secondary 1	SCHOOL LEVEL 4 Secondary 2	Total
Age Level 1 (7-13 yrs.)	106	21	2	-	127
Age Level 2 (14-15 yrs.)	27	61	46	-	144
Age Level 3 (16-17 yrs.)	5	14	80	23	124
Age Level 4 (18-22 yrs.)	-	5	53	75	133
Total	138	101	181	98	518

By considering percentages of correct responses in each verb, if we focus on the Italy-Serbia comparison, we observe a decreasing order which shows both analogies and differences between the two countries. In the Italian sample the hierarchy was the following: *to admit, to conclude/to remember, to assume, to predict, to doubt.* In Serbia the following decreasing order was found: *to admit, to conclude, to assume, to predict/to remember, to doubt. To admit,* an affirmative verb expressing certainty, is in the first position (that is, it is well recognised) in both countries, whereas the verb *to doubt*, expressing a mental state of uncertainty, appears at the bottom of the hierarchy both in Italy and in Serbia. By contrast, the verb *to remember* belongs to the best recognised verb in Italy but not in Serbia. If we consider similarities and differences between the two countries in identification rates of each verb at various school levels and/or with respect to the specific domain of knowledge, we notice the following relations: the recognition of the verb *to admit* increased regularly through school level both in Italy and in Serbia, while *to doubt* increased progressively along school level in Serbia but not in Italy. *To assume* was better recognised in Grade 5 of the Primary School and in the Grade 7 of the Secondary School in Italy but only in the Primary School in Serbia. *To conclude* was better understood in history in Serbia and in folk psychology in Italy. It is above all in Serbia that the verb *to remember* appeared to be highly recognised in mathematics as compared to the other domains, thereby indicating the association between such a discipline and memory. *To predict* is better identified in history in Serbia, and in folk psychology in Italy.

If we focus on the Tanzanian sample, we observe the following trend: in all verbs percentages of correct recognition were homogeneously low. In general, if we collapse responses given to all verbs, we notice that Serbian students performed similarly to Italian students, while in Tanzania response rates were near to the chance level (see Figure 1).

If we distinguish among the domains of knowledge, verbs were better identified within folk psychology and worse identified in mathematics both in Italy and in Serbia. However, in Serbia performance in folk psychology was worse and in history and mathematics was better than in Italy. In Tanzania no differences among domains were found.

As regards the school level, in Italy response rates increased progressively; in Serbia the difference between the Grade 5 of the Primary School and the Grade 7 of the Secondary School is smaller than in Italy. In Tanzania no developmental trend emerged.

If we analyse the interaction between the domains of knowledge and the school level, in Italy percentages of correct answers in history and mathematics were similar (and lower than in folk psychology), whereas in Serbia correct answers in history were, at the 5th Grade of Primary School, even higher than in folk psychology and, in the 3rd Grade, only slightly lower than folk psychology.

In Tanzania no interaction effects occurred. Nevertheless, in no country were interactions between domains and grade of schooling statistically significant.

The puzzling finding of the third study was the uniformity of incorrect responses recorded in Tanzania. A possible explanation is that the task was meaningful for the western countries but not for other cultures.

Maybe the metarepresentational verbs included in the task are too unusual or technical in Tanzania or that in such a country the use of the verbs proposed by the task is differentiated on the basis of indigenous linguistic and conversational conventions rather than on the actual understanding of the terms. It is unlikely that metarepresentational activity fails to occur.

It is worth noticing that in Italy and Serbia, as well as Canada, similar rates of comprehension of metacognitive and metalinguistic verbs occur, both in reference to school level and to domain of knowledge. Differences found between Italy and Serbia as regards the domain can be explained by making reference to differences in the school systems or in the present socio-political conditions. This, for instance, could explain why verbs were better recognised in history in Serbia than in Italy: the ethnic conflicts and the consequent socio-political instability could make people more sensitive to the past events of their country and to the interpretation of the current facts and actions from a historical perspective. Nevertheless, a common way of understanding the mental activity underlying the meaning of the metarepresentational verbs seems to characterise performance in western countries, perhaps because of the similarity of their school systems.

2.6   CONCLUSIONS

A first finding of our investigation regards the developmental trend. Total scores computed revealed that in each domain metarepresentational competencies increase across school levels. However, significant differences in mean total scores emerged in all domains only between Primary School Grade 3 children and the older ones. We can hypothesise that Primary School Grade 3 children significantly differed in performances from the pupils of subsequent levels of schooling because performances we are dealing with are strongly connected with two important kinds of events occurring at this age level. On one side, in the first school years children are confronted with the formal processes of instruction and the connected ways of managing the questions of knowledge and mind from a "meta" level. That is to say that the child meets with a new or almost new way of thinking whose frameworks lie in the epistemological structures of the various disciplines. These structures induce students to grasp the role of the specificity of the different symbolic systems and to reflect on the different modes of representing reality. This way of thinking will be systematically applied during compulsory schooling, as opposed to what happens in the family or in nursery school. For these reasons, during the first years of school, metarepresentational performances become commonplace.

Anyway, it is reasonable to assume that after three or four years of age a kind of apprenticeship begins in which the child's participation in the activity of thinking and talking about the topics of knowledge and mind takes on a form which will be maintained for the whole school period. On the other hand, we must think that for eight-year-olds (age which corresponds to the Grade 3 of Primary School) second order metarepresentational ability (X believes that Y believes p) represents a very recent acquisition (emerging between five and seven years of age; see Wimmer & Perner, 1983) and thus it is not well mastered, while older pupils have mastered that ability. The acquisition of this ability would positively affect learning in disciplines as ways of thinking, since it is significantly associated to epistemological development, particularly with competence in reasoning about evidence and understanding inference (Astington, Pelletier & Homer, 2002). Furthermore, improved recursive thinking might significantly influence the metarepresentational ability involved in mental verb identification. The observed developmental trend can be also be interpreted in terms of advance from implicit understanding (often contextually based) to explicit knowledge of the metarepresentational verbs (very seldom completely achieved in our sample) (Olson, 1994).

A second finding concerns knowledge domains. As only one item tested each domain any inferences must be seen as conjectures. The higher increase in performances in folk psychology and history in comparison with mathematics - which is evident in western countries - might depend on the fact that the former are more strictly connected than the latter with everyday discursive practices. In fact, the lexicon of psychology and history, but not of mathematics, greatly overlaps common language; furthermore, psychological and historical but not mathematical thinking tends to include features of narrative, rather than paradigmatic, thought which is privileged by the ordinary speech. Moreover the best and most precocious performance in folk psychology in comparison with the performance in the other two domains of knowledge can be connected with the fact that we could refer to folk psychology as the first domain of knowledge children become familiar with. In fact, by considering the development of theory of mind, one may hypothesise that, if children are able to deal with desires psychology from two years of age (and consequently to master some mental verbs), then they may have a familiarity with the folk psychology domain at the ages here considered. Later on, other domains will appear, such as history and mathematics, that will be shaped by curricula encountered in the school environment. Between these two domains, mathematics as taught at school represents the field which is least like the narrative thought of everyday psychology, while history is the most.

A third line of evidence emerging from our studies concerns the differences among countries. The most relevant difference separates European and North American countries, on one side (Italy, Canada and Serbia), from Tanzania, on the other side. In fact in western countries we can observe changes in performances depending on age (developmental trend) as well as on domains of knowledge (folk psychology, history, and mathematics). On the contrary, in Tanzania performances remain at chance level. This suggests that the mental language task proposed is not culture-free. We can hypothesize that Tanzanian pupils find our task puzzling and unmeaningful. These were the only groups of subjects who were tested in a foreign language.

We must remember that in Tanzania secondary school pupils study English (Malmberg, Wanner, Sumbra & Little, 2001), so have the opportunity to meet Western thought, while in primary school the language of instruction is Swahili; nonetheless, even secondary school students gave responses at the chance level similar to primary school children. Lillard's (1998) review of theory of mind across cultures showed relevant differences between Western *vs.* non-Western cultures in concepts as "mind", "relationship between mind and behaviour" and "influences on mind". These differences would make the learning of English terms for "mind" quite different and would explain poor test performance.

A last consideration is about methodology. We found a remarkable range of variability in the acquisition of mental verbs even within the same domain of knowledge or the same group of subjects. It can partially depend on the heterogeneous nature of the verbs considered: in fact the epistemic verbs included in our task are not classified on the basis of use frequency in a specific country or domain of knowledge and, more in general, on the basis of criteria that can be used to establish relationships among the verbs. This problem should be taken into account in further studies.

To conclude, we would like to point out that the research on the acquisition of mental verbs would profit from the knowledge of the language really spoken at home and at school in the curricular subjects or, to say it with other words, from the knowledge of the use of mental language in the different school subjects in different school levels and in different countries. This knowledge would give us the picture of the mental language that the school proposes to the child and which it asks him/her to take part in.

APPENDIX
Instructions

The words "think" and "say" are very common and we use them all the time to refer to various ways in witch we do or think something. For instance, if I say "I think I will be late" it is not understood whether or not I am certain to be in late; whereas if I say "I know I will be in late" it is clear that I am positive about it. Instead if I say "I foresee that I will be in late" it means that I am not totally sure about it.

In the following pages you will find a series of short stories in which a character thinks or says something. The situations refer to day-to-day life, history, or mathematics. First of all, you should read the short story and then the four possible answers. In each answer the word "think" or "say" (which are underlined in the story) are substituted by a more precise word. Therefore, you should choose which of the four sentences is the one in which the word "think" or "say" is best replaced. Please mark your choice with a cross.

The questionnaire is anonymous and you will not be evaluated for it. In other words, it is not a test and you will not get a mark at the end. However, you should answer each question accurately and make sure that you have marked one answer per story.

Folk Psychology

1. John and Claire, a brother and sister, are playing in their room with a toy train. At some point Claire feels thirsty and goes to the kitchen to get a drink. While Claire is in the kitchen, John takes the toy train to the living room because there is more room to play there. Claire comes back and looks for the toy train in her room where she had left it. Indeed, Claire thinks that the toy train is in their room.
a) Indeed Claire remembers that the toy train is in their room
b) Indeed Claire hypothesises that the toy train is in their room
c) Indeed Claire demonstrates that the toy train is in their room
d) Indeed Claire discovers that the toy train is in their room

2. Marc and Anne have to look after their younger brother, Peter because their mother has gone out. At some point Pier starts to cry. Anne says: "As a child when I use to cry, my mother sang and I stopped. Let's sing a song for Pier to make him stop crying". Marc, instead thinks that the song will not make Pier stop crying. Anne sings but Pier keeps on crying.
a) Marc assumes that the song will not make Pier stop crying
b) Marc discovers that the song will not make Pier stop crying
c) Marc demonstrates that the song will not make Pier stop crying

d) Marc doubts that the song will not make Pier stop crying

3. Simon notices that his brother Paul always stops in front of the windows of shops where video games are sold. On Paul's birthday his parents say to Simon: "For Paul's birthday we have bought a video game. We wonder if we have made a good choice". Simon says that Paul will be very pleased.

a) Simon predicts that Paul will be very pleased
b) Simon confirms that Paul will be very pleased
c) Simon suggests that Paul will be very pleased
d) Simon defines that Paul will be very pleased

4. Carl and some of his friends are playing hide-and-seek. Now it's Carl turn to seek his friends who are hiding. Lucy wants to trick Carl. So, she lets her red scarf fall in front of the bathroom door and then she goes to hide in the kitchen. Carl thinks that Lucy is hiding in the bathroom if her scarf has fallen in front of the bathroom door.

a) Carl infers that Lucy is hiding in the bathroom
b) Carl believes that Lucy is hiding in the bathroom
c) Carl knows that Lucy is hiding in the bathroom
d) Carl hypothesises that Lucy is hiding in the bathroom

5. It is the last day of school. Monique's mother goes to pick her up at school and she thinks that Monique is happy because the holidays are about to begin. When Monique comes out her mother sees that she is not smiling and so she asks her what has happened. Monique says that she is happy because the holidays are about to begin, but she is also sad because she won't see her schoolmates for three months.

a) Her mother remembers that Monique is happy because the holidays are about to begin.
b) Her mother assumes that Monique is happy because the holidays are about to begin.
c) Her mother understands that Monique is happy because the holidays are about to begin.
d) Her mother believes that Monique is happy because the holidays are about to begin.

6. Magdaleine is watching a movie on TV. There is a thunderstorm and the movie is interrupted just before the policeman was to find out who had robbed the bank. So Magdaleine tries to guess who is guilty and it seems to her that the postman might be the one. Next day, Magdaleine meets Tom who has watched the whole movie and she says to him that in her opinion the postman is guilty. Tom says that she is right: the postman was guilty.

a) Tom confirms that the postman was guilty

b) Tom concludes that the postman was guilty
c) Tom asserts that the postman was guilty
d) Tom explains that the postman was guilty

7. Laurie asks her mother if she can go to the park with her friends. Her mother gives her permission but she forbids her to eat ice cream and candies because Laurie has had stomach ache the whole morning. When Laurie comes back her mother sees that she has a chocolate stain on her T-shirt and therefore her mother thinks that Laurie has eaten an ice cream.
a) Her mother doubts that Laurie has eaten an ice cream
b) Her mother infers that Laurie has eaten an ice cream
c) Her mother knows that Laurie has eaten an ice cream
d) Her mother understands that Laurie has eaten an ice cream

8. Samuel's mother tells him that he can go out with his friends, but he has to be home by six o'clock. Samuel comes home at eight o'clock and his mother scolds him for having disobeyed her. At first Samuel says that he had not heard his mother ask him to come back by six o'clock, but then Samuel says that he has disobeyed.
a) Samuel concludes that he has disobeyed
b) Samuel explains that he has disobeyed
c) Samuel concedes that he has disobeyed
d) Samuel suggests that he has disobeyed

9. Claudia shares a secret with George and tells him not to tell anybody. The next day at school another classmate mocks Claudia telling her that he knows everything about her secret. Since Claudia had told it only George, she says that it was George who revealed her secret.
a) Claudia concedes that it was George who revealed her secret
b) Claudia defines that it was George who revealed her secret
c) Claudia concludes that it was George who revealed her secret
d) Claudia asserts that it was George who revealed her secret

History

1. Last week his teacher had explained to Bruce that at some point in European history people began to move to cities from the countryside to find work. This week there is a test. The first question is: "Why did people begin to move to cities from the countryside?". Bruce thinks that this happened because people could find jobs in the cities.
a) Bruce remembers that this happened because people could find jobs in the cities.

b) Bruce hypothesises that this happened because people could find jobs in the cities.

c) Bruce demonstrates that this happened because people could find jobs in the cities.

d) Bruce discovers that this happened because people could find jobs in the cities.

2. Jennifer and Duane are looking through a history book on Ancient Egypt. On one page there is the picture of a strange statue. According to Duane the statue represents a tiger, whereas Jennifer thinks that it is not a tiger. While they are discussing it, Jennifer and Duane realise that beneath the picture it is explained that the statue represents the Sphinx.

a) Jennifer assumes that it is not a tiger

b) Jennifer discovers that it is not a tiger

c) Jennifer demonstrates that it is not a tiger

d) Jennifer doubts that it is a tiger

3. The teacher has explained that Napoleon used to win battles because he had a great deal of military experience. Now the students are reading in class the story of a battle fought by two armies, one led by a general with much experience, and the other led by a young general. The teacher asks: "In your opinion who's going to win the battle?" Luis says that the battle will be won by the older general.

a) Luis predicts that the battle will be won by the older general

b) Luis confirms that the battle will be won by the older general

c) Luis suggests that the battle will be won by the older general

d) Luis defines that the battle will be won by the older general

4. Strolling along the lake shore, Charles and his father get to the CN tower. Charles looks at the top of the tower and his father tells him that it is 512 meters high. His father also says that the CN tower is the tallest building in the world. The next day, Charles's teacher asks: "What is the tallest building in the world?" Charles says that the CN tower is the tallest building.

a) Charles infers that the CN tower is the highest building

b) Charles believes that the CN tower is the highest building

c) Charles knows that the CN tower is the highest building

d) Charles hypothesises that the CN tower is the highest building

5. The teacher tells the students that the Vikings were capable of building sailing ships. Since Claire thinks that the Vikings lived in the middle of the desert, she asks: "What did they build those ships?" The teacher explains to Claire that the Vikings used to live along the coast and they used the ships for war.

a) Claire remembers that the Vikings lived in the middle of the desert

b) Claire assumes that the Vikings lived in the middle of the desert
c) Claire understands that the Vikings lived in the middle of the desert
d) Claire knows that the Vikings lived in the middle of the desert

6. A class is visiting the Museum of steam engines. The guide explained that these locomotives worked by burning coal; this is the reason they produced so much smoke. Victoria then remarks that the walls of the old stations must have been black with smoke. Jim says that is exactly the case: in a picture which hangs on one of the museum walls one can see clearly how dirty the smoke made the stations.
a) Jim confirms that is exactly the case
b) Jim concludes that is exactly the case
c) Jim asserts that is exactly the case
d) Jim explains that is exactly the case

7. In studying history, Terry has learned that when a group of people does not like where they live, they move and settle in a better place. Furthermore, he has read that during the Middle Ages Italy was invaded by a barbarian population that came from northern Europe. Terry thinks that they have settled in Italy because they liked it there.
a) Terry doubts that they have settled in Italy because they liked it there
b) Terry infers that they have settled in Italy because they liked it there
c) Terry knows that they have settled in Italy because they liked it there
d) Terry understands that they have settled in Italy because they liked it there

8. Manuela is asked some questions on history. The teacher asks her in which year America was discovered and she answers: "In 1429". The teacher corrects her: "You mean in 1492". "No, no, it was discovered in 1429" Manuela insists. "No, Manuela you are wrong. America was discovered in 1492", the teacher corrects her again. "I am not wrong; the book says 1429". When all her classmate show her that the book actually says that America was discovered on 1492, Manuela says that she is wrong.
a) At the end Manuela concludes that she is wrong
b) At the end Manuela explains that she is wrong
c) At the end Manuela concedes that she is wrong
d) At the end Manuela suggests that she is wrong

9. In history class the teacher invited the students to look at the map of the United States carefully in order to answer her questions. "Where was the city of New York built?" Joseph answers: "On the coast of the Atlantic Ocean". "Where was the city of Los Angeles built?" On the coast of the Pacific Ocean, Paula answers. "Where was the city of Chicago built?" "It was built on the coastline of Lake Michigan", Christine answers. At this

point Mike says that the biggest cities in the USA have been built on the coast of either an ocean or a large lake.

a) Mike concedes that the biggest cities in the USA have been built on the coast of either an ocean or a large lake.

b) Mike defines that the biggest cities in the USA have been built on the coast of either an ocean or a large lake.

c) Mike concludes that the biggest cities in the USA have been built on the coast of either an ocean or a large lake.

d) Mike asserts that the biggest cities in the USA have been built on the coast of either an ocean or a large lake.

Mathematics

1. Last week the teacher explained to David that to double 6 one can multiply 6 by 2. Today the teacher asks David: "How do you double 6?". David thinks that he can multiply 6 by 2.

a) David remembers that he can multiply 6 by 2

b) David hypothesise that he can multiply 6 by 2.

c) David demonstrates that he can multiply 6 by 2.

d) David discovers that he can multiply 6 by 2.

2. Mary and George are studying the multiplication tables. When they have to multiply seven by eight, Mary says the answer is 54; however George thinks that 54 is wrong. Therefore they look into the book and see that 7 times 8 is 56.

a) George assumes that 54 is wrong

b) George discovers that 54 is wrong

c) George concludes that 54 is right

d) George doubts that 54 is right

3. The teacher is asking the children some questions. She has a question for each student. The teacher asks Carl: "Without doing any calculations, if you earn three times seven tokens and I earn twice seven tokens, which one of us will have fewer tokens? Carl says that the teacher is going to have fewer tokens.

a) Carl predicts that the teacher is going to have fewer tokens.

b) Carl confirms that the teacher is going to have fewer tokens.

c) Carl suggests that the teacher is going to have fewer tokens.

d) Carl defines that the teacher is going to have fewer tokens.

4. John has in front of him a set of hockey cards. He counts the cards from the first to the last: there are six. After that, John recounts them from the last to the first: there are six. Then, he throws them and while they are falling down he counts them one after the other and again there are six.

Therefore, John thinks that, in whatever ways he counts his cards, the order does not matter.
a) John, therefore, infers that the order does not matter
b) John, therefore, believes that the order does not matter
c) John, therefore, knows that the order does not matter
d) John, therefore, hypothesise that the order does not matter

5. Katy has a younger sister who likes counting. Usually, the younger sister counts to 10 correctly. Now she is counting and when she gets to 10 she stops and asks Katy: "What number comes after 10?". Katy thinks that her sister can't learn this. Therefore, she answers: "Don't worry about it. When you are older, you will learn it.
a) Katy remembers that her sister can't learn this.
b) Katy assumes that her sister can't learn this.
c) Katy understands that her sister can't learn this.
d) Katy believes that her sister can't learn this.

6. Robert is counting the numbers from 1 to 20 aloud in front of his mother. When he gets to 16, he stops and thinks for a while. He asks his mother: "Mom, does 17 come after 16?" His mother says that after 16 comes exactly 17.
a) His mother confirms that after 16 comes exactly 17
b) His mother concludes that after 16 comes exactly 17
c) His mother affirms that after 16 comes exactly 17
d) His mother explains that after 16 comes exactly 17

7. Janet and Sara are preparing some coloured - paper masks to celebrate the Carnival. Janet has cut out three red paper-masks and she shows them to Sara. Sara looks at them and then she says: "I haven't cut out as many masks as you have!". Therefore, Janet thinks that Sara must have cut out one or two masks.
a) Janet doubts that Sara must have cut out one or two masks.
b) Janet infers that Sara must have cut out one or two masks.
c) Janet knows that Sara must have cut out one or two masks.
d) Janet understands that Sara must have cut out one or two masks.

8. Dorothy and Peter are discussing the best way to double 7. Dorothy want to multiply 7 by 2; on the other hand, Peter claims that it is better to add 7 and 7 because it is easier to add the numbers. Dorothy says that it is true that it is easier to add the numbers, but she is going to multiply them.
a) Dorothy concludes that it is true that it is easier to add the numbers, but she is going to multiply them.

b) Dorothy explains that it is true that it is easier to add the numbers, but she is going to multiply them.

c) Dorothy concedes that it is true that it is easier to add the numbers, but she is going to multiply them.

d) Dorothy suggests that it is true that it is easier to add the numbers, but she is going to multiply them.

9. Three children have started collecting stamps. Steven wonders who has collected the most stamps. He knows that he has 4 stamps and Joseph tells him that he has 25 stamps and Anne has even more then he has. Steven says that Anne has collected the most stamps.

a) Steven that Anne has collected the most stamps.

b) Steven says that Anne has collected the most stamps.

c) Steven says that Anne has collected the most stamps.

d) Steven says that Anne has collected the most stamps.

REFERENCES

Antonietti A., Liverta-Sempio O., Marchetti A. Lo sviluppo del linguaggio mentale in psicologia ingenua, storia e matematica. Studi di Psicologia dell'Educazione 1998(a); 17: 170-203

Antonietti A., Liverta-Sempio O., Marchetti A. Mental verbs on language and thought: A developmental study in three domains of knowledge. XV Biennial Meeting of the ISSBD; 1998(b) July 1-4; Bern.

Astington, J.W. "What is theoretical about the child's theory of mind? A Vygotskian view of its development". In *Theories of Theories of Mind*, P. Carruthers, P.K. Smith, (Eds.), Cambridge University Press, Cambridge, 1996.

Astington J.W. Theory of mind goes to school. Educational Leadership 1998; 56, 3: 46-48.

Astington J.W., Gopnik A. Theoretical explanations of children's understanding of the mind. British Journal of Developmental Psychology 1991; 9: 7-31

Astington J.W., Olson D.R. Metacognitive and metalinguistic language: learning to talk about thought. Applied Psychology: An International Review 1990; 39: 77-87

Astington, J.W., Pelletier, J. "The language of mind: Its role in teaching and learning." In *The handbook of education and human development. New models of learning, teaching and schooling*, D.R. Olson, N. Torrance (Eds.) Cambridge, MA: Blackwell, 1996.

Astington J.W., Pelletier J., Homer B. Theory of mind and epistemological development: The relation between children's second-order false-belief understanding and their ability to reason about evidence. New Ideas in Psychology 2002; 20: 131-144

Bartsch, K., Wellman, H.M., *Children talk about the mind*, New York: Oxford University Press, 1995.

Booth J.R., Hall W.S. Role of the cognitive internal state lexicon in reading comprehension. Journal of Educational Psychology 1994; 86: 413-422.

Bretherton I., Beeghly M., Talking about internal states: the acquisition of an explicit theory of mind. Developmental Psychology 1982; 18: 906-921.

Bruner, J., *Actual Minds, Possible Worlds*. Cambridge: Harvard University Press, 1986.

Burr J.E., Hofer B.K. Personal epistemology and theory of mind: Deciphering young children's beliefs about knowledge and knowing. New Ideas in Psychology 2002; 20: 199-224.

Camaioni L., Longobardi E. Referenze a stati interni nella produzione linguistica spontanea a venti mesi. Età Evolutiva 1997; 56: 16-25.

Camaioni L., Longobardi E., Bellagamba F. Evoluzione dei termini di stati mentali nelle storie di fantasia scritte da bambini in età scolare. Età Evolutiva 1998; 60: 20-29.

Dunn, J. "Changing minds and changing relationships." In *Children's Early Understanding of Mind*, C. Lewis, P. Mitchell (Eds.), Hillsdale, NJ, Erlbaum, 1994.

Dunn J. Bretherton I., Munn P. Conversations about feeling states between mothers and their young children, Developmental Psychology 1987; 23: 132-139.

Dunn J., Brown J., Slomkowsky C., Tesla C., Youngblade L. Young children's understanding of other people's feelings and beliefs: individual differences and their antecedents. Child Development 1991; 62: 1352-1366.

Furrow D., Moore C., Davdige J., Chiasson L. Mental terms in mothers and children speech: Similarities and relationships. Journal of Child Language 1992; 19: 617-631.

Groppo M., Antonietti A., Ardino V., Liverta-Sempio O., Marchetti A., Olson D.R. The development of metarepresentational concepts in folk psychology, history and mathematics, Cognitive Processing 2000; 1: 99-117.

Groppo M., Antonietti A., Liverta-Sempio O., Marchetti A. Metalinguistic-metacognitive competence and literacy: A developmental study, *Redefining Literacy*, On-line, autumn, 1999; 1 5.

Hambleton R.K. Guidelines for adapting educational and psychological tests: a progress report, European Journal of Psychological Assessment (Bulletin of the International Test Commission) 1994; 10: 229-244.

Homer B., Olson D.R. Literacy and children's conception of language. Written Language and Literacy 1999; 2,1: 113-140.

Jenkins J.M., Turrell S.L., Kogushi Yuiko, Lollis S., Ross H.S. A longitudinal investigation of the dynamic of mental state talk in families. Child Development 2003; 74, 3: 905-920.

Lillard A. Ethopsychologies: Cultural variations in theories of mind? Psychological Bulletin 1998; 123, 1: 3-32.

Luria, A.R. *Cognitive development: Its cultural and social foundations.* Cambridge: Cambridge University Press, 1976.

Malmberg L.E., Wanner B., Sura S. Little T.D. Action-control beliefs and school experiences of Tanzanian primary school students. Journal of Cross-Cultural Psychology 2001; 32, 5: 577-596.

Misciones J.L., Marvin R.S., O'Brien R.G., Greenberg M.T. A developmental study of preschool children's understanding of the words "know" and "guess". Child Development 1978; 49: 1107-1113.

Olson, D.R. *The world on paper.* Cambridge University Press, Cambridge, 1994.

Olson D.R. Towards a psychology of literacy: on a relations between speech and writing. Cognition 1996; 60, 1: 83-104.

Olson, D.R. Critical thinking: Learning to talk about talk and text. In *Handbook of academic learning. Construction of knowledge,* G.D. Phye (Ed.), San Diego, CA: Academic Press, 1997.

Olson, D.R. *Psychological theory and educational reform. How school remakes mind and society.* Cambridge: Cambridge University Press, 2003.

Olson D.R., Astington J.W., Thinking about thinking: Learning how to take statements and hold beliefs. Educational Psychologist 1993; 28, 1: 7-23.

Olson D.R., Homer B. The child's conception of "word". Paper presented at the XXVI International Congress of Psychology, Montreal, 1996.

Olson D.R., Torrance N. Language, literacy, and mental states. Discourse Processes 1987; 10: 157-167.

Olson D.R., Torrance N. (Eds.), *Modes of thought. Explorations in Culture and Cognition.* Cambridge, MA: Cambridge University Press, 1996.

Shatz M. Theory of mind and the development of social-linguistic intelligence in early childhood. In C. Lewis, P. Mitchell (Eds.), *Children's early understanding of mind: origins and development*, LEA, Hillsdale 1994.

Shatz M., Wellman H.M., Silber S. The acquisition of mental verbs: a systematic investigation of the first reference to mental state, Cognition 1983; 14: 301-321.

Siegal, M., Peterson, C.C. "Conversazione, sviluppo cognitivo e teoria infantile della mente." In *Il pensiero dell'altro. Contesto, conoscenza e teorie della mente*, O. Liverta-Sempio, A. Marchetti (Eds.), Milano: Raffaello Cortina Editore 1995.

Sperber A.D., Devellis R.F., Boehlecke B. Cross-cultural translation: methodology and validation, Journal of Cross-Cultural Psychology 1994; 25, 4: 501-524.

Wellman H.M., Bartsch, K. Before belief: children's early psychological theory. In *Children's early understanding of mind: Origins and development*, C. Lewis, P. Mitchell (Eds.). Hillsdale, NJ: LEA, 1994.

Wellman H.M., Johnson C.N., Understanding mental processes: a developmental study of "remember" and "forget". Child Development 1979; 50: 79-88.

Wimmer H., Perner J. Beliefs about beliefs: Representation and constraining function of wrong beliefs in young children's understanding of deception. Cognition 1983; 13: 103-128.

Zanobini M., Scopesi A., Cattani A. L'uso dei termini mentali in differenti contesti interattivi. In *Processi comunicativi e linguistici nei bambini e negli adulti: prospettive evolutive e sociali*, A. Scopesi, M. Zanobini (Eds.), Milano: Angeli 1998; 75-92.

Chapter 3

THE SOCIALIZATION OF THEORY OF MIND
Cultural and Social Class Differences in Behaviour Explanation

Angeline Lillard
University of Virginia

A great deal of research suggests that European-Americans prefer to explain behaviour in terms of the mental states and traits of the individual (Heller & Berndt, 1981; Wellman, 1990; Ross & Nisbett, 1991; Lillard, 1998). Our tendency to construe behaviours in terms of underlying personality traits is apparently automatic. Winter & Uleman (1984) presented participants with descriptions of people, like "The librarian carries the old woman's groceries across the street." After viewing many such sentences, people were asked to recall as many descriptions as they should on a recall sheet that cued each sentence by either a trait word ("helpful"), or a semantic cue ("books"). Although participants reported that they were unaware of having made trait inferences, the trait cues were associated with significantly better recall than were the semantic cues. As Ross & Nisbett (1991) have concluded, "The evidence to date thus suggests that people automatically--and unconsciously--provide a dispositional interpretation to behavioural information" (p. 121). This tendency to view others' behaviours in terms of internal attributes has been regarded as "fundamental" (although erroneous) (Ross & Nisbett, 1991), universal (Gilbert & Malone, 1995), and due to innate schemas (Brown & Fish, 1983).

The developmental literature involving European and American children suggests that the tendency to consider mental constructs (in general) increases with age (Eder, 1989; Yuill, 1993). Historically, young children have been considered behaviourists, describing people and explaining actions in external terms (Shantz, 1983). When asked, for example, why they or others perform certain actions, children of ages 3 through 7 tend to refer more often to external than internal causes (for example, Curtis & Schildhaus, 1980). Some have even argued that when young children do resort to traits, they are using traits to describe *behaviour patterns* more so than to describe *people* (Ruble & Dweck, 1995). With age, children become more likely to consider the mental states and traits underlying behaviours (Flapan, 1968; Livesley & Bromley, 1973; Peevers & Secord, 1973; Barenboim, 1981; Miller, 1987).

More recent research in developmental psychology highlights that children, like adults, are capable of considering various psychological states (Miller & Aloise, 1989; Flavell & Miller, 1998; Heyman & Gelman, 1998; Wellman & Gelman, 1998). Preschoolers do sometimes spontaneously talk about others' mental states and infer psychological causes (Hood & Bloom, 1979; Bretherton & Beeghly, 1982; Bartsch & Wellman, 1995). When given carefully constructed examples of human mistakes and intended acts (like a girl putting either chocolate sauce or ketchup on her ice cream), even 3-year-olds gave psychological explanations for the behaviour (Schult & Wellman, 1997). And although children's spontaneous descriptions of others are often external (Livesley & Bromley, 1973; Peevers & Secord, 1973), when given a forced choice between an external description ("This boy is wiping up his spilled milk") and an internal one ("This boy is feeling sad about his spilled milk"), 3-year-olds showed a slight but significant preference for describing people with reference to internal features (Lillard & Flavell, 1990; Youngstrom & Goodman, 2001). Toddlers apparently even attribute intentions by 18 months of age (Meltzoff & Moore, 1995) and possibly earlier (Woodward, 1998).

In sum, evidence regarding young American children is in flux. The traditional picture of them as behaviourists has been giving way to a new view, that they have some insight into minds quite early, and even prefer to interpret behaviours in terms of mental states by age 3. With age, American children increasingly discuss and attend to internal states, and American adults are very psychological in their explanations for others' behaviour. Some would claim that with development people are increasingly able to interpret the underlying causes of behaviours (Livesley & Bromley, 1973; Selman, 1980); others would claim they have merely learned cultural scripts and schemas (D'Andrade, 1984; Nelson, Plesa & Henseler, 1998). The present chapter examines both possibilities by looking at the development of behaviour interpretation in different cultures.

3.1 ATTRIBUTION ACROSS CULTURES

Adults from other cultures do not discuss internal features of people as frequently as American adults do (Shweder &, Bourne, 1984; Lillard, 1998). Cousins (1989), for example, found that Americans responded to the question "Who am I?" with three times as many trait descriptions ("I am easygoing") as did Japanese, but with about one third as many social category and context descriptions ("I am in the gymnastics club"; "I am one who swims often") (see also Bond & Cheung, 1983). In explaining behaviours, Asians have also been shown to rely more on external factors. Morris & Peng (1994) found that, for the same murder cases, American newspaper reports tended to report internal causes and Chinese papers tended to report external causes. Al-Zahrani & Kaplowitz (1993) compared Saudi with American attributions for eight behaviours, and coded the attributions as internal (referring to traits, mental states, etc.) or external (referring to situation or context). Americans were significantly more internal than were Saudis in behaviour attribution. Similar findings were obtained in another study for Koreans and Americans (Cha & Nam, 1985).

Such patterns hold even when attributions are made for nonhumans' behaviours. Morris & Peng (1994) showed American and Chinese high school students, and American and Taiwanese graduate students, Michotte-like stimuli in which several fish (considered social stimuli) moved to a single fish and stopped, whereupon the single fish moved forward. In other displays, circles (nonsocial stimuli) performed the same maneuvers. Respondents were asked to rate, on Likert scales, the extent to which the movement of the single item (fish or circle) was caused by internal and by external factors.

Importantly, all groups performed similarly for the nonsocial displays. Also, for the social displays, the American and Taiwanese graduate student samples performed similarly. There were significant differences for the American and Chinese high school students on the social displays, however, with Americans scoring significantly higher on the internal scale, and lower on the external scale. Whether the discrepancies across age groups (high school versus graduate student) were an effect of cultural differences between Taiwan and China, or due to the discrepant levels of education or age, is uncertain. Taiwan and China clearly share strong Confucian roots (for a discussion of such values, see Menon, Morris, Chiu & Hong, 1999), and most Taiwanese are ethnically Chinese, but Taiwan may be more influenced by western values than mainland China (Fiske, Kitayama, Markus & Nisbett, 1998).

3.2 DEVELOPMENT OF ATTRIBUTION ACROSS CULTURES

Given the differences in adults, and the fact that development occurs in this domain for U.S. children, cross-cultural developmental studies of behaviour attribution are of particular interest. One pertinent study, by Iyengar & Lepper (1999), speaks to the issue of value for internally versus externally motivated activities. They found that whereas European-American children preferred to engage in activities that they, as opposed to their mothers, had chosen, Asian-American children preferred the activities that their mothers had picked. By age 9, then, Euro-American children place higher value on internally-motivated activities, whereas Asian-American children place higher value on activities motivated by an important external source. In another study of Asian (Korean and Chinese) versus American children, Han and colleagues (Han, Leichtman & Wang, 1998) found that, when asked to provide descriptions of life events, American 4- and 6-year-olds provided more references to internal states than did the Asian children. These studies, although indirectly related to attribution, do suggest that cultural differences in attribution might even appear by early elementary school.

Miller (1984) examined behaviour attributions in India and the United States. She asked Hindu and American (Chicago) children, ages 8, 11, and 15, to think of two prosocial and two antisocial behaviours engaged in by someone they knew, and to explain why those people had done the behaviours. Adults in both cities were also tested. The main adult samples were middle class, like the children, but comparison adult samples from lower-class, less educated groups were also obtained.

For the adults, the typical cultural difference was found: Americans tended to refer to dispositional causes of behaviour, whereas Indian adults tended to refer to contextual ones. Among 8-year-olds, in contrast, there was little difference across cultures: both groups tended to use somewhat more situational than dispositional explanations, especially for good behaviours. This changed gradually at each age level, and by adulthood, Indians were more situational for both good and bad behaviours, whereas Americans were more dispositional for both. Miller examined three possible explanations for her findings: (1) that respondents named different behaviours in each culture, so that explanation differences stemmed from having chosen different behaviours; (2) that the ability to abstract was at root; and (3) that education and social class differences across the cultures were responsible. Further experiments suggested that none of these factors explained the main result, and Miller concluded that Hindu versus American cultural conceptions of the person were responsible.

Miller's method is particularly apt in terms of its cultural portability. Rather than impose events on participants, Miller asked participants to come up with culturally meaningful behaviours of particular valence, and then explain them. This results in better functional equivalence than one might obtain were one to impose the event itself. For more discussion of the rationale for this method, see Miller (1984, p. 965).

The primary purpose of the present study was to extend research on the development of behaviour interpretation to different American and Asian samples. In addition, in response to Miller's (1997) and others' calls to consider subpopulations in the same culture, we also tested rural children in both countries. Finally, because of current interest in theory of mind, we analysed explanations according to whether they explicitly considered a range of "theory of mind" explanations (mental states like beliefs and desires, and traits; see Wellman, 1990). In contrast, Miller analysed only the use of dispositional versus contextual explanations.

3.3   EXPERIMENT 1

Children from rural and urban settings in the United States and Taiwan participated in these experiments. All were selected as convenience samples. Ideally SES would have been equated across cultures but this was not possible. Indeed, it was not possible to obtain precise SES information for the samples, as the schools considered this too intrusive. To the best of our ability, using census and other information, we estimate that the Taiwanese subjects were all of the middle class, whereas the urban American ones were of middle to upper-middle class and the rural American ones were mainly of the lower class (a significant percentage of children at each rural school was on the free lunch program).

Participants were 7-, 9-, and 11-year-olds. The ns were 31, 33, and 40 children in each age group in Taipei; 31, 35, and 35 from a rural community in Taiwan; 15, 29, and 14 from an urban area of the US; and 37, 25, and 14 from a rural area of the US.

All children were tested in their schools using a paper-and-pencil questionnaire. On the front side, children were directed to think of someone they knew well, like a classmate or a neighbour, who recently did something that was a good thing to do, and to describe what they did. They were asked to do the same for a different person who did something bad. At the bottom of the sheet they were instructed to turn their paper over and explain, for each event, why the person did it. Taiwanese questionnaires were translated from English into Mandarin and then back translated by a new translator from Mandarin into English. Taiwanese responses were translated into English twice, each time by fluent Mandarin speakers. No meaningful differences were found across the translations, so the first set of translations and codes was used. All data were entered into data files listing the behaviour and its explanation as provided by the child. When a child provided more than one explanation for a behaviour, each explanation was coded separately. Explanations were coded into 20 subcategories which were placed into three major categories: internal (focused on character traits and mental states), external (the actor's physical circumstances, an enduring behaviour pattern of the actor, a relationship to another person, another person's mental or physical state, God or other supernatural forces, physical situations not specific to the person, and social laws and norms), and other. The interrater agreement was 88%; Cohen's kappa was .87.

The types of behaviours children cited in each culture were similar in type and proportion, with most children everywhere citing helping others as a prototypical good behaviour, and acts of physical aggression as prototypical bad behaviours. Children's explanations were evaluated in terms of their internality. As the measure of internality, the number of external explanations each child provided was subtracted from the number of internal explanations. A repeated measures analysis of variance (ANOVA) was run on these scores, with three between factors (age: 7, 9, and 11; community: rural vs. urban; and country: Taiwan vs. US) and one within factor (valence: good vs. bad behaviour).

A main effect was found for community, $F(1, 327) = 14.57, p < .0005$. Children in urban communities were more likely to give internal responses than were children in rural communities. Examples of internal responses are, "Grace [...] cheers me up because she is a very nice person," (UA 7, or Urban American 7-year-old) and, "A friend did something bad and this something was lying [...] because she was trying to cover up something else." (RA 9). There was also a main effect for country, $F(1, 327) = 4.56, p < .05$, with American children giving proportionately fewer internal responses, overall, than Taiwanese children. This was entirely due to the rural American children, and it was also reflected in a community by country interaction, $F(1, 327) = 3.93, p < .05$. Rural American children were much more likely to provide external reasons for behaviours than were any of the other groups. There was also a trend for age, $F(2, 327) = 2.82, p = .06$, with older children providing proportionately more internal explanations than did younger ones. An interaction of valence by community resulted from rural children being especially likely to provide external reasons for good behaviours ($F[1, 325] = 5.49, p < .01$).

The rural American findings were novel and interesting enough to pursue in a second experiment, described below. Taiwanese responses were not pursued further and thus are discussed here. The Taiwanese data were surprising in their lack of difference from the urban American children. This lack of difference fits with some other results suggesting more westernized Asian people might in some ways be similar to western people. Bond &

Cheung's (1983) 20 statements study showed that Hong Kong respondents did not differ from Americans in terms of ascribing traits to themselves. Like Hong Kong, Taiwan is capitalistic, industrialized, and westernized relative to the People's Republic of China, although all three share a Confucian/Buddhist/Taoist heritage. Morris & Peng (1994) also showed that Taiwanese graduate students tended to give external explanations for behaviours as often as did American graduate students.

However, closer inspection revealed that although often internal, Taiwanese explanations were often of a different character than those of American children. In particular, Taiwanese children often stated that people do things because they *think* it is good ("He thinks that it is right to help others"; "My teacher thinks that we should help others"), or because they *know* that helping others is the source of happiness. American children were more apt to refer to others' desires and preferences in their internal explanations. Clearly the children were socialized to think in different terms about the causes of behaviours.

When discussing bad behaviours, Taiwanese children also showed a "Pollyanna" tendency not seen in American children. Statements like the following appeared in Taiwanese explanations: "There is a classmate in our class with bad temper because he always screams loudly. I hope he will make improvements." (UT 9). This seems to reflect taking responsibility for others' behaviour, as discussed by Lewis (1995) for children in Japanese schools. Especially at age 11, bad behaviours were frequently ascribed to Taiwanese parents: "His parents do not control him, that is why he is not polite"; "His parents have not taken a good control on him from his early childhood"; "His parents have not told him that kids shouldn't use swear words"; "He is not educated well."

There also appeared to be much more coding of "laws to live by" in Taipei, especially among 11-year-olds, for example, "He must want to accumulate some credits for his parents" (so that they will go to heaven after death); "The teacher always says that 'I cannot be missed for doing the good things;'" "Because our teacher is always saying things like, 'You gain more if you work more, you lose more if you do less.'" (all UT 11s); "Because when you have something good, you shall share it with others" (UT 9). The rural Taiwanese and American children offered fewer moral guideposts.

In sum, although there were interesting differences in the Taiwanese and American children, Taiwanese children were similar to urban American ones in their of internal interpretations of behaviour. The most striking findings in how behaviours were explained in Experiment 1 were found across rural and urban dimensions within the United States. This novel finding was pursued in a second experiment.

3.4   EXPERIMENT 2

Experiment 2 was conducted to determine if the urban-rural difference in behaviour explanation that was seen in Experiment 1 would replicate with new American samples. In addition to the questions asked in Experiment 1, children were asked to explain 4 pre-determined behaviours, two good and two bad. These were "A boy gave his gingerbread house to another child," "A girl helped another girl with her schoolwork," "A boy pushed a girl away right when she was going to catch a ball," and "A girl broke another girl's necklace." The purpose of these was to establish whether children from the two contexts would preserve their style of explaining behaviours even when the targets of those explanations were strangers and engaged in the exact same behaviours. Responses were entered and coded as Experiment 1. Participants were 41 seven- (mean 7;6) 48 nine- (mean 9;5), and 15 eleven-year-olds (mean 11;5), (respectively) from a rural area of the US, and 18 seven- (mean 7;6) 14 nine- (mean 9;4), and 16 eleven- year-olds (mean 11;5) from an urban area of the eastern United States.

A repeated measures ANOVA was performed on the difference scores, with two between factors (age: 7, 9 and 11; community: rural vs. urban) and one within factor (valence: good vs. bad behaviour). For the responses to the open-ended question, this yielded significant main effects for community ($F[1, 146] = 6.79$, $p = .01$) and valence ($F[1, 146] = 13.8$, $p < .01$), but not for age. There were no significant interactions. The main effect reflected the fact that rural children were once again more external in their explanations, overall, than were urban children. For example, one rural child said, "Angie, she took me ice-skating because she is my mom's friend" (R9). Regarding the main effect for valence, children were more likely to give an external response when the behaviour was good than when it was bad. For example, one urban child gave this external reason for a good behaviour: "Steven helped me glue my ghost in my book cause I was having trouble" (U9). A rural child explained a bad behaviour with this internal reason: "My brother threw a plastic toy at my head because he was mad" (R9).

For the preselected behaviours, an ANOVA revealed a main effect for valence ($F[1, 146] = 84.31$ $p < .01$), with subjects again tending to give internal responses for bad behaviours much more so than for good behaviours. There was also a trend towards an interaction of community and behaviour type, $F(1, 146) = 2.79$, $p < .10$. Whereas for bad behaviours, the two types of community did not differ, for good behaviours, children in the urban community were more likely to provide internal explanations than were children in the rural community, $t(150) = 2.04$, $p < .05$. Thus even when the behaviours are provided, and the characters are completely unknown to the children, there is still some tendency for rural children to provide more external reasons for good behaviours than do urban children.

Urban children were slightly more likely to give internal reasons even when the person was entirely unknown to them.

In sum, children's explanations for bad behaviours tended to focus relatively more on internal factors than do explanations for good behaviours, regardless of how well children know the protagonists. This is consistent with other work on attribution. New to this work is the finding that children from a more rural area of the United States were more likely that urban ones to use external explanations for good behaviours, especially when the actor was well known to the child and the child provided the behaviour.

3.5   DISCUSSION

Cultural differences are usually a matter of degrees, of different patterns and frequencies of behaviours occurring in different cultural contexts (Ochs. 1988). Thus children in rural areas do give internal explanations and children in more urban areas do give external ones, but the frequencies of each type are rather different in the two communities, as found in both experiments described here. Across both experiments, lower SES children from rural areas in the eastern United States gave more external explanations for behaviours than did higher SES children from more urban areas in that region. These differences were greater at age 7 than age 11, with rural children becoming more internal with age.

This finding can be explained in terms of children's language socialization in different cultural contexts. Seven-year-olds are still very much influenced by their parents; as children get older, the larger culture plays a greater role in socialization. Perhaps lower SES parents are likely to be more focused on external explanations. This conjecture is based on prior work in other domain. For example, in a study examining SES and values, Kohn & Schooler (1969) found that higher SES respondents valued autonomy, personal causation, independent judgment, and an interest in how and why things happen. In contrast, lower SES respondents valued respectability and ability to get along. Such values might lead lower SES respondents to focus on situational determinants of behaviours, such as how one's relationship to other people would make one behave a certain way. In contrast, higher SES respondents would show more internal orientation, linked as it is to autonomy and personal causation. Likewise, other research has found that more educated Americans, who are also likely to be of higher income, are more agenic and thus see the self and internal factors as being more responsible for behaviours (Herzog, Franks, Markus & Holmberg, 1998).

Perhaps corroborating this conjecture, other work shows that lower-income children within the United States are slower to reach theory of mind milestones than children in more urban areas (Holmes, Black & Miller, 1996; Cole & Mitchell, 1998). Theory of mind acquisition is apparently assisted by parent's mental state talk with children: children who pass mental state tasks earlier have parents who talk to them more about mental states (Dunn & Brown, 1994), and evidence suggests this relation might even be causal, with mother internal state talk at an early age leading to child understanding later (Ruffman, Slade & Crowe, 2002). Whereas our higher SES children were already quite focused on internal reasons already at age 7, this orientation was slower to develop in more rural children. We speculate that it develops in the rural children more through exposure to media and perhaps teachers in school, rather than parents.

Future work should more carefully examine cultural variations in how theories of mind are used to explain behaviours. This work is part of a growing body of work showing within culture differences (Cohen, Nisbett, Bowdle & Schwarz, 1996; Plaut, Markus & Lachman, 2002), and suggests some interesting differences, even within cultures, that could shed light on how children come to interpret the behaviours of themselves and those around them.

REFERENCES

Al-Zahrani S.S.A., Kaplowitz S.A. Attributional biases in individualistic and collectivistic cultures: A comparison of Americans with Saudis 1993; 56: 223-233.

Barenboim C. The development of person perception in childhood and adolescence: From behavioural comparisons to psychological constructs to psychological comparisons. Child Development 1981; 52:129-144.

Bartsch, K., Wellman, H. M. *Children talk about the mind.* Oxford: Oxford University Press, 1995.

Bond M. H., Cheung T.-s. College students' spontaneous self-concept: The effect of culture among respondents in Hong Kong, Japan, and the United States. Journal of Cross-Cultural Psychology 1983; 14: 153-171.

Bretherton I., Beeghly M. Talking about internal states: The acquisition of an explicit theory of mind. Developmental Psychology 1982; 18: 906-921.

Brown, A. L., Bransford, J. D., Ferrara, R. A., Campione, J. C. "Learning, remembering, and understanding." In *Handbook of child psychology: Vol.3 Cognitive development*, J.H. Flavell, E.M. Markman (Eds.), New York: John Wiley, 1983.

Cha J.K., Nam K.D. A test of Kelly's cube theory of attribution: A cross-cultural replication of Mc Carthur's study. Korean Social Science Journal 1985; 12: 151-180.

Cohen D., Nisbett R., Bowdle B., Schwarz N. Insult, aggression, and the southern culture of honor: An "experimental ethnography". Journal of Personality and Social Psychology 1996; 70: 945-960.

Cole K., Mitchell P. Family background in relation to deceptive ability and understanding of the mind. Social Development 1998; 7: 181-197.

Cousins S. D. Culture and self-perception in Japan and the United States. Journal of Personality and Social Psychology 1989; 56: 124-131.

Curtis R.C., Schildhaus, J. Children's attributions to self and situation. The Journal of Social Psychology 1980; 110: 109-114.

D'Andrade, R. G. "Cultural meaning systems." In *Culture theory: Essays on mind, self, and emotion*, R.A. Shweder, R.A. LeVine (Eds.), Cambridge, England, 1984.

Dunn J., Brown J. Affect expression in the family, children's understanding of emotions, and their interactions with others. Merrill-Palmer Quarterly 1994; 40, 120-137.

Eder R. A. The emergent personologist: The structure and content of 3 1/2-, 5 1/2-, and 7 1/2-year-olds' concepts of themselves and other persons Child Development 1989; 1218-1228.

Fiske, A., Kitayama, S., Markus, H., Nisbett, R. "The cultural matrix of social psychology." In *The handbook of social psychology*, D.T. Gilbert & F.S.T. (Eds.), Vol. 2, Boston, MA, USA: Mcgraw-Hill, 1998.

Flapan. *Children's understanding of social interaction*. New York: Teacher's College Press, 1968.

Flavell, J.H., Miller, P.H. "Social cognition." In *Handbook of child psychology: Vol. 2. Cognition, perception, and language development. (5th Ed.)*, D. Kuhn, R.S. Siegler (Eds.), New York: Wiley, 1998.

Gilbert D.T., Malone P.S. The correspondence bias. Psychological Bulletin 1995; 117: 21-38.

Han, J.J., Leichtman, M.D., Wang, Q. Autobiographical memory in Korean, Chinese, and American children. Developmental Psychology 1998; 34: 701-713.

Heller K.A., Berndt T.J. Developmental changes in the formation and organization of personality attributions. Child Development, 1981; 52: 683-691.

Herzog A.R., Franks M.M., Markus H.R., Holmberg D. Activities and well-being in older age: Effects of self-concept and educational attainment. Psychology & Aging 1998; 13, 2: 179-185.

Heyman G.D., Gelman S.A. Young children use motive information to make trait inferences. Developmental Psychology 1998; 34, 2: 310-321.

Holmes H., Black C., Miller S. A cross-task comparison of false belief understanding in a Head Start population. Journal of Experimental Child Psychology 1996; 63: 263-285.

Hood L., Bloom L. What, when, and how about why: A longitudinal study of early expressions of causality. Monographs of the Society for Research in Child Development 1979; 44, 6, Serial No. 181.

Iyengar S.S., Lepper M.R. Rethinking the value of choice: a cultural perspective on intrinsic motivation. Journal of Personality and Social Psychology 1999; 76: 349-366.

Kohn, M.L., Schooler C. Class, occupation, and orientation. American Sociological Review 1969; 34: 657-678.

Lillard A.S. Ethnopsychologies: Cultural variations in theory of mind. Psychological Bulletin 1998; 123: 3-33.

Lillard A.S., Flavell J.H. Young children's preference for mental-state over behavioural descriptions of human action. Child Development 1990; 61: 731-742.

Livesley, W.J., Bromley, D.B. *Person perception in childhood and adolescence*. London: Wiley, 1973.

Meltzoff, A.N., Moore, M.K. "Infants' understanding of people and things: From body imitation to folk psychology." In *The body and the self*, J.L. Bermudez, A. Marcel, N. Eilan (Eds.), Cambridge: MIT Press, 1995.

Menon T., Morris M.W., Chiu C.-y., Hong Y.-y. Culture and the construal of agency: Attribution to individual versus group dispositions. Journal of Personality & Social Psychology 1999; 76, 5: 701-717.

Miller J.G. Cultural influences on the development of conceptual differentiation in person description. British Journal of Developmental Psychology 1987; 5: 309-319.

Miller, J.G. "Theoretical issues in cultural psychology." In *Handbook of cross-cultural psychology* (Vol. 1). J.W.P.Y.H. Berry (Ed.), Boston, MA, USA: Allyn & Bacon, Inc., 1997.

Miller P.H., Aloise P.A. Young children's understanding of the psychological causes of behaviour: A review. Child Development 1989; 60: 257-285.

Morris M.W., Peng K. Culture and cause: American and Chinese attributions for social and physical events. Journal of Personality and Social Psychology 1994; 67, 6: 949-971.

Nelson K., Plesa D., Henseler S. Children's theory of mind: An experiential interpretation. Human Development 1998; 41: 7-29.

Ochs, E. *Culture and language development.* Cambridge: Cambridge University Press, 1988.

Peevers B.H., Secord P.F. Developmental changes in attribution of descriptive concepts to persons. Journal of Personality and Social Psychology 1973; 27: 120-128.

Plaut V.C., Markus H.R., Lachman M.E. Place matters: Consensual features and regional variation in American well-being and self. Journal of Personality & Social Psychology 2002; 83, 1: 160-184.

Ross, L., Nisbett, R.E. *The person and the situation: Perspectives of social psychology.* New York: McGraw-Hill, 1991.

Ruble, D.N., Dweck, C.S. "Self-conceptions, person conceptions, and their development." In *Social development,* N. Eisenberg (Ed.), Thousand Oaks, CA: Sage, 1995.

Ruffman T., Slade L., Crowe E. The relation between children's and mothers' mental state language and theory-of-mind understanding. Child Development 2002; 73, 3: 734-751.

Schult C., Wellman H. Explaining human movements and actions: Children's understanding of the limits of psychological explanation. Cognition 1997; 62: 291-324.

Selman, R.L. *The growth of interpersonal understanding.* New York: Academic Press, 1980.

Shantz, C.U. (1983). Social cognition. In J. H. Flavell, E.M. Markman (Eds.), *Cognitive development* (Vol. III, pp. 495-555). New York: Wiley.

Shweder, R.A., Bourne, L. "Does the concept of the person vary cross-culturally?" In *Culture theory: Essays on mind, self, and emotion,* R.A. Shweder, R.A. LeVine (Eds.), Cambridge, England: Cambridge Unversity Press, 1984.

Wellman, H.M. *The child's theory of mind.* Cambridge, MA: Bradford Books/MIT Press, 1990.

Wellman, H.M., Gelman, S.A. "Knowledge acquisition in foundational domains." In *Handbook of child psychology: Vol. 2. Cognition, perception, and language development. (5th Ed.)* D. Kuhn, R.S. Siegler (Eds.), New York: Wiley, 1998.

Winter L., Uleman J.S. When are social judgments made? Evidence for the spontaneousness of trait inferences. Journal of Personality & Social Psychology 1984; 47: 237-252.

Woodward A.L. Infant's selectively encode the goal object of an actor's reach. Cognition 1998; 69: 1-34.

Youngstrom E.A., Goodman S. Children's perceptions of other people: mentalistic versus behaviouristic descriptions of peers and adults. Developmental Science 2001; 4: 165-174.

Yuill, N. "Understanding of personality and dispositions." In *The development of social cognition: The child as psychologist,* M. Bennett (Ed.), New York: Guilford, 1993.

Zarate M.A., Uleman J.S., Voils C. Effects of culture and processing goals on the activation and binding of trait concepts. Social Cognition 2001; 19: 295-323

Chapter 4

RELATIONS AMONG THEORY OF MIND, METACOGNITIVE LANGUAGE, READING SKILLS AND STORY COMPREHENSION IN L1 AND L2 LEARNERS

Janette Pelletier
Institute of Child Study, OISE, University of Toronto, Canada

This research was supported by a Connaught New Faculty Matching Grant, and a Social Sciences and Humanities Research Council of Canada Institutional Grant. The author would like to express appreciation to collaborators in related research, John Morgan and Janet Astington, to graduate assistants Marla Endler, Jennifer Lasenby and Stacey Ordon, and to the children in the Toronto Catholic District School Board.
This chapter describes how reading skill and reading comprehension were shown to relate to metacognitive factors such as theory of mind and metacognitive language in two empirical studies in Toronto, Canada. L1 children spoke English as a first language and L2 children spoke English as a second language. Study 1 examined these factors in Grade 4 (8-9 year olds) who spoke English or Portuguese as a first language. Study 2 examined these factors in L1 and L2 Kindergarten-Grade 2 (4-7 year olds) who spoke English, Cantonese, Tagalog or Ukrainian as a first language. All children were being schooled in English.

4.1   BACKGROUND TO STUDY 1 AND STUDY 2

Research in theory of mind is increasingly moving in the direction of applications to education such as how theory of mind relates to children's early success in school (Astington, 1998; Astington & Pelletier, 1999). For example, we know that theory of mind is related to children's ability to infer intentions and behavior, including the mental states and behaviour of story characters (Pelletier & Astington, 2004; Peskin & Astington, 2004). Theory of mind has likewise been shown to relate to children's epistemological understanding such as realizing that evidence is a reason for knowing (Astington, Pelletier & Homer, 2002). This kind of prerequisite ability is in turn required for scientific understanding (Kuhn & Pearsall, 2000).

We also know that children's general language development is closely related to theory of mind understanding and in some studies has been shown to predict theory of mind performance (Astington & Jenkins, 1999; Cutting & Dunn, 1999). Ruffman et al. (2003) showed that features of language development such as syntax and semantics predict theory of mind understanding. Many studies report the primacy of vocabulary development to theory of mind understanding (e.g. Astington & Pelletier, 1999; Lohmann & Tomasello, 2003). A specialized form of language development, one that relates to mental state understanding, may be necessary for children to describe the mental states of others, such as those of story characters. It is this "language of mind" (Astington & Pelletier, 1996) that allows children to understand characters' beliefs and intentions and at higher levels, authorial intention.   Indeed, a study that empirically examined the relation between Bruner's (1986) 'landscapes of action and consciousness' showed that children are able to coordinate mental state understanding with story action when they understand and use metacognitive language in retelling stories (Pelletier & Astington, 2004). Specifically, this metacognitive language gives labels to mental states such as thinking, knowing, believing, wondering and dreaming. It is related to children's ability to take sentential complements, for example, knowing "that X believes something to be true" or "thinking that a character doesn't know something" (Naigles, Hohenstein & Marsland, 1997; de Villiers, 2000; Hale & Tager-Flusberg, 2003; Lohmann & Tomasello, 2003).

For second language learners there are certain predictors of reading success that relate to specific factors in second language oral proficiency (Cummins, 1979; Clarke, 1980; Saville-Troike, 1984; Wong Fillmore & Valdez, 1986). An additional factor explored in the present studies was the level of metacognitive awareness. Carrell, Gajdusek & Wise (1998) based their work on the belief that L2 learners require explicit metacognitive training in reading. Tang & Moore (1992) showed that providing English Second Language (ESL) emergent readers with metacognitive training was more effective in raising reading comprehension levels than providing pre-reading activities, and in fact was associated with higher levels of retention. Gernsbacher, Hallada & Robertson (1998) showed that readers require high levels of metacognitive understanding in order to make inferences about story characters' emotional states. High-knowledge readers generate richer mental state models than low-knowledge readers, pointing to the importance of having language to talk about mental states (Barry & Lazarte, 1998). It has been shown that mental state inferencing is difficult in reading comprehension activity (Bahri & Al-Hussein, 1997). One reason for this may be that while children are expected to know about reasoning, teachers may not necessarily be given instructions in how to teach children to talk about thought (Franks, Mulhern & Schillinger, 1997). This is particularly salient for teachers of second-language learners who may not "pick up" this kind of language outside of the classroom. Children require language-specific knowledge before they can be expected to employ higher-level metacognitive strategies during reading; specifically, it has been shown that metacognitive knowledge is related to reading comprehension in both first and second languages (Schoonen, Hulstijn & Bossers, 1998). Fitzgerald (1995) claims that second language readers do recognize and use metacognitive vocabulary and metacognitive strategies in monitoring their reading comprehension. However, Jimenez, Garcia & Pearson (1995) argue that unknown vocabulary obstructs comprehension for L2 readers.

These findings point to the important role of metacognitive factors in L2 children's ability to carry out higher order comprehension processes in reading and in listening to stories. In order to access story characters' thoughts and intentions, children need to understand the language that gives labels to mental states, language such as think, plan, trick and so on. This type of language may be particularly difficult for L2 learners to acquire as there is no simple pairing of vocabulary with object, agent or action. In Canada specifically, and for most of North America more broadly, many children begin school speaking a language other than English, which is typically the language of schooling. In fact, in many areas in Toronto, Canada, at least 50% of school-age children do not speak English as a first language. Thus it is important to understand how language development in general, and metacognitive language in particular, relate to reading comprehension among L2 learners. In this way, educators can provide compensatory metacognitive instruction to better prepare children for reading. The two studies described in this chapter were carried out in Toronto, Canada, to examine this relation among Grade 4 children who spoke English or Portuguese as a first language, and among Kindergarten to Grade 2 children who spoke English, Cantonese, Tagalog and Ukrainian as a first language.

4.2 STUDY 1

The aims of Study 1 were to examine how theory of mind, metacognitive language, phonological processing and reading comprehension related to each other among L1 and L2 learners. In the province of Ontario, all school children undergo standardized achievement testing in Grades 3, 6 and 9. This study was designed to examine how metacognitive factors related to children's performance on the wide-scale reading achievement test in Grade 3. It was important to examine this relation for L1 and L2 learners in order to address the issue of whether L2 learners encounter more difficulty on standardized reading achievement tests because they do not understand the metacognitive language upon which many test items are based. In a related example, many items on the wide-scale mathematics achievement test ask children to "explain their thinking," "predict", "estimate", or "hypothesize". Children who do not understand the mental activities for which these labels stand have greater difficulty on such test items. On the reading comprehension subscales, test items may ask children to "infer" a character's "intention" based on the character's actions or "predict" what a character would do in another situation. These questions require children to have a theory of mind about story characters and to understand and use metacognitive language to make evaluations and inferences related to the story characters' actions. Thus it is important for educators to understand L2 children's understanding of both theory of mind and metacognitive language, as well as the relation between them vis-à-vis reading comprehension.

Study 1 was designed to include children who spoke either English as a first language or Portuguese as a first language from each of four achievement levels on the wide-scale achievement test taken the preceding year. All children were schooled in English and were drawn from 8 schools representing socioeconomic and cultural diversity. There were 79 Grade 4 children (mean age 9.5 years at time of study) (36 English FL – 20 girls and 16 boys, 43 Portuguese FL – 22 girls and 21 boys). The breakdown by achievement level was as follows: Level 1 (lowest) = 18, Level 2 = 22, Level 3 = 22, Level 4 = 17. The measures in Study 1 included:

- the province-wide Reading Achievement Scores (Levels 1 - 4)
- the Peabody Picture Vocabulary Test (standardized receptive vocabulary)
- the Woodcock Reading Mastery Test (standardized) (word attack, word identification and passage comprehension subtests)
- theory of mind: second order task (modified to make more difficult for older children) (e.g. one will character X think character Y will say?)

- the Metacognitive Language Task (Astington & Pelletier, 2004): 12 metacognitive terms in forced choice format
- Fables Task (Pelletier & Beatty, 2004): 2 story comprehension items. An example of a fable is as follows: A fox had fallen down a well. A thirsty goat walked by and the fox called out: "Come down here and taste this delicious water." The goat jumped right in and the clever fox climbed on the goat's back and got out of the well. The fox said, "Silly goat, if you had paid attention to where you were going you would not be stuck in the well." Children were asked 4 questions representing levels of understanding: Knowledge (who had fallen in the well?) Comprehension (why did the goat jump in the well?) Understanding of deception (is someone playing a trick? who?) Higher-level comprehension/evaluation (what is the moral/lesson of the story?)

4.2.1 Procedure

All English-speaking children were tested in English. All Portuguese-speaking children were tested both in English and Portuguese (on different days). Experimental tasks were translated into Portuguese. The Portuguese equivalent versions of standardized tests were given. Tasks were administered by English-speaking and Portuguese-speaking psychometrists and clinical graduate students. The wide-scale achievement test was given in English to all children in Ontario; data from the Grade 3 sample were used in this study.

Study 1 Examples and Coding. A few examples of children's responses to the experimental tasks were coded in the following ways:

Theory of mind (see Astington, Pelletier & Homer, 2002)
- "Mom thinks Lisa will say fruit because that's what she told her"
- "Mom thinks Lisa will say fruit because Mom doesn't know that Lisa saw the ice cream and now Lisa knows what it is"
- Score 1/0 for correct/incorrect responses (3 control + 1 first order)
- Score of 0-5 for second order
- Maximum score of 18 (for both stories)

English/Portuguese fables task (Pelletier & Beatty, 2004)
- "If you trick a person, don't expect not to be tricked back" (E)/ "If you do something to someone, then they will do it back" (P)
- "Never give food to strangers" (P)/ "Never take food from strangers" (E)
- Score of 1/0 for correct/incorrect responses (Q 1-3 facts)
- Score of 0-5 for moral of story

- Maximum score of 16 for both fables

Metacognitive Language Task (Astington & Pelletier, 2004) (example, modified for older children)

- "John goes to school. There is a new kid in class. John says, 'Hi, what's your name?' The kid says his name is Daniel. John and Daniel play together. When John gets home, he says to his dad, 'There was a new kid in my class today.' Dad asks, 'What's his name?' John says, 'Er...D...D...' John couldn't tell Dad the new kid's name. Tell me, does John conclude what the new kid's name is, or does John forget what the new kid's name is?'
- Score of 1/-1 for correct/incorrect (x 12)

4.2.2   Results
Comparison of Means

Across all measures in both language groups, there were few differences in means when all children were included in the comparison. However, not surprisingly, Portuguese-speaking children scored significantly lower on the English vocabulary test. Overall in both language groups, high-achieving (levels 3/4) children were similar to each other and low-achieving (levels 1/2) children were similar to each other. For example, there was a significant difference between high- and low-achieving groups in performance on theory of mind and fables ($p < .005$) but no difference between language groups (see Figures 1 and 2). The exception to this finding was that low-achieving Portuguese speaking children performed somewhat lower on English reading skill and reading comprehension subtests than did low-achieving English speaking children. This suggests that differences for second language learners are more pronounced for lower-achieving but not higher-achieving students.

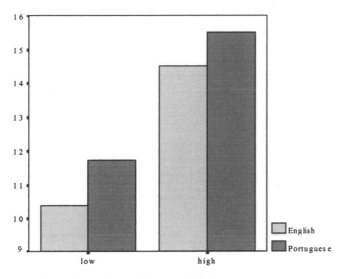

Wide Scale Reading Achievement Level

Figure 1. Low- and high-achievement groups and theory of mind scores

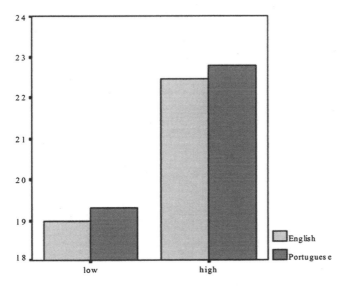

Wide Scale Reading Achievement Level

Figure 2. Low and high achievement levels and fables task performance

Correlations

For Portuguese-speaking children who were tested in both languages, paired samples correlations showed significant relations between their Portuguese decoding and English decoding skills (r=.82, p<.001); their Portuguese theory of mind and English theory of mind (r=.33, p<.05); their Portuguese fables and English fables (r=.59, p<.001), but not Portuguese vocabulary and English vocabulary. On the English measures alone there were significant relations between English decoding skills and Metacognitive Language Task performance (r=.52, p<.001); between English decoding skills and fables task performance (r=.38, p<.001); between English skills and theory of mind (r=.27, p<.05).

Analyses of Variance

English theory of mind and metacognitive language scores were summed to give a total "metacognitive" score. This variable was then re-coded by way of a median split into high and low performance groups. Children's general vocabulary was also re-coded by a median split to make high and low language groups. Given the research showing the importance of general language ability to theory of mind and metacognitive language development (e.g. Astington & Jenkins, 1999), analyses of the contribution of metacognitive factors to story comprehension was carried out for the low language group, to control for the effects of general language development. Group analyses showed that for the low-language children, metacognitive factors were more important in overall reading ability (Reading) and story comprehension (Fables) than for high language children. Specifically within the low language group, children who were in the higher metacognitive group performed significantly better on both the standardized reading comprehension task and on the fables task. See Figures 3 and 4.

Low language group

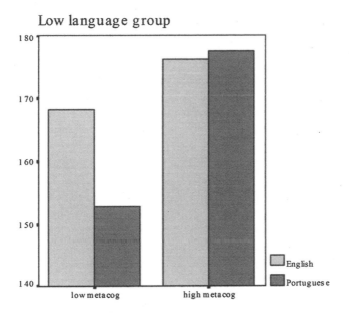

Figure 3. Reading scores for low and high metacognitive groups in low language children.

Low language group

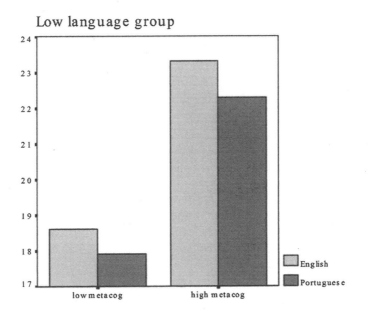

Figure 4. Fables scores for low and high metacognitive groups in low language children.

Regressions

What predicted fables task performance for L1 and L2 children? A stepwise regression on fables task performance with vocabulary, standardized reading (WRMT), theory of mind and metacognitive language as the independent variables showed that across all children, only English vocabulary (PPVT) predicted fables task performance (that is, the ability to make inferences). There were no differences for English and Portuguese groups in these analyses.

The next question asked what predicted performance on wide-scale provincial reading tests. A stepwise regression on the standardized reading achievement test with vocabulary, standardized reading total score on the WRMT, theory of mind and metacognitive language as the independent variables showed that across all children, only the passage comprehension subtest on the standardized reading test (WRMT) predicted performance on the wide-scale reading test (that is, contributed unique variance). This finding is not surprising as one would expect a standardized reading test to predict performance on a wide-scale achievement test.

It was then important to know what predicted performance on the standardized reading test (passage comprehension subtest). A stepwise regression on the passage comprehension score was carried out with vocabulary, metacognitive language, and theory of mind as the independent variables. Results showed that there were differences for English (L1) and Portuguese (L2) children. Specifically, for L1 learners, only vocabulary and word identification skill predicted comprehension on the standardized test. Interestingly, for L2 learners, beyond word identification skill, theory of mind and metacognitive language predicted comprehension. That is, theory of mind and metacognitive language were more salient for L2 learners in reading comprehension.

A final question in Study 1 asked what differences there would be for high- and low-achieving L2 children. Regression analyses were carried out for the L2 group alone. It was found that for low-achieving L2 children, only metacognitive language accounted for unique variance in reading comprehension. For high-achieving L2 children, only vocabulary and word identification predicted comprehension, the same pattern as in the L1 children. Thus, metacognitive language development was most salient for L2 low-achieving children.

4.3   STUDY 2

Study 2 was an extension of Study 1, carried out with younger children from Kindergarten-Grade 2 (4-7 years). The goal was to examine whether the relation between metacognitive factors and story comprehension would continue to be more salient for L2 learners, who were also younger and were just beginning to read and understand stories. In this study, a random sample was employed, rather than a convenience sample selected according to levels. Most of same measures were employed (theory of mind, fables, metacognitive language, general vocabulary), and in Study 2, a short-term memory measure was included; the Digit Span Task from the Wechsler Intelligence Scale for Children-Revised was used for this purpose. Study 2 participants included 61 Kindergarten children (4/5 years old), 86 Grade 1 children (6 years old), and 81 Grade 2 children (7 years old). There were 73 children who spoke English as a first language, 54 who spoke Cantonese as a first language, 42 children who spoke Tagalog as a first language, and 59 who spoke Ukrainian as a first language. As in Study 1, children were drawn from schools serving a range of socioeconomic and cultural backgrounds. Most L2 children were tested in both their first language and in English; however only the results of the English language measures for L2 learners are presented here with the exception of paired L1-L2 correlations.

4.3.1   Results
Comparison of Means

Not surprisingly, significant differences were found in all measures across grade levels (see Table 1).

Table 1. Means and Standard Deviations across Measures and Grade Levels

Task	Grade	N	Mean	Std. Deviation	Minimum	Maximum
Vocab	K	59	79.37	15.23	40.00	105.00
	Gr 1	86	89.89	15.37	47.00	124.00
	Gr 2	76	104.51	17.33	61.00	153.00
	Total	221	92.11	18.80	40.00	153.00
MCL	K	110	8.02	1.92	4.00	12.00
	Gr 1	144	9.04	1.80	4.00	12.00
	Gr 2	135	9.62	1.84	2.00	12.00
	Total	389	8.95	1.95	2.00	12.00
ToM	K	110	8.91	4.79	.00	21.00
	Gr 1	144	10.51	4.69	1.00	22.00
	Gr 2	135	13.71	5.52	.00	25.00
	Total	389	11.17	5.38	.00	25.00
Fables	K	110	6.10	4.25	.00	14.00
	Gr 1	144	8.22	3.81	.00	14.00
	Gr 2	135	9.65	3.84	.00	16.00
	Total	389	8.12	4.18	.00	16.00
Dig Span	K	110	8.00	2.86	.00	14.00
	Gr 1	144	10.17	2.91	2.00	18.00
	Gr 2	135	10.77	3.17	.00	24.00
	Total	389	9.76	3.19	.00	24.00

Likewise, significant differences were found across language groups. English first language children scored higher on vocabulary and theory of mind. This is not surprising for two reasons: English first language children would be expected to understand more English vocabulary than their English second language counterparts. Second, given the strong relation between language development and theory of mind, English first language children might be expected to perform better on theory of mind tasks. Cantonese first language children scored highest on the memory task (Digit Span). Tagalog first language children scored lower on all measures. There were no gender differences in these analyses and gender was not considered further.

Table 2. Means and Standard Deviations across Measures and Language Groups

Task	Language	N	Mean	Std. Deviation	Minimum	Maximum
Vocab Eng 1	English	73	97.30	18.15	60.0	141.0
	Cantonese	47	89.21	19.38	53.0	129.0
	Tagalog	42	86.28	19.20	40.0	120.0
	Ukranian	59	92.15	17.54	48.0	153.0
	Total	221	92.11	18.80	40.0	153.0
Vocab L2	English	0	.	.	.	.
	Cantonese	60	8.18	2.38	2.0	12.0
	Tagalog	47	.57	1.19	.0	5.0
	Ukranian	60	9.85	2.28	4.0	14.0
	Total	167	6.64	4.38	.0	14.0
Digit Span	English	73	6.71	1.58	3.0	11.0
	Cantonese	107	8.12	1.95	4.0	12.0
	Tagalog	90	5.16	2.07	.0	10.0
	Ukranian	119	6.52	1.85	.0	12.0
	Total	389	6.68	2.15	.0	12.0
Megacoglang	English	73	9.61	1.63	6.0	12.0
	Cantonese	107	9.03	1.84	4.0	12.0
	Tagalog	90	7.83	2.06	2.0	12.0
	Ukranian	119	9.32	1.79	4.0	12.0
	Total	389	8.95	1.95	2.0	12.0
Tom 1st Order	English	73	5.19	1.07	2.0	6.0
	Cantonese	107	5.11	.97	2.0	6.0
	Tagalog	90	3.94	1.74	.0	6.0
	Ukranian	119	5.41	.84	3.0	6.0
	Total	389	4.94	1.30	.0	6.0
Tom 2nd Order	English	73	4.15	2.06	.0	8.0
	Cantonese	107	3.57	2.18	.0	9.0
	Tagalog	90	1.73	1.95	.0	7.0
	Ukranian	119	3.73	2.03	.0	8.0
	Total	389	3.30	2.23	.0	9.0
Tom 3rd Order	English	73	3.75	3.34	.0	11.0
	Cantonese	107	3.36	3.01	.0	12.0
	Tagalog	90	1.18	2.16	.0	10.0
	Ukranian	119	3.31	2.77	.0	11.0
	Total	389	2.92	2.98	.0	12.0

Correlations

Across all groups, children's performance on the vocabulary test was related to performance on all other measures. Furthermore, performance on the Metacognitive Language Task was related to performance on all other measures, especially on theory of mind and fables. Theory of mind performance was related to performance on the fables task (r=.49, p<.001). On this experimental measure that was directly translated into Cantonese, Tagalog and Ukrainian, it appears from initial analyses that children who performed well in theory of mind in their first language, also performed well in English. This pattern held for children's performance in the fables. Specifically, English fables task understanding was related to fables understanding in Cantonese, Tagalog, and Ukrainian.

Regressions

Hierarchical stepwise regressions of the English language measures showed that children's theory of mind performance was predicted by vocabulary development. That is, children who performed well on the vocabulary test likewise had higher theory of mind development. This result supports previous findings that general language ability may precede or predict theory of mind understanding (Astington & Jenkins, 1999). The next regression analysis showed that vocabulary, metacognitive language and theory of mind scores each independently predicted children's performance on the fables task. Interestingly for each of the L2 groups (Cantonese, Tagalog and Ukrainian), fables task performance was predicted by metacognitive language development. That is, metacognitive language was more salient in L2 children's ability to understand the deeper meaning of the fables than it was for L1 children. Digit span, the measure of memory ability, made no contribution to fables task understanding.

4.4   SUMMARY AND CONCLUSIONS

These two studies examined the relations among theory of mind, metacognitive language, reading skills, and higher order story comprehension in L1 and L2 learners. Study 1 examined these relations among Grade 4 children who spoke either English or Portuguese as a first language. Study 2 examined these relations among Kindergarten – Grade 2 children who spoke either English, Cantonese, Tagalog or Ukrainian as a first language. There was a clear pattern that emerged from both studies. General vocabulary development contributed most to reading comprehension and fables understanding for L1 children and high-achieving

L2 children. That is vocabulary, more than any other factor, predicted how well L1 and high-achieving L2 learners would do on the reading and story comprehension tasks. However, the metacognitive factors of theory of mind and metacognitive language contributed more to reading and story comprehension for lower-achieving L2 children in Grade 4 and for lower-language L2 children in Kindergarten – Grade 2. It is noteworthy that children in these studies were deemed to be L2 learners, and not bilingual children. This is important to keep in mind, as effects of bilingualism have actually been associated with increased cognitive performance in general and with theory of mind in particular (Bialystok, 1988; Goetz, 2003). Nevertheless more detailed analyses of the L2 children's English language capabilities may show further interaction effects between metacognitive factors and reading.

The results of these studies point to the need for educators to consider the differential needs of first and second language learners as well as higher and lower achieving children, a need that has been raised previously regarding vocabulary and metalinguistic development of L2 learners (Carlisle, Beeman, Davis & Spharm, 1999). Children's achievement may also be related to family background which has been shown to be associated with children's theory of mind development (Cutting & Dunn, 1999). Most studies make recommendations for educational practice based on age, grade and special needs status. However, within normative populations of children, being somewhat higher or lower achieving or speaking a first or second language in school can make a difference in skills that are most important for learning, in this case, reading and story understanding. General vocabulary is important for children's reading achievement among English first language learners and among high-achieving first and second language learners. This suggests the need to provide explicit vocabulary training from an early age as some researchers are showing (e.g. Biemiller, 1998). Although metacognitive factors such as theory of mind and metacognitive language are also important in L1, they are less salient than general vocabulary. However, for second language learners, particularly lower achieving L2 children, metacognitive language and theory of mind are important in children's comprehension and inferencing ability; that is, they make unique contribution to children's understanding. This finding suggests the importance of targeting theory of mind and metacognitive language instruction for L2 learners, particularly those who are struggling in reading. Understanding the specific needs of both L1 and L2 learners in reading will help educators to tailor their instructional practices.

REFERENCES

Astington J. Theory of mind goes to school. Educational Leadership 1998; 56, 3: 46-48.

Astington J., Jenkins J. A longitudinal study of the relation between language and theory of mind development. Developmental Psychology 1999; 35: 1311-1320.

Astington J., Pelletier J. Language and metalanguage in children's understanding of the mind. Poster presented at the meetings of the Cognitive Development Society; 1999; Chapel Hill, NC.

Astington, J., Pelletier, J. "The language of mind: Its relation to teaching and learning." In *Handbook of Psychology in Education: New models of learning, teaching and schooling*, D. Olson, N. Torrance (Eds.), Basil Blackwell, 1996.

Astington, J., Pelletier, J. *Theory of mind and metacognitive vocabulary development in first and second languages.* Unpublished manuscript, University of Toronto, 2004.

Astington J., Pelletier J. Homer B. Theory of mind and epistemological development: The relation between children's second order understanding and their ability to reason about evidence. New Ideas in Psychology, Special Issue on Folk Epistemology 2002; 20, 2-3.

Bahri T., Al-Hussein A. Question type and order of inference in inferential processes during reading comprehension. Perceptual and motor skills 1997, 05, 2. 655 664.

Barry S., Lazarte A. Evidence for mental models: How do prior knowledge, syntactic complexity, and reading topic affect inference generation in a recall task for non-native readers of Spanish? Modern Language Journal 1998; 82, 2: 176-193.

Bialystok E. Levels of bilingualism and levels of linguistic awareness. Developmental Psychology 1988; 23, 4: 56-567.

Biemiller A. Oral vocabulary, word identification, and reading comprehension in English second language and English first language elementary school children. Paper presented at the annual meeting of the Society for the Scientific Study of Reading; 1998; San Diego, CA.

Bruner, J. *Actual minds, possible worlds.* Cambridge, MA: Harvard University Press, 1986.

Carlisle J., Beeman M., Davis L.H., Spharm G. Relationship of metalinguistic capabilities and reading achievement for children who are becoming bilingual. Applied Psycholinguistics 1999; 20: 459-478.

Carrell P., Gajdusek L., Wise T. Metacognition and EFL/ESL reading. Instructional Science 1998; 26: 97-112.

Clarke M. The short circuit hypothesis of ESL reading - or when language competence interferes with reading performance. Modern Language Journal 1980; 64: 203-209.

Cummins J. Linguistic interdependence and the educational development of bilingual children. Review of Educational Research 1979; 49: 222-251.

Cutting A., Dunn J. Theory of mind, emotion understanding, language, and family background. Individual differences and interrelations. Child Development 1999; 70, 4: 853-865.

De Villiers, J. "Language and theory of mind: What are the developmental relationships." In *Understanding other minds: Perspectives from developmental cognitive neuroscience*, Second Edition, S. Baron-Cohen, H. Tager-Flusberg, D. Cohen (Eds.), Oxford: Oxford University Press, 2000.

Fitzgerald J. English-as-a-second-language learners' cognitive reading processes: A review of research in the United States. Review of Educational Research 1995; 65, 2: 145-190.

Franks B., Mulhern S., Schillinger S. Reasoning in a reading context: Deductive inferences in basal reading series. Reading and Writing 1997; 9, 4: 285-312.

Gernsbacher M.A., Hallada B., Robertson R. How automatically do readers infer fictional characters' emotional states? Scientific Studies of Reading 1998; 2, 3: 271-300.

Goetz P. The effects of bilingualism on theory of mind development. Bilingualism: Language and Cognition 2003; 6, 1: 1-15.

Hale C., Tager-Flusberg H. The influence of language on theory of mind: A training study. Developmental Science 2003; 6, 3: 346-359.

Jimenez R., Garcia G., Pearson D. Three children, two languages, and strategic reading: Case studies in bilingual/monolingual reading. American Educational Research Journal 1995; 32, 1: 67-97.

Kuhn D., Pearsall S. Developmental origins of scientific thinking. Journal of Cognition and Development 2000; 1: 113-129.

Lohmann H., Tomasello M. The role of language in the development of false belief understanding: A training study. Child Development 2003; 74, 4: 1130-1144.

Naigles L., Hohenstein J., Marsland K. Learning that thinking is not knowing. Paper presented at the Biennial Meeting of the Society for Research in Child Development; 1997, April; Washington, DC.

Pelletier, J., Beatty, R. *"Look before you leap": A school-wide study of children's understanding of fables.* Manuscript submitted for review. Toronto, Ontario, Canada: OISE/UT, 2004.

Ruffman T., Slade L., Rowlandson K., Rumsey C., Garnahm A. How language relates to belief, desire, and emotion understanding. Cognitive Development 2003; 18: 139-158.

Saville-Troike M. What really matters in second language learning for academic achievement? TESOL Quarterly 1984; 18: 199-219.

Schoonen R., Hulstijn J., Bossers B. Metacognitive and language-specific knowledge in native and foreign language reading comprehension: An empirical study among Dutch students in grades 6, 8 and 10. Language Learning 1998; 48, 1: 71-106.

Tang H.N., Moore D. Effects of cognitive and metacognitive pre-reading activities on the reading comprehension of ESL learners. Educational Psychology 1992; 12, 3-4: 315-331.

Wong Fillmore, L., Valdez, C. "Teaching bilingual learners." In *Handbook of research on teaching*, M.C. Witrock (Ed.), 1986.

Chapter 5

CULTURE AND MENTAL STATES
A Comparison of English and Italian Versions of Children's Books

Marilyn Shatz,[1] Jennifer Dyer,[2] Antonella Marchetti,[3] Davide Massaro.[3]

[1]*University of Michigan;* [2]*California State University, Monterey Bay;* [3]*The Theory of Mind Research Unit, Department of Psychology, Catholic University of the Sacred Heart of Milan.*

5.1   INTRODUCTION

As adults, we typically interact with each other according to the standards and practices of our own communities. In most--if not all--cultures, folk understandings about unobservable motives based on internal mental states form an important part of adults' shared knowledge about the how and why of people's behaviour. Rather than being explicitly explained, these culturally-sanctioned understandings about mental states and the attendant ways to interact are often conveyed subtly through indirect means. One possible source of such information for children is in the books written for them. In this chapter, we summarize the previous research of the first two authors and their colleagues on the mental state information available in children's books; we then report on our recent research comparing books written in English to their translations into Italian, as we ask whether the books contain culture-specific cues to mental state understanding.

Many researchers have investigated children's developing understandings of their own and others' mental states, such as thoughts, feelings, desires, and motivations (e.g., Wellman, 1990; Astington, 1993; Shatz, 1994). Although they still have much to learn about others, children by the ages of 5 or 6 have acquired, without explicit instruction, a solid foundational understanding about mental states. As toddlers, they have begun to use the terms that express mental states (Bretherton & Beeghly, 1982; Shatz, Wellman & Silber, 1983), and by age 4 or 5, they understand that people will sometimes speak or act wrongly because of ignorance or erroneous beliefs (e.g., Perner, Leekam & Wimmer, 1987). Many factors appear to contribute to their developing understanding, including emotional state talk by mothers (Brown & Dunn, 1991) and social class (Shatz, Diesendruck, Martinez & Akar, 2003). In addition, children who have older siblings perform better on typical theory-of-mind tasks (e.g., false belief tasks) (Ruffman, Perner, Naito, Parkin & Clements, 1998), and 4-year-old bilingual English-Chinese speakers have been shown to perform better on some false-belief tasks than monolinguals in either language (Goetz, 2003).

5.2   BOOKS AS A SOURCE OF MENTAL STATE INFORMATION

To assess whether children's storybooks were another feasible source of mental state information for preschoolers, Dyer, Shatz and Wellman (2000) selected 90 narrative books written in English for 3-6-year-olds and considered the frequency and variety of terms connoting emotional states, cognitive states, desires and volitions, and moral evaluations and obligations. The expressions they coded included a list of terms generated from past research on children's use of mental state words ("child-generated terms), as well as terms from the books that connoted mental state ("book-generated" terms). The 90 books were indeed rich sources of information about mental state; there was one mental state reference for every three sentences. They found emotional and cognitive state terms to be the most frequent among the different kinds of terms.

5.3   COMPARING JAPANESE AND U.S. BOOKS

Following this study, Dyer, Shatz, Wellman, & Saito (2004) asked whether children's books in the U.S. were unique or whether books written in other languages in other countries might similarly include frequent references to the mental states of their characters. They chose Japanese children's books as a comparison case because, whereas children's books are common in both industrialized societies, cultural differences in beliefs about and practices governing personal relationships might affect the frequency and variety of references to mental state. For example, past work had shown that middle-class, European-Americans in the U.S. tend to construe the self as more individualistic than middle-class Japanese, who tend to construe the self as more interdependent (Markus & Kitayama, 1991). To test for similarities and differences in the kind and frequency of mental state terms in children's books, they compared a sample of 40 narrative picture books originally written in Japanese and published in Japan to a 40-book sub-sample of the previous 90 U.S. books, these 40 matched for age appropriateness and length to the Japanese books. The earlier list of terms to be coded in English was not simply translated into Japanese for use with the Japanese books. Rather, native speakers of Japanese helped develop a more comprehensive list that included both the words and phrases from the English, where appropriate, as well as apt additions based on native speakers' language knowledge. Native speakers of each respective language then identified instances of the lists' terms and coded them into the categories from the previous study (i.e., emotional states, cognitive states, desire and volition, moral evaluation and obligation), as well as two additional categories: cognitive emotion and traits. In addition, to begin to address possible cultural differences in the two samples of books, the authors examined the sentential contexts of each mental state term from the two largest categories, emotional states and cognitive states, to determine whether they supported an individual or an interpersonal or group-oriented stance. (See Dyer, et al., 2004, for details of this coding).

The results revealed that the Japanese children's books were very similar to the U.S. books. Both were rich in references to mental state; there was a mental state word for every two sentences. Both sets of books most frequently contained emotional and cognitive state terms. Moreover, five of the six most frequent emotional state terms in each language referred to the same state or action: *cry*, *happy*, *laugh*, *like*, and *scare*; and four of the five most frequent cognitive state terms in each language referred to the same state or action: *know*, *maybe*, *seem*, and *think*. Furthermore, our coding of emotional and cognitive state terms into individual or group-oriented contexts did not reveal any differences by culture. Thus, with these sorts of analyses, children's books from two cultures deemed to have some cultural differences in beliefs and practices governing personal relationships were nonetheless similar in their references to mental states: they used largely the same sorts of terms to refer to the same sorts of mental states in relatively similar contexts.

5.4   JAPANESE TRANSLATIONS OF BOOKS IN ENGLISH

However compelling the findings of the Dyer (2004) study, they are, of course, limited by the nature of the analyses on the sets of different books in the two languages. Shatz, Dyer and their colleagues also examined translations of children's books because they surmised it might be easier to discover subtle differences when overall textual content was held constant. That is, they asked whether the very same books were true to the original audience's standards, or whether the books might be modified in subtle ways to make the translated versions more attuned to the culture of the new intended audience. Of course, translation must always accommodate to differences in languages' semantic and syntactic structures, but the authors were concerned with whether there were more culturally motivated, stylistic changes that might reflect a culture's standards, practices, or beliefs. To begin to address these questions, they conducted a study using ten storybooks written in English for American children that had been translated into Japanese and published in Japan (Shatz, Dyer, Wellman, Bromirsky & Hagiwara, 2001). They examined the two versions (English and Japanese) of these books using largely the same codings as in Dyer, et al. 2004).

One methodological difference was that in examining the books for instances of the mental state words or phrases, Shatz et al. utilized a "double translation" method that allowed them to work with four versions of each book: two versions were the two published versions of the story, one in the original language and one in the language of translation; the other two "researcher" versions were obtained by having bilingual speakers translate the published versions, with a native English speaker translating the Japanese volume, and a native Japanese speaker translating the English volume. Comparing these various versions allowed them to discuss in detail the differences found across versions and to explore their import. Thus, non-native researchers doing the translations could note when the professional translators had translated something in a way that seemed unusual to them, and all the researchers could focus on possible motivations for the professionals' choices.

The results revealed that the overall frequency of mental state terms was about the same. Nonetheless, whereas the illustrations remained the same, the texts in the supposedly very same books were sometimes modified. The locations of the terms sometimes differed, as did some of the specific terms. And, in some cases, modifications seemed to have been made to accommodate the cultural values of the Japanese audience. As an example of such a case, consider this instance from *Madeline* by Ludwig Bemelmans. Madeline is an adventuresome little girl who regularly tests her teacher's patience and sense of control. On one page Madeline and her schoolmates are crossing a bridge. Whereas her schoolmates are obediently following their teacher, Miss Clavel, Madeline, at the end of the line, is seen walking on the wall overlooking the river, and the text in English is, "and nobody knew so well how to frighten Miss Clavel". But in the Japanese version, though the picture remains the same, the text reads, "sensei no misu kuraberu ha, nanigotonimo odorokanai hitodeshita" [the teacher, Miss Clavel, was a person who wouldn't be surprised by anything.]. The text was apparently modified because Japanese children are not expected to get the better of their elders.

Equally revealing of cultural differences were those cases where words that are considered in both cultures to be child-appropriate and are found in both book versions nonetheless appear in different locations depending on the contexts each culture deems appropriate. So, emotion terms are sometimes found in one version and not another. For example, in *Swimmy*, the adventuresome little fish who wants to investigate the world makes his invitation to explore "happily" to other fish in the English version; the emotion term is omitted in the Japanese. Possibly the Japanese translator considered it inappropriate for Swimmy's adventurousness to make him happy. But, it certainly was not omitted because the Japanese avoid explicit use of emotion terms, as the next example illustrates. In the English version of *No Roses for Harry*, Harry the dog begs Grandma to take him for a walk. She responds, "All right, Harry…after I've had my lunch and a nap, we'll go for a walk." One has to make the admittedly easy inference that going for a walk will make the dog happy. But in the Japanese, Grandma explicitly recognizes Harry's likely emotional state by saying "I'll let you have the pleasure of my taking you for a walk." From numerous examples such as these, the authors concluded that translations into Japanese do contain some modifications motivated by culture-specific practices and beliefs.

5.5 UNIVERSAL AND CULTURE-SPECIFIC FACTORS IN UNDERSTANDING OF MIND

Why did the analysis of books translated from English into Japanese reveal cultural differences whereas the comparative analysis of the two original languages' books did not? Dyer et al. (2004) suggest that there are both universal and culture-specific aspects to acquiring an understanding of mental states. In virtually any culture with linguistic expressions for these states, books need to provide a basic vocabulary for expressing mental states in a variety of contexts, both individual and interpersonal. At the same time, children need some exposure to the culturally-mitigated ways of expressing such states. In relatively general analyses, similarities of use may mask differences, especially for cultures with many commonalities. In more content-held-constant analyses, subtle differences of expression may be more readily discoverable.

5.6   EXPLORING THE GENERALITY OF CULTURAL INFLUENCES

Despite their similar status as economically advantaged, industrialized countries, the U.S. and Japan are vastly different, in the heterogeneity of their populations, in their histories, and in their beliefs and practices about personal relations. The various analyses of children's books in these two such different countries revealed both similarities and differences in the representation of mental states. To determine the generality of this finding, we asked whether a comparison of books written in English with their translations into Italian, the language of another western culture, would reveal the same pattern of similarities and culturally-mitigated differences as the U.S.-Japan studies or whether there would be no discernible differences in the ways children's books express mental states.

We already knew of one example of English-Italian differences occurring in translation that suggested we might indeed find differences even between similar cultures. In the book written by Shatz (1994) on toddler development about ten years ago, her grandson had provided many examples, especially about his mental state understanding. So, his picture had graced the book's cover. Four years later, the book was translated into Italian, and surprising to the author, both the title and the cover photo were changed. The original title, *A toddler's life: Becoming a person*, became *Diario dei primi passi* [Diary of first steps] in the Italian translation. Figure 1 illustrates how different the two covers are. When asked about the changes, the American editor speculated that perhaps the Italian publisher had intended to make the book more appealing to an Italian audience, but she could be no more specific[8]. Guided by this anecdote, and because the translation method had been the more revealing of culturally-mitigated differences in the earlier study, we used the translation method for the comparative U.S.-Italy study, examining Italian translations of children's books written in English for possible modifications consistent with culture-specific beliefs or practices.

---

[8] In the Farnese Palace in Piacenza some years later, the first author came upon a painting of an old man and a toddler by Emilio Longoni. The painting is entitled, "I primi et ultimi passi" [First and last steps.]. Possibly the painting was the inspiration for the title change.

Figure 1. English and Italian Versions of the Cover of a Book by Marilyn Shatz.

5.7 THE PRESENT STUDY
5.7.1 Method

We gathered 10 narrative picture books for children aged 3 to 6 that were originally written in English for children in the U.S. and then translated into Italian and published in Italy (see Table 1 for the titles). The coding protocol of mental state terms followed Dyer, et al. (2000). Five categories of terms were used: emotional states (e.g., *happy, sad*), cognitive states (e.g., *think, know, remember*), desire and volition (e.g., *want, need*), moral evaluations and obligations (e.g., *naughty, had to, should*), and cognitive emotions (e.g., *surprise*). A native speaker of English and a native speaker of Italian identified and coded the mental state terms in the English and Italian versions respectively. For the double translation method, an Italian-English bilingual translated the published English versions into Italian, and another Italian-English bilingual translated the published Italian versions into English, resulting in 4 versions of each book, 2 published and 2 researcher versions. We then discussed whether the versions differed, and if so, whether differences in the translations of mental state terms resulted from lexical gaps or something more interesting culturally.

Table 1. English and Italian Titles of Target Books

English Title	Italian Title
Emma's Pet	Nina vuole un amico
Frederick	Frederick
Harold and the Purple Crayon	Harold e la matita viola
If You Give a Mouse a Cookie	Se dai un biscotto a un topo
Just a Minute!	Aspetta un minuto!
Little Bear	Storie di orsacchiotto
Madeline	Madeline
Spring Story	Storia di primavera
Swimmy	Guizzino
There's a Nightmare in my Closet	Brutti sogni in ripostiglio

Note: All the books originated in the U.S. and were written in English. The Italian versions were published in Italy and translated into Italian.

5.7.2 Results

First, we present the overall frequencies of mental state expressions in the books in the two languages. Then we present some of the intriguing differences by language in the books and discuss the various data analyses. In tabulating the frequencies of the mental state terms and phrases, we counted both types and tokens. A type is, for example, the root word *think*, and a token is one instance of that word in any of its morphological forms. Thus, two instances of *think* in a book would be calculated as one type and two tokens, as would one instance each of the two terms *think* and *thinking*.

Table 2 presents overall data across the books on tokens, types, and ranges of mental state terms. It shows that there were relatively small, non-significant differences in the total number of mental state types and tokens when tallied across the books; nor is the range of frequencies of the different mental state terms very different by language across all ten books. Thus, just as Japanese translations do, Italian translations have amounts of mental state terms roughly comparable to those in the English originals. Yet, Table 3 shows that there were differences across the ten books by language in the frequency of mental state tokens in the various categories. This suggested that sometimes the very same story, expressed in two different languages, could differ with regard to the use of mental state expressions. Indeed, a non-parametric related sample Wilcoxon test revealed that the Italian translations contained significantly more mental state tokens than did the versions in English ($Z = -2.32$, $p < .05$).

To explore within-book differences further, we examined the different sorts of correspondences between mental state expressions in the books across the two languages. We categorized each mental state term according to one of the following five categories: 1) the same word was used in both versions (e.g., *happy* in English and *contento* [*happy*] in Italian), 2) a different word was used, but the meaning of the original was preserved (e.g., *want* in English and *piacerebbe* [*would like*] in Italian), 3) a different word was used and the meaning was different (e.g., *think* in English and *inventare* [*to invent*] in Italian), 4) a mental state term was used in one version and a phrase with the same general meaning (although no easily identifiable mental state term) was used in the other version (e.g., *hugged* in English and *lancia tra le braccia dell'amico* [*threw herself into the arms of*] in Italian), and 5) a mental state word or phrase was used in one version but there was no discernable term or phrase in the other version (e.g., The Italian version of *Frederick* used the term *allegri* [*cheerful*] with no corresponding word or phrase in the English version. The English version of *Frederick* used the term *lucky* with no corresponding word or phrase in the Italian version.).

Table 2. Frequencies of Mental State Tokens, Types, and Range of Frequencies of Mental State Tokens

Kinds of Terms	Frequency of Mental State Tokens		Frequency of Mental State Types		Range of Frequencies of Mental State Tokens	
	English	Italian	English	Italian	English	Italian
Emotional State	87	86	47	56	1-21	1-20
Cognitive State	86	92	41	39	0-19	2-22
Desire and Volition	39	42	6	4	0-10	0-13
Moral Evaluation and Obligation	15	24	11	11	0-5	0-6
Cognitive Emotion	12	12	3	3 .	0-6	0-7
Total	239	256	108	113		

Table 3. English and Italian Frequencies (Tokens) by Book

			Mental State Term		
Book	ES	CS	D&V	ME&O	CE
Emma's Pet	*13, 15	1, 3	2, 3	0, 0	0, 0
Frederick	8, 8	10, 9	0, 3	1, 3	0, 0
Harold and the Purple Crayon	7, 6	19, 22	5, 4	2, 0	0, 0
If You Give a Mouse a Cookie	1, 1	11, 9	9, 10	1, 1	0, 0
Just a Minute	1, 1	0, 2	7, 4	1, 3	0, 0
Little Bear	8, 6	17, 16	10, 13	2, 3	1, 1
Madeline	15, 16	1, 3	1, 1	2, 2	1, 0
Spring Story	21, 20	16, 18	4, 4	5, 6	2, 2
Swimmy	8, 8	9, 8	1, 0	1, 5	2, 2
There's a Nightmare in my Closet	5, 5	2, 2	0, 0	0, 1	6, 7
Total	87, 86	86, 92	39, 42	15, 24	12, 12

*Numbers are English and Italian frequencies, respectively. ES = emotional state, CS = cognitive state, D&V = desire and volition, ME&O = moral evaluation and obligation, CE = cognitive-emotion.

Table 4 shows that nearly half of all the terms used directly translatable words, for example, *contento* for *happy*. However, it is the instances from the other categories that represent some of the interesting differences between these books. We believe these cases represent some of the cultural differences between the groups for whom these books are targeted. One of the differences we found repeatedly was an increased intensity of expression in the Italian over the English. Sometimes, this took the form of a stronger emotional expression than was present in the original. For example, from *Emma's Pet*, the word *hugged* in the English, is replaced in Italian by a phrase with the same meaning, albeit somewhat stronger in feeling, *lancia tra le braccia dell'amico* [*threw herself into the arms of...*]. Since there is an Italian word for *hugged, abbracciato*, which is fairly common and likely understood by young children, it is improbable that the translator made the change simply to avoid the direct translation.

Table 4. English and Italian Frequencies (Tokens) of Word Correspondences

			Mental State Term		
Book	ES	CS	D&V	ME&O	CE
Same word	34	44	29	10	9
Different word/same meaning	19	16	2	1	1
Different word/different meaning	11	11	4	2	0
MS word/ms phrase	2	0	0	0	0
MS word/no corresponding ms word or phrase	*21, 22	15, 21	6, 9	4, 11	2, 2

*Numbers are English and Italian frequencies, respectively. ES = emotional state, CS = cognitive state, D&V = desire and volition, ME&O = moral evaluation and obligation, CE = cognitive emotion.

Another example comes from text in *Madeline*, in the very same place that we noted earlier had been modified from the English in the Japanese version. Here we see a modification in the Italian version too, but now the strong emotional description in the English is made even stronger in the Italian. Recall that the original English is, "And nobody knew so well how to frighten Miss Clavel." In Italian, the phrase is, "e faceva impazzire la signorina Artura ["She made Miss Artura crazy."]. As with the *hugged* example, the change was very probably not mandated by lexical decisions per se; although rhyme is a constraining factor in both versions, it is unlikely the sole reason for the change. Another example from *Harold and the Purple Crayon* similarly reveals increased intensity from the English to the Italian, this time with the implication of emotional frustration added to a cognitive state. The English phrase, *tried to think where* is somewhat neutral in emotion, but in the Italian, the emotionally richer locution *chissà dove sarà* [*who knows where?*] seems to index the character's frustration with not knowing where to look.

In addition to the intensity of expression, there were two other ways we found the books differed. For one, Italian versions were sometimes more explicit or precise regarding mental states than were the English versions. Consider an example from *Just a Minute*. During the first part of the story, whenever a little mouse asked others to join her in activities, they would always say, "just a minute!" Later on, the English reads, "Now, if I'm watching television, and my mom says, 'Dinner is ready,' I say just a minute!" The implication in the English version, carried not by a cognitive state verb but by 'now,' is that the mouse has learned from experience how to put others off. In contrast, the Italian version makes the implication explicit with a fuller explanation and a mental state term, *imparato* [*learned*]. It reads, "Ma adesso ho imparato come fare. Quando sto guardando la televisione, e la mamma dice: - A tavola! ...anch'io dico: - Tra un minuto!, ["But now I learned how to do it. When I'm watching television and my mom says, 'come to the table,' I say, 'just a minute!'"]

For another, we observed that the Italian versions sometimes used terms that expressed or implied a greater sense of social responsibility or awareness. For example, in *Spring Story*, all of the mice in the village are preparing a surprise birthday party for Wilford. Each mouse has a different job to do to prepare for the surprise. In the Italian, this notion of "doing one's duty," is made explicit in the following excerpt, "Nel frattempo il signor de' Topis stava facendo il suo dovere lungo il fossato." [Meanwhile, the signor was doing his duty...]. In the English, there is no notion of "duty." Indeed, there is no mental state reference at all. The excerpt is, "Lord Woodmouse, meanwhile, was making his way down the stream."

A stronger sense of social awareness in Italian versions is also depicted in *Frederick*. Here, the ending in the Italian version showcases more respect for others' work and modesty regarding one's own talents than does the English, in which the main character shows pleasure in the others' applause for him with no mention of appreciating their work. The English version reads, "When Frederick had finished, they all applauded. "'But Frederick,' they said, 'You are a poet.' Frederick blushed, took a bow, and said shyly, 'I know it.'" The Italian reads, "Quando Federico ebbe finito, i topolini scoppiarono in un caloroso applauso. Federico arrossì, abbassò gli occhi confuso, e timidamente rispose: - 'Non voglio applausi, non merito alloro. Ognuno, in fondo, fa il proprio lavoro.'" ["When Frederick was finished, they exploded into warm applause. Frederick blushed, confused, lowered his eyes, and shyly he answered: 'I do not want applause, I do not deserve laurel. Everybody, after all, does his own job.'"]

5.8   SUMMARY AND DISCUSSION

In sum, we discovered three ways in which the Italian translations differed from the English originals: heightened emotional intensity, more specific expression of mental states, and more explicit expression of social awareness or responsibility. Although the finding of more or heightened emotionality in the Italian versions may seem simply to confirm a stereotype of Italian social behaviour, our other findings of more specificity of mental state terms and more explicit social awareness and responsibility seem less obvious as possible differences between the two cultures. Indeed, we contend that all three kinds of examples illustrate that the Italian translations reflect beliefs or practices common in Italian culture, and we offer two kinds of support for our contention. First, we offer additional confirmatory statistical analyses. Recall that the by-book analysis confirmed a greater use of mental state terms in the Italian than in the English versions. When by-book related sample tests were conducted by category on the proportions of mental state verbs in each category, there were significantly more emotional state terms in Italian than in English ($Z = -2.701$, $p < .05$), and a tendency for more evaluation and obligation terms in Italian than in English versions ($Z = -1.836$, $p < .066$). Moreover, when we asked, using Cohen's K analyses (Cohen, 1960), whether there was a systematic tendency for translators either to maintain or to modify each mental state term in each book, we found no significant results. Thus, the differences in occurrence rates of mental state terms are just those compatible with the putative cultural differences.

Second, Eco's recent discussion of translated texts (Eco, 2003) provides inside into why cultural differences are to be found in translated works. Eco proposes that a translator acts as a negotiator between the cultural assumptions necessarily embodied in the original text by its author and the cultural expectations of the readers of the text the translator is creating. How much the translator is conscious of this process of negotiation between two possibly divergent cultural stances as she chooses the expressions for her translated text I an interesting question and a matter for further research. Thus, although we acknowledge that word choice, rhyming considerations, and other factors may affect translators' decisions, our findings support Eco's argument, and we agree with him that translations are not straightforward transfers from one linguistic system to another but rather involve processes of interpretation influenced by cultural understandings, whether explicit or implicit.

5.9   CONCLUSIONS

We do not want to overemphasize the differences we found because there were many commonalities among the versions as well. As with the Japanese translations of a mostly different set of books, we found all the versions had an abundance of mental state terms, Indeed, across all books, the total numbers of terms and types are not very different. Still, the differences are striking. Translators in both Japan and Italy found ways to modify stories according to the styles and cultural values of their intended audiences. Thus, the suggestion that books offer culture-specific, as well as universally-relevant, information about mental states (Dyer, et al., 2004) finds support in the comparisons of books from different cultures.

Finally, the modifications found in translations raise an important question about the role of translated books in the education of young children. When translations change the originals to accommodate to the styles and values of the intended audience, then those translations are NOT teaching children about other cultures' styles of expression and values. Rather, the styles and values of the translation's culture are being re-enforced. Whether or not translators do this purposely, either for didactic purposes or to make the books more palatable for consumers, the consequence is that we cannot assume that children exposed to translations will gain from them a good understanding of a varied, multi-cultural world.

ACKNOWLEDGMENTS

We thank Michael Siegal for suggestions for additional analyses. The work was supported in part by a Rackham Merit Fellowship and a National Science Fellowship to the second author and grants to the first author from the Office of Vice President for Research, and the Dean's office, the College of Literature, Science, and The Arts, University of Michigan. Jennifer Dyer is now at California State University, Monterey Bay.

This research was supported in part by a Collaborative Fellows Grant from Boston College. Portions of this research were presented at the meetings of the Cognitive Development Society Oct '03 and AERA April '04.

REFERENCES

Astington, J.W. *The child's discovery of the mind*. Cambridge, Mass.: Harvard University Press, 1993.

Bretherton I., Beeghly M. Talking about internal states: The acquisition of an explicit theory of mind. Developmental Psychology 1982; 18, 6: 906-921.

Brown J.R., Dunn J. "You can cry, mum": The social and developmental implications of talk about internal states. British Journal of Developmental Psychology 1991; 9: 237-256.

Cohen J. A coefficient of agreement for nominal scales. Educational and Psychological Measurement 1960; 20: 37-46.

Dyer J.R., Shatz M., Wellman H.M. Young children's storybooks as a source of mental state information. Cognitive Development 2000; 15, 1: 17-37.

Dyer, J.R., Shatz, M., Wellman, H.M., Saito, M. *Mental state references in U.S. and Japanese children's books*. Manuscript under review, 2004.

Eco, U. *Dire quasi la stessa cosa. Esperienze di traduzione*. Milano: Bompiani, 2003.

Goetz P.J. The effects of bilingualism on theory of mind development. Bilingualism: Language & Cognition 2003; 6, 1: 1-15.

MarKus H., Kitayama S. Culture and the self: Implications for cognition, emotion, and motivation. Psychological Review 1991; 98,2: 224-253.

Perner J., Leekam S.R., Wimmer H. Three-year-olds' difficulty with false belief: The case for a conceptual deficit. British Journal of Developmental Psychology 1987; 5, 2: 125-137.

Ruffman T., Perner J., Naito M., Parkin L., Clements W.A. Older (but not younger) siblings facilitate false belief understanding. Developmental Psychology 1998; 34, 1: 161-174.

Shatz, M. *A toddler's life: Becoming a person*. New York: Oxford University Press. 1994, It. Tran. *Diario dei primi passi,* Bologna: il Mulino, 1998.

Shatz M., Diesendruck G., Martinez-Beck I., Akar D. The influence of language and socioeconomic status on children's understanding of false belief. Developmental Psychology 2003; 39, 4: 717-729.

Shatz, M., Dyer, J.R., Wellman, H.M., Bromirsky, C., Hagiwara, N. "English and Japanese versions of children's books: Uncovering pragmatic relations between language and culture." In *Research on child language acquisition. Proceedings of the IASCL - VIII International Congress for the Study of Child Language, San Sebastian, Spain*, M. Almgren, A. Barrena, M.-J. Ezeizabarrena, I. Idiazabal, B. MacWhinney (Eds.), Somerville, MA: Cascadilla Press, 2001.

Shatz M., Wellman H.M., Silber S. The acquisition of mental verbs: A systematic investigation of the first reference to mental state. Cognition 1983; 14: 301-321.

Wellman, H.M. *The child's theory of mind*. Cambridge, MA: MIT Press, 1990.

Chapter 6

MIND OVER GRAMMAR
Reasoning in Aphasia and Development

Michael Siegal,[1] Rosemary Varley,[2] Stephen C. Want.[3]

[1]*Department of Psychology, University of Sheffield, Western Bank, Sheffield S10 2TP, UK;* [2]*Department of Human Communication Sciences, University of Sheffield, Sheffield S10 2TA, UK;* [3]*Department of Psychology, University of British Columbia, Vancouver, Canada V6T 1Z4*

In this chapter, we examine the relation between language and cognition in the light of recent evidence for reasoning without mediation by grammatical knowledge. Research on propositional reasoning (involving "theory of mind" understanding) in adult patients with aphasia reveals that reasoning can proceed in the absence of explicit grammatical knowledge. Conversely, evidence from deaf children shows that the presence of such knowledge is not sufficient to account for reasoning. These findings are in keeping with recent research on the development of naming, categorization, and imitation, indicating that children's reasoning about objects and actions is guided by inferences about others' communicative intentions. We discuss the extent to which reasoning is supported by, and tied to, language in the form of conversational awareness and experience rather than grammar.

It is widely acknowledged that language plays a fundamental role in the development of human reasoning (Bowerman & Levinson, 2000; Carruthers, 1998). One key proposal is that certain forms of reasoning can only take place in explicit sentences of a natural language (Segal, 1996; Smith, Apperly & White, 2003). Grammatical capacity is seen to be necessary to reason out solutions to particular problems, such as ones involving theory of mind (ToM) understanding in which the task is to determine the relation between others' mental states (e.g., beliefs and desires) and behaviour. For example, in a 'changed contents' ToM task

(Perner, Wimmer & Leekam, 1987), the subject is shown a familiar container (e.g., a Smarties tube) and is asked to indicate what it holds. Then the unusual contents are revealed (e.g., pencils) and the subject is asked what a person who has not seen the contents would say is inside the container).

Some features of a ToM involving eye gaze and emotion interpretation have been viewed as involving a "social-perceptual" component that is language-independent and has its own developmental trajectory (Tager-Flusberg & Sullivan, 2000). By contrast, it has been claimed that ToM reasoning on a changed contents task involves a "social-cognitive component" that depends upon language, specifically the grammatical capacity to embed one proposition within another statement ('Mary knows that John (falsely) thinks Smarties are in the tube') (De Villiers & Pyers, 2002). Astington & Jenkins (1999) carried out a longitudinal study of the relation between language and ToM reasoning in children who were mostly 3-years-old at the first time of testing. The children were tested twice more at 3.5 month intervals. Language ability in the form of syntax was moderately correlated with later performance on changed contents and other ToM reasoning tasks involving the ability to predict the behaviour of a person with a false belief. On this basis, it has been concluded that grammar is instrumental in ToM development.

In this article, we examine the extent to which ToM and other forms of reasoning are supported by grammar. We consider an alternative account that language serves to support reasoning in terms of conversational awareness and experience of others' intentions in communication.

6.1   REASONING IN AGRAMMATIC APHASIA

One profitable avenue for investigation into the relation between grammar and reasoning concerns the study of people who have severe forms of aphasia - an acquired disorder of language, resulting from damage to language-mediating regions of the cortex and associated sub-cortical structures.

In aphasia, there can sometimes be dramatic excisions of components of the language system, as in the case of severe agrammatic aphasia where the patient shows little or no ability to understand or construct sentences in any modality of language use (spoken or written). Even more extensive impairment is found in global aphasia where in addition to loss of grammatical ability there can also be substantial impairment of lexical knowledge. It is widely acknowledged that cognition is retained in many cases of aphasia (Kertesz, 1988). However, previous research has not investigated sufficiently precise questions about the forms of thinking that are mediated by grammar; the nature and degree of language impairment in the patients studied was equally non-specific. If the claim is that language propositions supported by grammar are necessary for ToM and causal cognition, a test then requires that aphasic patients have no access to propositional language in any modality of language use. Similarly, questions of disruption of cognition in aphasia have been addressed through administering tests from non-verbal intelligence scales with no clear rationale as to why language might be implicated in, for example, visuo-spatial problem solving. It is only now that claims of specific forms of language mediation (e.g., language propositions) in specific types of reasoning (e.g., ToM) have been tested.

Recent studies have adopted this more focused approach to the relation of grammar to cognition in aphasia (Varley & Siegal, 2000; Varley, 2002; Varley, Siegal & Want, 2001). These have revealed that patients with severe agrammatic aphasia, who have minimal access to propositional language, are capable both of ToM understanding and simple causal reasoning. For example, SA is a man in his fifties who has extensive damage to left hemisphere language zones following a focal bacterial infection of the brain. Following the lesion, SA displayed severe aphasia. He retained a large amount of vocabulary, but he had minimal grammatical ability. His difficulties in grammatical processing included a severe impairment in the understanding of spoken and written sentences, and he was unable to construct sentences in either speech or writing output. SA also had problems in understanding and using verbs. In psycholinguistic theories of sentence processing, the ability to understand and retrieve verbs is seen as a key process in both decoding and constructing grammatical language (Garrett, 1982). These grammatical processing deficits could not be accounted for by auditory and visual short-term memory constraints as SA showed grammatical comprehension difficulties on structures within his three-item retention limit (Martin, 1993). Despite these difficulties with language, SA's everyday activities included driving, playing chess, and financial planning, and these activities indicated that he remained capable of sophisticated cognition. This impression was confirmed by neuropsychological tests assessing abstract thinking and causal reasoning. In comparison to control subjects, SA's score on the Wisconsin Card Sorting Test (Heaton, 1993) was at the 91st percentile, and on the Story Arrangement Test of the Wechsler Adult Intelligence Scale at the 84th percentile. SA's ability to infer causes of events was shown by his perfect score on 15 trials of a 'causal association' test. This ability extends to reasoning about novel or unseen causes in tasks that demand the application of inductive reasoning in scientific problem-solving (Varley, 2002).

SA was also tested on a series of 'changed container' ToM tasks involving inferring the knowledge of others in instances where that knowledge was different from reality and also from the knowledge possessed by self (Wimmer & Perner, 1983). Despite his profound impairment of propositional language, SA demonstrated retained theory of mind understanding. Thus, reasoning about beliefs, together with other forms of sophisticated cognition, involve processes that are independent of grammar. By contrast, patients without aphasia, but who have had lesions to the right (non-language dominant) hemisphere display impaired ToM reasoning, as well as difficulties in understanding sarcasm, jokes, and the conversational implications of questions (Happé et al., 1999; Surian & Siegal, 2001). This double dissociation between grammar and cognition indicates that grammatical language is neither a necessary or sufficient condition for causal reasoning and ToM understanding. At least in adults, there is a dedicated neural substrate to theory of mind reasoning that is autonomous from grammar (Siegal & Varley, 2002; Saxe, Carey & Kanwisher, 2004).

People with aphasia have had normal competency in language prior to brain injury. Grammar might then be unnecessary for ongoing reasoning as instead it has served to configure reasoning in early development. However, the evidence from children with specific language impairment (SLI) indicates that they succeed as readily as normal children on ToM tasks (Leslie & Frith, 1988). Moreover, Van der Lely et al. (1998) report a case study of a child having a subtype of SLI specific to grammar who was able to perform well on a range of abstract nonverbal tasks at a level similar to that of normal children. But given that grammatical SLI does not result in the radical excision of grammar and the child is able to construct simple language propositions, it is unclear whether SLI studies represent a genuine test of the role of grammatical mediation in reasoning.

6.2 REASONING BEYOND GRAMMAR: EVIDENCE FROM NATIVE AND NON NATIVE SIGNING DEAF CHILDREN

Clearer evidence for the position that grammar is insufficient for reasoning can be found from research involving deaf children from hearing families who achieve proficiency in the syntax of sign language only after school entry. These children are reliably outperformed on ToM tasks by native signing children from families with a deaf signing member.

To examine the effects of access to language on cognitive development, Peterson and Siegal (1999) compared groups of severely and profoundly deaf children aged 5 to 12 years in their performance on theory of mind tasks. One group of children consisted of "native signers" from households with fluently signing deaf conversational partners. Another consisted of children from hearing families who learned sign language later from sources outside the home. All children were given tasks in which they were asked to predict the behaviour of a person with a false belief about the appearance, contents, or location of an object. For example, the children received a "changed location" ToM task following the procedure used by Baron-Cohen et al (1985). This consisted of two trials, each beginning with a girl hiding a marble in a basket and leaving the scene. While she was gone, a boy shifted the marble to a covered box (Trial 1) or the experimenter's pocket (Trial 2). The girl returned. Then the children were asked a belief test question ("Where will the girl look for her marble?"), followed by two control questions ("Where is the marble now?" and "Where did the girl put the marble in the beginning?").

Deaf children from signing families scored at a level similar to those of hearing children. However, the deaf from signing families outperformed deaf children from hearing families who in turn scored at a level similar to a group of children with autism. Recent research (Woolfe et al., 2002) has replicated this finding using a newly developed test of syntax and morphology in British Sign Language (Herman et al., 1999) and "thought-picture" measures that minimize the need for the use of language in ToM tasks (Custer, 1996). The two deaf signing groups were equivalent in their syntax as well as on measures of spatial intelligence and executive functioning in shifting attention. Nevertheless, the native signers again excelled in their ToM performance compared to their late signing counterparts. This pattern is consistent with that shown in other studies on the relation between language and cognition in deaf children (Peterson & Siegal, 2000).

By the age of 9-15 years both native and late signers can often ascribe beliefs to themselves and others in story narratives (Marschark et al., 2000). Nevertheless, the difficulties of late signers on ToM reasoning tasks can linger even at 13-16 years of age (Russell et al., 1998). These results attest to the importance of early access to a language for cognitive development, specifically with regard to understanding the minds of others. Such differences cannot be attributed to syntax given that the syntax of late signers is equivalent to that of native signers at the time of testing. The difficulties of late signing children on ToM tasks do not generalize to causal reasoning in the physical and biological domains (Peterson & Siegal, 1997), and are specific to the representation of false beliefs rather than the representation of false photographs (Peterson & Siegal, 1998).

In indicating that ToM reasoning extends beyond grammar, these findings establish the critical role of early access to conversational input. A deaf child growing up with a signing deaf family member may have the same access to conversation, and to an explicit ToM, as do normal hearing preschoolers, even though the medium for communication is sign language rather than speech. By contrast, up to the point of entering a signing classroom at school, the communication of deaf children with hearing family members can be limited to topics with a visual reference (Meadow, 1975). Thus late signers may not profit by the focus on mental states that occurs in the dialogues between hearing children and their mothers (Brown et al., 1996) and lack awareness in understanding the basic shared grounding for communication - the mutual beliefs, knowledge, and assumptions underpinning conversational exchanges (Clark & Brennan, 1991). Despite their proficiency in the syntax of sign language, they have difficulties in displaying their knowledge about the causal effects of holding false beliefs in ToM reasoning tasks. In this respect, many deaf children with cochlear implants may experience barriers to conversation similar to those of late signers. Although a small group of "oral deaf" children with cochlear implants in Peterson & Siegal's (1999) study scored similarly to hearing children, more recent research has pointed to variable performance among children with implants (Peterson, in press). A substantial number of children with cochlear implants have persistent difficulties in speech intelligibility to the extent that these difficulties interfere with their abilities to engage in conversations that provide insight into others' beliefs (Tye-Murray, 2003).

There are other reasons to maintain that grammar in the form of sentence complementation is insufficient for success on ToM reasoning tasks. As observed elsewhere (Astington & Jenkins, 1999; Siegal & Surian, 2003), 3-year-olds who fail ToM tasks spontaneously produce sentence complements in their speech. They correctly answer questions involving sentence complementation if those sentences take the structure [person]-[pretends]-[that x] (e.g., "He pretends that his puppy is outside"). By contrast, 3-year-olds do poorly when given sentences that take the form [person]-[thinks]-[that x] (e.g., "He thinks that his puppy is outside"). Both use the same complements yet children only pass when "pretend" is used. Moreover, there are many instances of sign languages and spoken Aboriginal Australian languages in which there is no sentence complementation (M.A. Baker, personal communication). Instead of clausal complements such as "John told everyone that Mary washed the car", users of such languages instead employ "clausal adjunct" forms such as "Mary having washed the car, John told everyone (it)." If complementation were necessary to instantiate ToM reasoning, no ToM would be possible in these language groups. Given these considerations, the syntax of sentence complementation falls short of providing a complete account of ToM performance, at least on pictorial tasks.

6.3   REFERENTIAL INTENT IN NAMING AND CATEGORIZATION

That grammar is not sufficient for reasoning raises issues about its role in conceptual development, particularly in the naming and categorization of objects. Whereas it has long been established that syntactic cues such as a speaker's use of definite and indefinite articles and present participles assist in children's word learning (Brown, 1957), very young children under the age of 3 years have not yet attained a level of grammatical ability that allows vocabulary items to be combined to create complex propositions. They do not normally utter sentences such as "Joe thought that there was candy in the jar" let alone more sophisticated propositions that refer to false beliefs such as "Joe thought that Jill knew that there was candy in the jar."

Nevertheless, in preferential looking tasks it has been shown that the "fast mapping" of words to objects occurs even before children have reached their period of maximal vocabulary development (Schafer & Plunkett, 1998). Children's spontaneous naming and categorization proceed rapidly in the absence of syntactic cues and a well-developed grammar; what is essential is an understanding of the speaker's referential intent (Bloom & Markson, 1999). To illustrate, Gelman & Bloom (2000) asked 3-year-olds, 5-year-olds, and adults to name a series of simple objects. In one condition, the objects were described as purposefully created (e.g., 'Jane went and got a newspaper. Then she carefully bent it and folded it until it was just right. Then she was done. This is what it looked like'); in another, the objects were described as having been created accidentally ('Jane was holding a newspaper. Then she dropped it by accident, and it fell under a car. She ran to get it and picked it up'). Even 3-year-olds were more likely to provide artifact names (e.g. 'hat') when they believed the objects were intentionally created and material-based descriptions (e.g. 'newspaper') when they believed the objects were accidentally created.

Young children's use of intention to guide their use of multiple names for the same object indicates that their early naming incorporates a ToM. At the same time, it serves to undermine the proposal of a Mutual Exclusivity assumption that cues in language learning initially constrain children to link objects to only a single label exclusive to the category in which these belong (Markman, 1984; Merriman et al., 1995). Deák & Maratsos (1998) gave naming tasks to children aged 3-4 years that involved contrasts and inclusiveness in pairs of words. Using this method, they found that children exhibited considerable flexibility in their representations of objects. For example, rather than linking an object such as a dinosaur-shaped crayon to a single label, children can use the speaker's intent in the context of a conversation to infer when the object should be labelled as a dinosaur or a crayon. The flexibility to use more than one label in object naming reflects young children's early knowledge of the distinction between the real and apparent properties of objects that is critical for reasoning about physical causality (i.e., that an apparently fresh drink may contain invisible contaminants) (Siegal, 1997; Sapp et al., 2000).

Sensitivity to the referential intent of the speaker emerges even in early word learning. For example, Akhtar et al. (1996) placed 24-month-olds in a situation where they played with three toys together with their mother and an experimenter. The mother then left the room while the child and experimenter played with a fourth toy. When the mother returned, she exclaimed looking at all four toys, "Wow! A gazzer!" Children reliably learned this word for the novel object, indicating the knowledge that adults use new words to express what is new. In acquiring words for objects, infants aged 19-20 months link an object to a new label as intended by the gaze of a speaker. They do this even while they have opportunity to handle another salient object before they see the one that is intended (Baldwin, 1993).

6.4   GOAL-DIRECTED REASONING BEFORE LANGUAGE

It has been maintained that children's naming shifts to a strong dependence on social cognition about others' intentions only at a late stage in their language development and is preceded by a reliance on the salience of objects (Hollich et al., 2000). However, the acquisition of the child's conception of other people's goals or intentions is developmentally prior to their acquisition of much word learning and grammar. Even young infants are sensitive to causal relations in the physical world (Scholl & Tremoulet, 2000) and recent studies indicate that, at 6 to 9 months, infants interpret goal directed actions in intentional terms depending on whether these involve animate or inanimate objects (Csbira et al., 1999; Woodward, 1999). For example, they expect a person's speech to be directed to another person rather than to an object, and a person's reaching with a sweeping movement to be directed at an object rather a person (Legerstee et al., 2000).

In addition, research on imitation suggests that children understand referential intent at an early age. This ability allows children to imitate effectively by watching others and keeping track of their goals. Meltzoff (1995) demonstrated that 18-month-old children can recognize the goal of a model (placing beads in a cup) and can themselves achieve that goal, after having seen only a failed attempt to produce it (dropping the beads outside the cup). Thus, rather than imitating the actions that a model actually demonstrated (dropping the beads outside the cup), the children imitated the actions that he *intended* (placing the beads in the cup). Moreover, children at 14 months are sensitive to verbal markers of intentional versus accidental action ('There!' vs. 'Woops!'), and they more readily imitate intentional than accidental actions (Carpenter et al., 1998). These studies converge to show that by the age of 12 months children are adept at monitoring people's intentions and at replicating a model's behaviour using intention, rather than simply action, as their guide.

As Carey (2000) has documented, research using techniques of habituation has shown that babies have "sortals" – concepts that pick out objects - before they have language and syntax. For example, infants can enumerate and individuate objects such that they display renewed attention in response to an object's unexpected appearance or disappearance. These distinctions represent a core, skeletal knowledge in early development (Gelman, 1990; Carey & Spelke, 1996). They serve to govern the coherence, function, and movement of objects and support language learning from the beginning, confirming the presence of a cognitive basis for naming and categorization (Macnamara, 1982; Mandler & McDonough, 1996; Clark, 1997).

6.5   CONCLUSION

Grammar generates elegance in communication. It is a powerful system that is critical for reducing mistakes in the transmission of knowledge (Nowak & Krakauer, 2000). It facilitates the maintenance of large numbers of social relationships and provides an efficient means to communicate feedback about potentially threatening events that are remote in time and space (Dunbar, 1993).

However, evidence from aphasia, deafness, and the development of naming and categorization converges to demonstrate that reasoning can occur largely independently from grammar. These findings reflect the emergence of knowledge about, and attention to, how language is used in social context. Language does permit the user to entertain propositions about the mental and physical world but its role involves the ability to make sense of communicative intentions and goes beyond competence in grammar.

The referential intent that is central to conversational understanding involves a domain of knowledge that has its own rules and maxims (Grice, 1975). It supports children's core knowledge of objects, facilitates the course of cognitive development, and sustains ongoing cognitive processing. Given this pivotal role, there is a recently recognized need to develop measures of this knowledge for both children and adults (Hilton, 1995; Bishop, 1998; Siegal, 1999; Surian & Siegal, 2001; Fritzley & Lee, 2003).

Whereas grammar has been seen as the driver of human reasoning (Bickerton, 1995), our account sees grammar as essential in enabling the effectiveness expression of ideas, rather than to think these through. This ability is separate and autonomous from referential intent and cognition (Chomsky, 1975; Bloom, 2000). The presence of grammar alone cannot guarantee understanding - and its absence can easily mask it.

ACKNOWLEDGMENTS

This chapter was adapted from an article in *Trends in Cognitive Sciences*, Volume 5, pp. 296-301 (2001) with permission from Elsevier. It was prepared with support from the Nuffield Foundation.

REFERENCES

Akhtar N. et al. The role of discourse novelty in children's early word learning. Child Development 1996; 67: 637-645

Astington J.W., Jenkins J.M. A longitudinal study of the relation between language and theory-of-mind development. Developmental Psychology 1999; 35: 1311-1320

Baldwin D. Early referential understanding: Infants' ability to recognize referential acts for what they are. Developmental Psychology 1993; 29: 832-843

Baron-Cohen S., Leslie A.M., Frith U. Does the autistic child have theory of mind? Cognition 1985; 21: 37-46

Bickerton, D., *Language and Human Behaviour.* Seattle: University of Washington Press, 1995.

Bishop D.V.M. Development of the children's communication checklist (CCC): A method for assessing qualitative aspects of communicative impairment in children. Journal of Child Psychology and Psychiatry 1998; 39: 879-891

Bloom P. Language and thought: Does grammar make us smart? Current Biology 2000; 10: R516-517

Bloom P, Markson L. Capacities underlying word learning. Trends in Cognitive Sciences 1999; 3: 286-288

Bowerman, M, Levinson, S.C., *Language Acquisition and Conceptual Development.* Cambridge, UK: Cambridge University Press, 2000.

Brown J.R. et al. Why talk about mental states? The significance of children's conversations with friends, siblings and mothers. Child Development 1996; 67: 836-849

Brown R. Linguistic determinism and the part of speech. Journal of Abnormal and Social Psychology 1957; 55: 1-5.

Carey, S., "Whorf versus continuity theorists: Bringing data to bear on the debate." In *Language Acquisition and Conceptual Development,* M. Bowerman, S.C. Levinson (Eds.), Cambridge, UK: Cambridge University Press, 2000.

Carey S., Spelke E.S. Science and core knowledge. Philosophy of Science 1996; 63: 515-533.

Carpenter M. et al. Fourteen-through 18-month-old infants differentially imitate intentional and accidental actions. Infant Behaviour and Development 1998; 21: 315-330

Carruthers, P. *Language, thought and consciousness: An essay in philosophical psychology.* Cambridge, UK: Cambridge University Press, 1998.

Chomsky, N., *Rules and representations.* Oxford, UK: Blackwell, 1975.

Clark E.V. Conceptual perspective and lexical choice in acquisition. Cognition 1997; 64: 1-37.

Clark, H.H, Brennan, S.E. "Grounding in communication." In *Perspectives on socially shared cognition*, L.B. Resnick, J.M. Levine, S.D. Teasley (Eds.), Washington, DC: American Psychological Association, 1991.

Csbira G. et al. Goal attribution without agency cues: The perception of 'pure reason' in infancy. Cognition, 1999; 72: 237-267

Custer W.L. A comparison of young children's understanding of contradictory representations in pretense, memory, and belief. Child Development 1996; 67: 678-688

de Villiers J.G., Pyers J.E. Complements to cognition: A longitudinal study of the relationship between complex syntax and false-belief-understanding. Cognitive Development 2002; 17: 1037–1060.

Deák G.O, Maratsos M. On having a complex representation of things: Preschoolers use multiple words for objects and people. Developmental Psychology 1998; 34: 224-240

Dunbar R.I.M. Co-evolution of neocortex size, group size and language in humans. Behavioural and Brain Sciences 1993; 16: 681-735.

Fritzley V.H., Lee K. Do young children always say yes to yes–no questions? A metadevelopmental study of the affirmation bias. Child Development 2003; 74: 1297-1313.

Garrett, M. "Production of speech: observations from normal and pathological language use." In *Normality and pathology in cognitive functions*, A. Ellis (Ed.), London: Academic Press, 1982.

Gelman R. First principles organize attention to and learning about relevant data – number and the animate-inanimate distinction. Cognitive Science 1990; 14: 79-106

Gelman S.A., Bloom P. Young children are sensitive to how an object was created when deciding how to name it. Cognition 2000; 76: 91-103

Grice, H. P. "Logic and conversation". In *Syntax and semantics, Vol. 3: Speech acts*, P. Cole, J.L. Morgan (Eds.), Academic Press, 1975.

Happé F. et al. Acquired 'theory of mind' impairments following stroke. Cognition 1999; 70: 211-240

Heaton, R.K. et al., *Wisconsin Card Sorting Test*. Psychological Assessment Resource, 1993.

Herman, R. et al., *Assessing BSL Development: Receptive Skills Test*. London: Forest Books, 1999.

Hilton D.J. The social context of reasoning: Conversational inference and rational judgment. Psychological Bulletin 1995; 118: 248-271

Hollich G.J. et al. Breaking the language barrier: An emergentist coalition model for the origins of word learning. Monographs of the Society for Research in Child Development 2000; 65: Serial No. 262

Kertesz, A., "Cognitive function in severe aphasia." In *Thought without language*, L. Weiskrantz (Ed.), Oxford, UK: Oxford University Press, 1988.

Legerstee M. et al. Precursors to the development of intention at 6 months: Understanding people and their actions. Developmental Psychology 2000; 36: 627-637

Leslie A.M., Frith U. Autistic children's understanding of seeing, knowing and believing. British Journal of Developmental Psychology 1988; 6: 315-324

Macnamara, J., *Names for Things*, MIT Press, 1982.

Mandler J.M., McDonough L. Drinking and driving don't mix: Inductive generalization in infancy. Cognition 1996; 59: 307-335

Markman, E.M., "The acquisition and hierarchical organization of categories by children." In *Origins of cognitive skills* , C. Sophian (Ed.), N.J. Hillsdale; Erlbaum, 1984.

Marschark M. et al. Understanding theory of mind in children who are deaf. Journal of Child Psychology and Psychiatry 2000; 41: 1067-1073

Martin R. STM and sentence processing: Evidence from neuropsychology. Memory and Cognition 1993; 21: 176-183.

Meadow, K.P. "The development of deaf children". In *Review of Child Development Research, Vol. 5*, E.M. Hetherington (Ed.), Chicago: University of Chicago Press, 1975.

Meltzoff A.N. Understanding the intentions of others: Re-enactment of intended acts by 18-month-old children. Developmental Psychology 1995; 31: 838-850

Merriman W. et al. How shall a thing be called? Journal of Child Language 1995; 22: 129-149

Nowak M.A., Krakauer, D.C. The evolution of language. Proceedings of the National Academy of Sciences 2000; 96: 8028-8033

Perner J. et al. Three-year-olds' difficulty with false belief: The case for a conceptual deficit. British Journal of Developmental Psychology 1987; 5: 125-137.

Peterson C.C. Theory of mind in children with cochlear implants. Journal of Child Psychology and Psychiatry, in press.

Peterson C.C, Siegal M. Insights into theory of mind from deafness and autism. Mind and Language 2000; 15: 123-145.

Peterson, C.C, Siegal, M., "Psychological, physical, and biological thinking in normal, autistic, and deaf children." In *The emergence of core domains of thought: New directions for child development, No. 75*, H.M. Wellman, K. Inagaki (Eds.), San Francisco: Jossey-Bass, 1997.

Peterson C.C, Siegal M. Changing focus on the representational mind: Deaf, autistic and normal children's concepts of false photos, false drawings, and false beliefs. British Journal of Developmental Psychology 1998; 16: 301-320.

Peterson C.C., Siegal M. Representing inner worlds: Theory of mind in autistic, deaf, and normal hearing children. Psychological Science 1999; 10: 126-129.

Russell P.A. et al. The development of theory of mind in deaf children. Journal of Child Psychology and Psychiatry 1998; 39: 903-910

Sapp F. et al. Three-year-olds' difficulty with the appearance-reality distinction: Is it real or is it apparent? Developmental Psychology 2000; 36: 547-560.

Saxe R., Carey S., Kanwisher N. Understanding other minds: Linking developmental psychology and functional neuroimaging. Annual Review of Psychology 2004; 55: 87-124.

Schafer G., Plunkett K. Rapid word learning by fifteen-month-olds under tightly controlled conditions. Child Development 1998; 69: 309-320

Scholl B.J., Tremoulet P.D. Perceptual causality and animacy. Trends in Cognitive Sciences 2000; 4: 299-309

Segal, G. "Representing representations", in *Language and thought: Interdisciplinary themes*, P. Carruthers & J (Eds.), Cambridge, UK: Cambridge University Press, 1996.

Siegal, M., *Knowing children: Experiments in conversation and cognition* (2nd Ed.). Hove, UK: Psychology Press, 1997.

Siegal M. Beyond methodology: Frequently asked questions on the significance of conversation for development. Developmental Science 1999; 2: 29-34

Siegal, M., Surian, L. Modularity in language and theory of mind: What is the evidence? Paper presented at the Conference on Innateness and the Structure of the Mind; Sheffield, UK; 2003.

Siegal M., Varley R. Neural systems underlying theory of mind. Nature Reviews Neuroscience 2002; 3: 463-471

Smith M., Apperly M., White V. False belief reasoning and the acquisition of relative clauses. Child Development 2003; 74: 1709-1719.

Surian L., Siegal M. Sources of performance on theory of mind tasks in right hemisphere damaged patients. Brain and Language 2001; 78: 224-232.

Tager-Flusberg H., Sullivan K. A componential view of theory of mind: Evidence from Williams syndrome. Cognition 2000; 76: 59-89.

Tye-Murray N. Conversational fluency of children who use cochlear implants. Ear and Hearing 2003; 24: 82S-89S.

Van der Lely H.K.J. et al. Evidence for a grammar-specific deficit in children. Current Biol. 1998; 8: 1253-1258.

Varley, R. "Science without grammar: scientific reasoning in severe agrammatic aphasia". In *Cognitive Bases of Science,* P. Carruthers, S. Stich, M. Siegal (Eds.), Cambridge: Cambridge University Press, 2002.

Varley R., Siegal M. Evidence for cognition without grammar from causal reasoning and 'theory of mind' in an agrammatic aphasic patient. Current Biol. 2000; 10: 723-726

Varley R., Siegal M., Want S. Severe impairment in grammar does not preclude theory of mind. Neurocase 2001; 7: 489-493.

Wimmer H., Perner J. Beliefs about beliefs: representation and constraining of wrong beliefs in young children's understanding of deception. Cognition 1983; 13: 103-128.

Woodward A.L. Infants selectively encode the goal object of an actor's reach. Cognition 1999; 69: 1-23.

Woolfe T., Want S.C., Siegal M. Signposts to development: Theory of mind in deaf children. Child Development 2002; 73: 768-778.

Chapter 7

THE SILENT UNDERSTANDING OF THE MIND
The Deaf Child

Antonella Marchetti,[1] Olga Liverta-Sempio,[1] Flavia Lecciso.[2]

[1]*The Theory of Mind Research Unit, Department of Psychology, Catholic University of the Sacred Heart, Milan;* [2]*The Theory of Mind Research Unit, Department of Psychology, Catholic University of the Sacred Heart, Brescia.*

This paper examines theory of mind in deaf children. It first outlines the conditions in which deaf child grow up. Then it examines the reasons for studying theory of mind development in deaf children, and the studies carried out up to now on the subject. It concludes with the results of a study on the development of false belief understanding in deaf children, which takes the affective relational context into consideration.

7.1 THE DEAF CHILD AND HIS DEVELOPMENT

Sacks' expression (1989) "*Seeing voices*", after which his book on deafness is entitled, can help the hearing to understand the phenomenon because it brings the unknown nearer to the known. "*Seeing voices*" refers to the deaf person's ability to transform sound into images, rendering voices visual, almost as if eyes translate movement into sound. Normally, when we become aware of an object our senses "converge" without our realising it; all five senses may be involved simultaneously and objects are seen, touched, smelled, "listened to", etc., at the same time, so when they are recognised, their shape, surface, smell and sounds merge. But when one of these senses is missing (hearing for example) the other senses substitute it or compensate for its absence, and become hyperactive in order to cope with the deficiency. In his book, Sacks identifies and stresses the importance of the compensatory channel of sight for the deaf who, as they are surrounded by air that does not vibrate with sound and voices, but is full of silent conversations or seeing voices, soon learn to translate these voices and sounds into movement and images.

According to official documents, the definition of a deaf child is a child whose hearing is insufficient to learn his own language, join in the usual activities for his age, and to take part successfully in normal schooling (OMS, 2001).

Hearing loss is divided into four categories according to its severity (Marcelli, 1989). These categories are, starting from the least severe cases: a) mild, below 40 dB, b) moderate, from 40 to 60 dB c) moderately severe, from 60 to 85 dB, and d) profound, over 90dB.

Those in the last category have to communicate with others by lip reading or sign language or both. A further way of classifying deafness is by its aetiology (Marcelli, 1989). The cause of deafness may be: 1) of congenital or degenerative genetic origin; 2) of prenatal origin, caused by embryo or foetus problems; 3) of neonatal origin, caused by, for example, premature birth or perinatal problems; or 4) caused by traumas, or be of infectious or toxic origin, in infancy.

It is known that the effects of deafness on a child's mental development are connected primarily with the communicational and linguistic functions and everything that is involved in their development. These effects depend both on the age of onset of deafness in the child and whether his caregiver or the people in his primary relational environment are deaf as well – things that are obviously closely connected with each other.

If deafness occurs from birth or straight afterwards, its effects are not diagnosed immediately. Studies carried out (see Freedman, 1971; Chess & Fernandez, 1980) show that in the first year of a deaf baby's life he can respond satisfactorily to external stimulation, imitate gestures and vocalise (this tends to diminish in time). So a baby with a hearing impairment does not, at the outset, demonstrate any particular problems, but they become very evident later in cognitive and linguistic development (Marcelli, 1989). The "onset age" can be crucial when linked with the age the baby starts to speak. Development problems in children who are either deaf from birth or have gone deaf before acquiring language skills (prelingual deafness), would seem to be different from those in children who lose their hearing after they have already developed language skills (postlingual deafness). The difference is described admirably by Sacks (1989) when he says that for those who have gone deaf after being able to hear, the world may till be full of sounds, even if they are «ghost» sounds, while a different situation occurs when a person has been deaf before developing language skills. For prelingual deaf, there will never be the illusion of sound. They live in a world where there is a total and uninterrupted absence of sound, a world of silence)[9] ".

As will be seen later, the difference between prelingual and postlingual deafness is particularly important in the study of theory of mind in children with hearing impairments.

Whether the parents or the caregivers in the child's primary relational environment are deaf also has an influence on his development. Problems occur in a mother-deaf child relationship especially when it is made up of a hearing mother and a deaf child, but a deaf mother-deaf child relationship can be likened to that of a mother and child with no loss of hearing. Various studies have been carried out (e.g. Schlesinger & Meadow, 1972; Meadow, Greenberg & Erting, 1983; 1985) which show that deaf children of hearing mothers actually spend less time, compared with deaf children of deaf mothers, interacting with their caregivers: these mothers seem to be less flexible and more intrusive, and their children less creative and less active, within the relationship. Mothers and children who are both deaf, on the other hand, are more capable of having "conversations" about themselves and each other, and on objects or things that are happening elsewhere. Several studies (Wood et al., 1986; Erting, Prezioso & Hynes O'Grady, 1989) stress the difference between deaf and hearing parents when communicating with their deaf child. Deaf parents, like deaf children, are also essentially "visual" beings, whilst hearing parents, who may be very sensitive and capable of visual interaction, are also "hearing" beings, who have to learn to communicate with their deaf child in a very special way, i.e. by "stressing" everything visually during activities, games, experiences and conversation.

More specifically, even as concerns affective mother-child relationships, research on attachment has not shown any substantial differences between couples of deaf mothers and deaf children and hearing mothers and hearing children (Meadow, Greenberg & Ertine, 1983). So this means that, also in these circumstances, the way child-caregiver relationships are built up is conditioned by how the mother and child communicate; the difficulties increase when they use different means of communication when "speaking" to each other. This gives us some important things to reflect on, which we refer to again later in this chapter: the quality of interaction between mother and child brings to mind the link found by Fonagy & Target (2001), between early affective communications

---

[9] Here some clarification is required concerning the use of some evocative images that are sometimes encountered in research on deafness. For example, to speak of a "silent world" for the deaf or of the "world in the dark" for the blind, as expressed by Sacks (1989), is not a completely accurate description of the deaf or blind person's world: these are only metaphors for their conditions, because in the same way as someone blind has never experienced the dark, someone deaf (or congenitally deaf) has no notion of what silence is. This is a further example of the projection of our world onto one that we simply do not know.

between child and caregiver and theory of mind development. Whether the caregiver can hear or not often influences the acquisition of a communication code or "language" by the child. Vygotsky (1934) maintains that acquisition of language is essential for mental development, as the connection between language and thought is indissoluble. Language's primary function is to communicate: it is borne out of interaction which allows the exchange of information and relations with others, but then it has a second function: language makes thought possible, or more specifically, it is language, the semiotic mediation tool that transmits culture and structures thought. One could rightly ask what effect there could be on the development of the mental functions in children that do not acquire the main tool to communicate and think, or do so very late. The parent's role is again crucial in this case. So, if we agree with Vygotsky's hypothesis, language cannot be learnt in solitude, but by interacting continuously with others.

Again, deaf children of deaf parents have fewer problems than the deaf children of hearing parents (Erting, Prezioso & Hynes O'Grady, 1989), as caregivers who are also deaf do not need to learn different ways, from the ones they are used to, to communicate satisfactorily with their deaf children, i.e. sign language: it is the language they use daily to communicate, think and help their children to get to know about their own lives and that of the child himself and the world around them. Hearing parents, on the other hand, even if they are sensitive and well prepared for the problems to be faced, will encounter difficulties at this stage, as that they can hear *and* see. The "language" that deaf children normally learn is made up of both speech and signs.

In the literature that we will shortly be examining, children that have learnt to understand and speak oral language, (i.e. spoken language) also with the help of technical auditory devices and sign language, are referred to as the "oral deaf"; children who have learnt to use sign language are referred to as signers. The hearing ability of the child's caregiver is also important in these circumstances. Children with deaf parents usually learn sign language from them (or from some close relation, such as a brother or sister or a grandparent, who is good at sign language) straight away, in the primary relational environment, which is why they are called native signers. Children with hearing parents usually learn sign language later than "native signers", around school age, with the help of the secondary relational environment, (e.g. school), as their parents either lack or are not good at sign language; these children are called "late signers". Late signers who grow up with hearing parents, who are not capable of communicating with them satisfactorily, actually suffer from conversational deprivation.

7.2 THEORY OF MIND IN ATYPICAL AND PATHOLOGICAL DEVELOPMENTAL CONDITIONS

Interest in studying theory of mind in children with hearing impairments began about ten years ago; in fact the first paper on it was published in 1995 (Peterson & Siegal, 1995). In addition to helping us to further understand deaf children, it deals fundamentally with two interconnected issues. The first concerns whether theory of mind deficit is specific or not to autism (Baron-Cohen, 1995; Baron-Cohen, Tager-Flusberg & Cohen, 2000; Corcoran, 2000). The second sees this research as a "test-bed" for the Vygotskian hypotheses on theory of mind development, which have emerged more recently, after the "classical" hypotheses, such as the modular mechanism (Astington, 1996). As can be seen later, of the two, the second issue is the most important for this research.

The first issue concerns the cognitive hypothesis, initially proposed by Baron-Cohen, Leslie & Frith (1985), that theory of mind deficit explains the core symptoms of autism (marked lack of social interaction, communication and pretend play). It is explained using a modular concept of the mind: damage to a specific component of a network of neuro-cognitive mechanisms results in a dysfunction in the theory of mind module (ToMM, Theory of mind mechanism) (Baron-Cohen, Leslie & Frith, 1985). The neurological damage is not only the cause of the typical autistic behaviour mentioned above, but also a delay in theory of mind development (Frith, 1989).

The specificity hypothesis is supported by the first studies on autistic children, in which the control groups consisted of people suffering from: Down's syndrome (Baron-Cohen, Leslie & Frith, 1985), with specific speech disorders (Leslie & Frith, 1988; Perner et al., 1989), were mentally retarded (Baron-Cohen, 1989, Reed & Peterson, 1990), had emotional disorders (Siddons et al., 1990) and had Williams syndrome (Tager-Flusberg, 1993). All these control groups carried out theory of mind tasks better than the autistic children. The studies on theory of mind later extended to other pathologies or critical situation in the developmental age, questioned the specificity hypothesis and now further research needs to be carried out on the subject (e.g. Repacholi & Slaughter, 2003). In fact research on children suffering from deficiencies such as behavioural disorders (Hobson, 1990; Happè & Frith, 1996), atypical development conditions, such as blindness (Brown et al., 1997) or deafness (e.g. Peterson & Siegal, 1995, 1997) has highlighted the serious problems in theory of mind development that also occur in disorders other than autism, even though in many cases these disorders are not as serious or deep-seated as in the syndrome described by Kanner. Further data are available with the numerous studies on schizophrenia in adults (Frith & Corcoran, 1996; Sarfati et al., 1999; Corcoran, 2000; Pickup & Frith, 2001; Mazza et al. 2001; Bruene, 2003), and in developmental age (Pilowsky et al., 2000). More specifically, even if these studies also show that, on the one hand, there are theory of mind difficulties in disorders other than autism, such as schizophrenia, on the other, they prompt further research into the specificity question, as it seems that the theory of mind deficit hypothesis could be extended to schizophrenia, and this is the issue being discussed at present (Davies & Stone, 2003; Gerrans & McGeer, 2003). Intense work is also being carried out, using the vast behavioural, neuro-anatomical and neuro-imaging research now available in the field of pathology, on modelling the different theory of mind disorders observed to date. In these models there is a specific explanation of theory of mind deficits in the different clinical conditions. For example Abu-Akel (2003) proposes a neuro-biological model in which theory of mind disorders are placed in a continuum: starting from a condition (1), characterised by the absence of the representational/conceptual understanding of mental states, such as in autism, going on to one (2) in which the representational understanding of mental states is present, but it is accompanied by the inability to express or apply it, as is seen in the Asperger syndrome and in schizophrenia with negative symptoms. It then goes on to a condition (3) in which, as well as the representational understanding of mental states, there is abnormal application of these states, as in schizophrenia from delusion or paranoia; it ends with the state (4) in which there is complete representational understanding of others' minds, but also a disturbed self, as in schizophrenia with passivity phenomena.

Research into theory of mind in deaf children has contributed, right from the start, to nourishing doubts as to the hypothesis concerning the specificity of theory of mind deficit in autism, and underlines the presence of anomalies in theory of mind development in these children (Peterson & Siegal, 1995, 1997; Russel et al., 1998). More specifically, what was immediately questioned was the modular concept of theory of mind development, tracing the anomalies to a socio-linguistic hypothesis (Peterson & Siegal, 1995, 1997). This is connected to the second fundamental issue, mentioned above, which underlies research into theory of mind of the deaf and that more directly concerns the relation between language, mentalistic ability and the developmental contexts this paper is based on. We will now examine the terms of the issues, and then look at the reference literature that has been used in the research on deaf children presented later in this chapter.

7.3 THEORY OF MIND IN DEAF CHILDREN

Whilst the modular view states that theory of mind development depends on the biological growth of neuro-cognitive genetic structures (Baron-Cohen, Leslie & Frith, 1985; Leslie, 1987; 1991; 1994; Frith, Happé & Siddons, 1994), thereby making environmental and cultural influences irrelevant, Vygotsky's contextual approach (Astington, 1996) argues that theory of mind develops as a result of the child's taking part, from birth, in activities typical of his own culture (Bruner, 1990; Bruner & Feldman, 1993). Research into deaf children is particularly difficult from this point of view, as there are obviously very limited opportunities, compared to those of hearing children, for them to participate with conversation in social interaction. The study is also of particular interest in the light of the empiric socio-constructivist research carried out on typical theory of mind development, which maintains that a positive connection exists between family interaction where mental state are expressed, and the successive development of theory of mind in children (Youngblade & Dunn, 1995; Brown, Donelan-McCall & Dunn, 1996; Hughes & Dunn, 1998; Ruffman, Perner & Parkin, 1999; Mcins ct al., 2002).

The main hypothesis proposed up to now in the research on theory of mind development in deaf children, the conversational hypothesis is in fact, contextual and was put forward by Siegal and Peterson (Peterson & Siegal, 1995; 1997; 1998; 1999; Woolfe, Want & Siegal 2002; Peterson, 2003). According to this hypothesis, for theory of mind to develop in children, mental states such as feelings, beliefs and desires must be commented on, discussed and explained during family interaction. Conversation is difficult for children with hearing impairments and this can cause problems in acquiring theory of mind. The authors encountered this in their research into theory of mind in deaf children, but they make a point that strongly supports the hypothesis of an important link between conversation and theory of mind development. In fact, deficit in theory of mind development does not occur in all deaf children, but only in those growing up in hearing families, i.e. late signers. Deficit in theory of mind development in late signers had already be noted in the first study carried out on theory of mind in deaf children (Peterson & Siegal, 1995), which examined late signer children: this was confirmed not only in later studies, but more importantly in research that compared the performance of late and native signers. These studies are examined below, using the first one in particular to further illustrate the socio-linguistic hypothesis.

Peterson & Siegal (1995) observed 26 late signer children, from 8 to 13, who were totally or profoundly deaf and prelingual. In the study, false belief understanding is assessed by using the unexpected transfer task (Wimmer & Perner, 1983) in the version adapted by Baron-Cohen and colleagues (1985) for autistic people, in which the language used to tell the story is simplified by using dolls: they do not need to have any linguistic ability to express themselves, as the replies to the test have to be given non-verbally (see Castelli, Lecciso & Pezzotta, 2003). Half of the group is given the test question as originally formulated by Baron-Cohen (Baron-Cohen, Leslie & Frith, 1985) - *Where will Sally look for her ball?* -, the other half is asked the question according to the conversational hypothesis proposed by Siegal & Beattie (1991) - *Where will Sally look for her ball first?* -[10]. The results show that 65% of deaf children do not usually manage to carry out the false belief task that normally developed hearing children of about four can carry out perfectly well. The test question is also understood better in conversational rather than standard form. Peterson and Siegel conclude that there is no significant difference between the deaf children's performance, and that of the autistic ones examined in some of their previous research, using the same type of task and questions, worded in the same way. Two factors are discussed by the authors: first of all the data do not support the hypothesis that difficulties in false belief understanding are specific to autism: deaf and autistic children show a similar deficit in false belief understanding, secondly, some results support the conversational hypothesis: the neurological explanation, as in the modular approach, put forward by Frith (1989) would not seem to be applicable to deafness. Moreover, according to Peterson and Siegel, children with hearing impairments do not have the same deficits as those Frith attributes to autism, such as mannerisms, problems with non-verbal communication and socialisation. They also affirm that delay in mentalizing is caused by the limited opportunities, early in development, for deaf children of hearing parents to have daily talks with their most significant partners. So it would seem that hearing mothers of deaf children limit their sign language, even when they are good at communicating in this way, to tangible and visible subjects (Harris, 1992; Marschark, 1993), drastically reducing opportunities to share emotions, beliefs, and desires with them and having conversations focused on abstract mental states. Peterson & Siegel (1995) see many similarities between deaf and autistic children in this. These similarities are supported by further research (Tager-Flusberg, 1992) which points out that there are more

---

[10] Siegal's hypothesis is that performance in the false belief question worded in the standard way cannot be explained in terms of the child's theory of mind, but on the basis of the linguistic, conversational and methodological approach used in the test. More specifically, the false belief test question in the standard version (*"Where will Sally look for her ball?"*) entails the child's making an inference and accepting that the aim of the examiner is to evaluate his ability to come to a conclusion on the false belief of the person. But a child who is not particularly good at conversation may not understand that the rule of quantity is being broken (Grice, 1975): the examiner's question is not detailed enough and does not make the question clear, so the smaller children would presumably interpret it as *"Where must Sally look for her ball to find it?"* and not in the terms tacitly intended by the researcher *"Where is the first place that Sally will look for her ball?"* (Siegal & Beattie, 1991).

references to mental states in conversations between Down's syndrome children and their mothers, than in those between autistic children and their caregivers. As can be seen from the above mentioned research carried out on normal children (Youngblade & Dunn, 1995; Brown, Donelan-McCall & Dunn, 1996; Hughes & Dunn, 1998; Ruffman, Perner & Parkin, 1999; Meins et al., 2002), late signers do not have the daily mother-child conversations which are considered essential to children's theory of mind development, in the first years of their lives.

Further research on later signers confirms this result. Peterson & Siegal (1998), for example, compared the performance of late signer children in the false belief and false photograph tasks (Zaitchik, 1990)[11] with those of high- functioning autistic ones (in one experiment) and autistic children (in another experiment), in addition to that of normal children. On the whole there was no difference between the performances of the deaf children and that of the high-functioning autistic and autistic children; the false belief task appeared to be more difficult than the false photograph one. The authors attribute these results to the conversational hypothesis, i.e. to the limited opportunities for these clinical groups to have enriching daily conversation. This lack of opportunity would make the human mind an inaccessible "black box" for these children, ruling out the prediction that people's behaviour can depend on false beliefs; on the contrary, it would not rule out correct understanding of a photographic image (taken by a camera and therefore more easily understood than the human mind) as opposed to reality.

The study carried out by Russell et al. (1998) examines false belief understanding (unexpected transfer, in Peterson & Siegal's conversational version, 1995) in late signers in three age groups: 4 to 7, 8 to 12 and 13 to 16. The findings show a significant difference between the best performance by the top age group and the poorest performance by the other two age groups, where there was no difference between them. Russel and his colleagues explain this particular developmental tendency in theory of mind ability in the light of the socio-linguistic hypothesis mentioned previously. On the one hand, the limited opportunities for these children to learn about states of mind through conversation can be seen from the difficulties in theory of mind development, on the other, the negative effects of the lack of conversation are not a permanent handicap to theory of mind, and diminish

---

[11] In his false photographic test, Zaitchik (1990) used real objects such as a mother doll, a baby doll, a toy house and a Polaroid camera, with which the child being tested photographed the baby doll in one of the rooms in the toy house. The researcher then got the mother doll to take the baby doll out of the room where it had been photographed and put it in another one. The child being tested was given a test question ("where is the baby in the photo?"); a memory-check control question ("where was the baby when the photo was taken?") and a reality-check control question ("where is the baby now?").

in adolescence, probably as a result of schooling and increased opportunities to meet other partners, things that have a long term effect on mentalizing abilities. A recent study by Peterson (2003), which compared late signers, from 4 to 13, with normal pre-school children, adds further details to the picture of the mentalizing ability and difficulties in these children. In fact Peterson extends her research further in the field of psychological understanding of children, adding false belief understanding, the awareness of perceptive and emotional perspective and the understanding of emotions and desires. Her results confirm the late signers' delay in false belief understanding, but also show that they have no difficulty in interpreting emotions and recognising facial expressions. They are, however, less capable than four year old hearing children, of seeing beyond their own point of view and reflecting on the different emotional-affective states of others, in order to predict how desires and emotions can guide behaviour. The results are attributed to the conversational hypothesis and the fact that the biggest discrepancy between hearing and deaf children is in their understanding of false beliefs and, only to a lesser extent, to acquisition of perspective based on desires and emotions is further confirmation that, in deaf children, theory of mind is not absent, but is being developed, even though it is later than in hearing children.

The studies carried out up to now provide us with useful data as to the conversational hypothesis, but the research on deaf children, that deals not only with late signers, but also with native signers, i.e. children with hearing impairments that learn sign language in their primary relational environment, delivers more significant data on the link between conversational experience and theory of mind development. These studies demonstrate Peterson's affirmation more clearly (2003, p. 172): "it is not deafness per se, but rather deafness in conjunction with a hearing family that predicts severe delays in ToM development". Research into false belief understanding, carried out by specialists from different countries (Peterson & Siegal, 1997, 1999: Australia; Courtin & Melot, 1998: France; Remmel, Bettger & Weinberg, 1998: U.S.A.), shows that native signers differ considerably from late signers in that they seem to develop the concept of false beliefs at about the same age as normal children. One study in particular, by Courtin (1999), further underlines the situation for native signers: according to Courtin, native signers can understand false beliefs earlier than hearing children because they use sign language, as use of multiple visual perspectives is required and therefore the authors thinks that it helps them to understand conceptual perspectives. The two studies carried out by Woolfe, Want & Siegal (2002) on late and native signers aged 4 to 8, "picture" tests, such as *thought pictures* (from Custer's version, 1996), in which talking is reduced to a minimum, were used as theory of mind tasks. They also confirm how much more difficult these tasks are for late as opposed to native signers and the control group of hearing children, even when there are no significant differences in mental age and syntactic ability between the two groups of deaf children. On the whole, the above studies seem to make the conversational hypothesis most plausible, as it can be presumed that it is the discrepancy in conversational experience between the two groups of children – native and late signers – that causes the differences in performance during mentalistic tasks. Deaf children and deaf parents create the right conditions for communicating with one another in the primary relational environment, by means of sign language, in which they can try out conversation which may include states of mind such as beliefs, desires, emotions and imagination, in the same way as for children and parents who are both hearers. In a deaf child and hearing parent relationships, where a mutual linguist code initially lacks, this occurs much later.

Whilst the results of the research carried out on late and native signers are consistent, this is not true of the studies on the oral deaf. In research by Courtin & Melot, (1998) the results for the oral deaf performance can be compared to those of late signers, but are poorer for both groups than for native signers. Peterson & Siegal (1999) maintain, however, that oral deaf performance is nearly the same, if not the same, as that of native signers and normal hearing children. Most probably these children's characteristics account for the difference in results. As there is a hearing residual, they have a good chance of being able to communicate satisfactorily with their hearing partners, even though this may not always be effective. Normal theory of mind development for the oral deaf seems closely connected to linguistic ability (Peterson & Siegal, 2000) or to the amount of delay in language development (de Villiers, 2000). Studies on the oral deaf also cover the relationship between grammatical and syntactic ability and theory of mind development. When studying 22 seven year old oral deaf children, de Villiers and his colleagues (1997) observed that only half of them passed the unexpected transfer task in story form, but also that their linguistic ability is significantly higher. In another study on the oral deaf, using non-verbal false belief tasks, de Villiers & de Villiers (1999) again found a delay in theory of mind acquisition, even if it was assessed by means of non-verbal tasks that four year old normal, hearing children can carry out successfully. The best predictor for succeeding in these tasks is linguistic ability, as in a good use of syntax and consideration of intentionality in describing the events. These results lead the authors to support the explicative hypothesis (which, in our opinion, is not an alternative to the conversational hypothesis proposed by Siegal and his colleagues), according to which the difficulties that deaf children encounter in false belief tasks are specifically connected to the syntactic problems, in the form of sentence complementation, which are necessary for false beliefs to be understood (X thinks that Z thinks that…). This hypothesis is not confirmed in other studies on deaf children, however, because in the research mentioned above, by Woolfe, Want and Siegal

(2002), no differences in syntactic ability were seen between later signers, who are not good at theory of mind tasks, and native signers, who do them better. Woolfe, Want and Siegal interpret the results in the light of the strong link between theory of mind and language, but from a different point of view from that of de Villiers & de Villiers' (1999, 2000) who limit linguistic ability specifically to syntactic ability. In the same way as in other papers (Garfield, Peterson & Perry, 2001; Siegal, Varley & Want, 2001) though, they consider the effects of the linguistic channel, apart from syntax: language, and the conversation it is used in, are the way the child acquires others' unperceivable mental states. Under normal conditions of development, without hearing impairments and the resulting linguistic problems, stories and conversational comments on people's unexpected behaviour appear spontaneously and are needed to direct the child's attention to mental states. But deaf children's chances of taking part in this kind of conversation in the family (dialogue, discussions, pretend play, and other forms of spontaneous daily conversation) is very limited if there is no common language. In her research in 2003, Peterson provides further data that weaken de Villiers' hypothesis. In this, she says that if the delay in the acquisition of theory of mind by deaf children had been caused by the delay in syntactic ability, as de Villiers asserts (2000), then they should have no difficulty in acquiring mentalistic concepts, such as perspective taking based on desires and emotions that, unlike false beliefs, do not need to be represented by means of syntactic structures, in the form of sentence complementation. But her study demonstrates that the late signers' performance is poor not only in the false belief phase, but also in this task, which suggests that there is more to the delay in these children's theory of mind than syntactic problems (Peterson, 2003).

To sum up, studies carried out up to now on theory of mind development in deaf children are important because they were carried out on totally and deep deaf children from different countries, cultures and educational systems, and with different systems of communication within their families. So they provide valuable socio-contextual information on various aspects of this disorder, such as the country they come from (Australia, France, USA, Scotland, England and Italy); the family environment (e.g. deaf or hearing parents); the main means of communication (sign language or oral language) and the educational approach to deafness (teaching of sign language or oral language).

Various papers have examined a wide age range (from 4 to 16) using slightly different tasks at different levels, to evaluate the children's understanding of false belief and/or acquisition of other concepts connected to theory of mind ability. Many of these studies have characteristics in common that it would bear in mind in later research, such as only referring to the chronological rather than mental age of the children being examined. Not all of those that explore theory of mind development in deaf children compare the performance of deaf children with the hearing children in the control group: researchers seem, in fact, to concentrate mainly on comparing one group of deaf children with another (see the next paragraph). In addition to this, even when there is a control group of hearing children, it is practically never compared with deaf children of the same chronological and/or mental age, but is made up of normal developed children aged four to five, an age at which false belief tasks are typically undertaken.

As far as the explicative hypotheses are concerned, the conversational hypothesis proposed by Peterson & Siegal (1995) seems to be most significant, as it stresses the existence of a close link between theory of mind development and the child's experience of family interaction in the primary relational environment, in which mental states such as beliefs, emotions, desires, motives are discussed. This contextual hypothesis is socio-cognitive, as it examines the child's social interaction in terms of communication and the language used in interpersonal relationships, but does not consider the emotional importance that the relationship between the child and the caregiver has for both of them, above all, in the child's infancy. Studies on theory of mind development in typical situations that focus on this aspect of interaction have found a close link between the quality of affective bond between child and caregiver and theory of mind development (Fonagy, Redfern & Charman, 1997; Meins, 1997; Meins et al., 1998; 2002; 2003; Symons & Clark, 2000; Liverta-Sempio & Marchetti, 2001; Meins et al. 2002; 2003). In these papers the affective quality of the relationship is defined according to the attachment theory (Bowlby, 1969; 1973; 1980; 1988; Ainsworth et al., 1974) and a positive association can be seen between secure attachment and better results in theory of mind tasks. In one of the explicative hypotheses in this result, that of Fonagy, Redfern & Charman (1997; Fonagy & Target, 1997), considers that secure attachment facilitates development of understanding of the mind in children. They also maintain that theory of mind, defined by them as mentalising ability, or reflexive function, develops with the help of the coherence and security in the first object relations. Consistency and security allow the child to feel safe in exploring the caregiver's mind, where he will find an image of himself that is a being motivated by intentions, desires and sentiments, i.e. as a mentalizer; an image that, when interiorised, will make up the nucleus of his reflexive self. A sensitive caregiver's behaviour helps him to understand his own behaviour and other people's reactions, and to realise that an interior layer of ideas, sentiments, beliefs and intentions are responsible for it (Fonagy & Target, 1997).

This is an intersubjective process, that takes place between caregiver and child, and that is part of theory of mind acquisition: whilst the mother sees her child as a being with a mind, and tries to understand his desires and beliefs, the child manages to think about others and himself in mentalistic terms. The research that follows is based on this relational-affective view of theory of mind development.

7.4 THEORY OF MIND AND AFFECTS IN DEAF CHILDREN

This paper analyses the development of theory of mind, from a relational-affective point of view (Liverta-Sempio & Marchetti, 2001) in a group of profoundly deaf children aged 6 ½ to 12, with hearing parents. They have been in a school for both hearing and deaf children, in the north of Italy, since the first class. The school aims to use the same language for everyone, so verbal language is gradually added to the deaf children's communicative system.

As we believe that theory of mind abilities develop in a combined process between the child and his caregivers, in this study we have examined deaf children by considering their theory of mind development to be closely connected to the child-adult emotional relationship, defined in terms of security of attachment. Given the particular way deaf children interact with other people, which is often characterised by difficulties and isolation, it is absolutely essential in this context to widen our research to figures other than parents, who are emotionally significant for the deaf children's growth, such as teachers.

We examined the following issues:
- the theory of mind ability in a group of deaf children, compared with a control group;
- the relation between theory of mind development and their receptive vocabulary;
- the affective dimension – in terms of the quality of attachment – of the relationship between deaf children and their caregivers (parents and teachers), compared with that of the children in the control group;
- the connection between theory of mind ability and affective relationships within the family and at school.

7.5 METHODOLOGY
7.5.1 Participants

34 children were examined. The clinical group consisted of 17 profoundly deaf children aged 6 ½ to 12, whose mental age, measured in Ravens, was within the norm. No other physical or psychological disorders had been diagnosed in them; the children either attended the Northern Italian elementary school mentioned previously. The group consisted of 11 boys

and 6 girls and their parents were hearers. All the children had hearing aids. The way most frequently used to communicate with each other was: 6 children used LIS - *Lingua Italiana dei Segni* (Italian Sign Language), 2 used *Italiano Segnato* (Signed Italian)[17]; 1 used spontaneous signs and 8 communicated verbally. The control group consisted of 17 hearing children, who were paired with deaf children of the same chronological age and the same sex. Deaf children and control group attended audio-phonetic elementary and middle schools.

7.5.2   Tools

The children were each provided with a set of tests. These were given verbally to each child in the three sessions, at a week's distance, in a quiet room and with the help of a translator[13], who translated the verbally given questions into either Signed Italian or LIS, depending on the way the subject usually communicated. Each of the tests was adapted according to the literature on the linguistic difficulties that deaf children encounter. The set consisted of:

- two first-order false belief tasks: the "unexpected transfer" test (Wimmer & Perner, 1983; in the version by Liverta-Sempio, Marchetti & Lecciso, 2002c) and the "deceptive box", in an acted version (Perner, Leekam & Wimmer, 1987) adapted by Liverta-Sempio, Marchetti & Lecciso, 2002c). In the "unexpected transfer" task, actual objects are used to carry out the test. The child is told a story in which the first doll has a ball which it puts in a box and then leaves the room. Whilst it is out of the room, another doll moves the ball to another box. The child is then first asked a test question on false belief and then a memory control question and a reality control question. When adapting the tests for deaf children (see also, Castelli, Lecciso & Pezzotta, 2003) to make the story and the questions more understandable, all the verbs were changed from the future to the present tense. The "deceptive box" task was set for the children in an acted version, involving the child and one of his classmates. The child is given a box of wax crayons with a tiny doll inside it. The child is then asked what there is in the box, both before and after he has opened it.
- When the three control questions are asked, there is a test question on others' false beliefs and further one on his personal false beliefs. The

---

[12] *Italiano Segnato* (Signed Italian) is a systematic manual representation of Italian or a transliteration in which Italian words and syntax are transformed into signs.
[5] The translator is a teacher at the audio-phonic school, but the children in the tests were not actually her pupils.

way the test questions (and not control questions) are asked had been modified as regards the standard version used on normal development children, in the same way as in the previous ones.

- Two separation anxiety tests: referred to as Family SAT (Klagsbrun & Bowlby, 1976; Fonagy et al., 1997; Slough, Goyette & Greenberg, 1988; Liverta-Sempio, Marchetti & Lecciso, 2001) – regarding the family and School SAT (Liverta-Sempio, Marchetti & Lecciso, 2001) regarding school. These are semi-projective tests and evaluate the child's answers to questions on separation from significant adults (parents and teachers). Each test involves three mild separation and three severe ones (Slough & Greenberg, 1990). Each test is given individually, recorded on audio media and then transcribed. The researcher first describes the situation to the child and then asks him three questions: one on the character's sentiments, another on how he justifies the sentiment and a further one on coping with it. In Slough, Goyette & Greenberg's classification system (1988), there are three scales: the attachment scale, or the child's ability to express vulnerability or needs in a separation; the self-reliance scale, or expression of being sure about dealing with separation personally; the avoidance scale or degree to which child side-steps or avoids talking about separation[14]. Some specific changes have been made to the two tests, in presenting the tasks and formulating the items and in asking the questions (e.g. future tenses and conjunctions have been removed, as well as all the terms that could have been difficult for the children to understand).
- The PPVT (*Peabody Picture Vocabulary Test-Revised*) in the original version by Dunn & Dunn (1981) is a tool for measuring the size of receptive vocabulary. The Italian version by Camaioni & Ercolani (1998) was used in this research. The first of the two existing parallel forms, M and L, was chosen. The test is based on 175 words that the child has to match with one of the four figures or numbers in each of the pages in the book. He is told that there are four figures on each page, each of which is numbered, and is asked to point to the one that he thinks best illustrates the word he is given.

---

[14] A total scale of attachment can also be calculated (Fonagy et al., 1997) by adding the scores resulting from the attachment and self-reliance scales and exchanging the avoidance scale scores obtained by deducting the maximum marks in the scale (18) from the resulting total [SAT Total = A + S + (18 − AV]. The sample distribution of attachment scale is divided into quartiles (Fonagy et al., 1997), so three groups can be formed: the secure, insecure and ambiguous (neither secure nor insecure) attachment groups.

7.6 RESULTS

7.6.1 Mentalizing Ability in the Deaf Children Compared to the Control Group

The group of deaf children was divided into two age groups: in the first there were 10 children aged 6 ½ to 10 and in the second 7 boys and girls aged 11 and 12.

The deaf children up to 10 gave random answers to various tasks: in fact, in the group of older children aged 11 and 12 only 71.4% of the answers to the deceptive box test - question on false beliefs in others - were correct and only 85.7% were correct in the same test - one own false beliefs-.

As can be seen from Table 1, the comparison between the performances of the group of deaf children and the control group, divided into age groups, shows that there are significant differences for younger children (6 ½ -10) in both the false belief tasks and, more specifically, the deaf children did not manage them as well as the control group of children. In the older children's age group (11-12 years old), however, the deaf children were less successful than hearing children in the unexpected transfer task, but there was little and no significant difference between the two groups in the deceptive box task.

Table 1: Means and ANOVA According to Tasks and Age Groups

Age groups		DEAF	CONTROL	$F_{(1,18)}$
6 1/2 – 10	UNEXPECTED TRANSFER	2,4	3,00	7,36*
6 1/2 – 10	DECEPTIVE BOX	4,00	5,00	11,25**
11 – 12	UNEXPECTED TRANSFER	2,14	3,00	10,8**
11 – 12	DECEPTIVE BOX	4,57	5,00	4,50 (n.s.)

(*$p < 0,05$; **$p < 0,01$)

By and large[15], the results confirm previous research (Peterson & Siegal, 1995; Russell et al., 1998; Woolfe, Want & Siegal, 2002) regarding a considerable delay in theory of mind development in deaf children. Whilst it is known that hearing children carry out first-order false belief tasks successfully around 4 years of age, the children in our research, of up to 10, gave random answers to the tests set for them. Finally, it is no coincidence that, in the deceptive box false belief test, the best performance by deaf children aged 11 and 12 was in understanding the own false belief questions, which shows that, as also demonstrated by Peterson (2003), the biggest difficulty for them was to assume the other person's point of view. This also seems to confirm the approach of the simulation proposed by Harris (1992) for theory of mind development in general: so theory of mind starts from preferential access to one's own mind, even in deaf people.

7.6.2   Language and Theory of Mind Ability

We would first underline the difference in data that has emerged from statistical analysis, between the receptive vocabulary of deaf children and control groups of hearing children: the control group children got higher average scores in the PPVT than deaf children in the two age groups – from 6 ½ to 10 ($F_{(1\ 18)}$= 33,64 $p < 0,001$), and 11 to 12 ($F_{(1\ 12)}$= 17,54 $p < 0,001$).

If, however, we look at the link between language and mentalizing ability in the clinical group, from the statistical analysis (ANOVA) carried out no significant link has been found between the false belief tasks and the linguistic ability of the children, as shown in the receptive language tests (PPVT), even though there seems to be a tendency in deaf children, that manage to carry out both the deceptive box and unexpected transfer tasks, to get higher average scores in the PPVT (93,43 vs. 64,14 for unexpected transfer; 83,90 vs. 66,14 for the deceptive box). It should be noted though

---

[15] Further, in reference to the total group of deaf children, using the t-test for paired samples, compared with the unexpected transfer test, the deceptive box task is much easier for older children, both for the own self belief (t = -3,87, df. 6, $p< 0,01$) and false belief in others questions (t = -2.,3, df. 6, $p< 0,05$). There are various ways of interpreting this data: the simplified acted version was easier to access (the unexpected transfer task is carried out using dolls, whilst the deceptive box test involves the examinee and a classmate); learning effects are linked to the way the tasks are presented (the unexpected transfer is always given to children before the deceptive box task; so it would be of interest to look into the effect order has on the results); more conceptual processes, linked to the different structures of the two tasks. In the deceptive box test, understanding the false belief is based on perception, but in the unexpected transfer test it is based on previous knowledge. In addition to this, the different sequences of the control and test questions in the tests used (control questions before the test question in the deceptive task/test question before the control questions for unexpected transfer test) could influence the way the answer is given, making it easier – in the deceptive box task – or making it more difficult – in the unexpected transfer task.

that the language test used measures the language, or rather the extent of the child's vocabulary.

Linguistic development and how it is linked to mentalizing ability should perhaps also examined from different points of view: it might be more advantageous to examine the deaf child's mental language, i.e. the vocabulary they use to refer to mental states. There are two reasons for going into this more thoroughly: first of all, various studies that have been carried out show a specific relation between that type of language and successful theory of mind tasks (Dunn, et al., 1991; Youngblade & Dunn, 1995; Brown, Donelan-McCall & Dunn, 1996; Hughes & Dunn, 1998; Ruffman, Perner & Parkin, 1999; Meins et al., 2002) and secondly, with specific reference to the deficit being examined, as has already been mentioned, hearing mothers of deaf children have difficulty in communicating with their children particularly on the abstract subjects that involve thought (Marshark, 1993; Peterson, Siegal, 1995), the mentalistic language that, according to Elizabeth Meins (Meins et al., 2002), has a fundamental role in the development of mentalistic ability in children. It would also be most interesting to go into more detail as to which mentalistic language is most difficult for deaf children to use. In fact research carried out by Rieffe & Meerum Terwogt (2000) shows that deaf children with hearing mothers talk about others' beliefs as often as hearing children do, but they talk more often about desires[16]. This is discussed in a paper now being published (Liverta-Sempio, Marchetti & Lecciso)

7.6.3 Attachment

If we consider the difference between the scores obtained by the clinical and control groups in the SAT scales, using the t-test, we can see that the deaf children had considerably lower scores than the control group, in the attachment scale (t-test= -6,49, df 32, $p<.001$), the Family SAT total scale (t-test= -2,27, df 32, $p<0,05$), and in the School SAT attachment scale (t-test= -2.90, df 32, $p<0,01$).

This confirms the deaf child's difficulty in establishing a secure attachment with his caregiver, in a situation in which the dyad is characterised by different sensorial conditions (deaf child-hearing caregiver) (Meadow, Greenberg & Ertine, 1983).

It also shows how the differences between the clinical and control groups are not limited to relations with the family caregiver, but extend, when there are severe separation situations, to affective relations with the

---

[16] The reason deaf children express their desires more frequently is interpreted by the authors (Rieffe & Meerum Terwogt, 2000) to mean that they need to make others understand their desires clearly (and therefore explicitly), as opposed to hearing children whose may also communicate their desires implicitly.

school caregiver, confirming that the representation of internal working models has been transferred to a different significant partner (van Ijzendoorn et al., 1992).

7.6.4   Mentalizing Ability and Affective Relationships

As far as the relation between mentalizing ability and affective relations is concerned (see Table 2 for the significant results), the ANOVA shows that deaf children who successfully carry out the unexpected transfer task, compared with those who do not, rely more on their own ability (self-reliance) to face mild separations, and get higher means scores in the total attachment scale, in their relation with both their parents and their teachers. They also get lower scores in the avoidance scale of the two SATs, which is proof of their ability to face the separation, without trying to avoid it. The results of the deceptive box test – others' false beliefs – seem to be linked more to the relationship with the school caregiver: children who can recognise and put a schoolmate's beliefs into words get higher marks in the School SAT than those who do not pass the test in the attachment, self-reliance and total attachment scales. The child's ability to recognise his own false belief is connected to higher scores in the attachment scale both for Family and School SATs; so children who, in the kind of separations shown in the SATs, are capable of putting suffering, discomfort and sadness into words can also recognise their own false belief in the test.

Table 2: Means for Family SAT and School SAT Scales Based on Carrying out the False Belief Tasks Successfully

SAT scale	Unexpected transfer		
Family SAT	Passed	Failed	$F_{(1\,15)}$
Self-reliance	9,57	6,90	5,33*
Avoidance	6,86	10,20	5,45*
Total attachment	29,14	21,40	6,48*
School SAT			
Self-reliance	9,43	6,30	6,31*
Avoidance	6,71	11,50	7,37*
Total attachment	29,57	19,30	6,07*
School SAT	Deceptive box (other's false beliefs)		
Attachment	8,90	5,43	4,63*
Self-reliance	8,90	5,71	6,64*
Total attachment	27,70	17,57	5,84*
School SAT	The deceptive box (own false beliefs)		
Attachment scale	8,45	5,50	8,73 **
School SAT			
Attachment scale	8,91	4,83	6,64*

(* *p.* <0,05; ** *p.* <0,01)

The connection found between the mentalistic tests and the level of attachment is of particular interest: success in the ToM tests appears to be closely connected to how secure the attachment is and, inversely, to the level of avoidance, in the child's relationship both with his parents and his teacher. This result is in line with those of the researchers (Fonagy, Redfern & Charman, 1997; Fonagy & Target, 1997; 2001) who consider theory of mind development to be a relational, intersubjective, affectively significant process.

7.7   "GETTING PAST THE WALL OF SILENCE"

The results stress the existence, specificity and depth of difficulties in the development of deaf children, which can be traced in the different aspects examine below.

In the mentalistic area, the situation is critical for deaf children who demonstrate a considerable delay, within which there is a significant difference between them and the control group of hearing children, at least up to the age of twelve (maximum age examined).

A situation of this sort is, at least partially, mitigated if we look at the performance of the older children aged 11 and 12 in the false belief task deceptive box test: the results do not differ significantly from those of the control group. This is symptomatic of the developmental potential of these children, provided (as in our research) that the research conditions are adapted to the group being examined (specially modified instruments, presence of a translator, etc.). This emphasises the necessity to use specially prepared procedures that take the specific development processes of deaf children into account. The results also underline how difficult these children find it to establish secure attachments: their physical impairment is undoubtedly a risk factor for deaf children when trying to build secure attachment patterns with parents and teachers.

This data, full of implications at both fact-finding and intervention levels, concerns the connection found between the mentalistic ability of children and the quality of the attachment they establish with their caregivers, whether they be parents or teachers.

The result of the relation between success in the false belief tasks and the affective tests allow us to support the idea of development of mentalistic ability as a process which is a mainly co-constructed, intersubjective process, based firmly on relevant affective relationships (Meins, 1997) This concept encourages us to abandon a straightforward standpoint to support complex causality: a specific sphere of a child's development can be enhanced (within a context), while directly or indirectly affecting the other spheres. From a perspective sensitive to the developmental potentialities of the relationships with multiple caregivers (van Ijzendoorn et al., 1992), teachers have a crucial role in shaping the course of the child's development in all its spheres, as well as facilitating cognitive development.

The school caregiver may represent an excellent emotional opportunity for the child, which interconnects with the emotional processes and ups and downs in the relationship he has established with his primary caregivers. In the light of more recent research carried out by Fonagy (Fonagy, Redfern & Charman, 1997; Fonagy & Target, 2001) and Meins (1997; Meins at al., 2003), if they are transposed from home to school, the resource represented by the school caregiver can be viewed in terms not only of the child's security, but also in terms of the mentalizing functions that the adult can carry out for, with and in support of the child. So facilitating security in the relations that are most important to the child has a series of repercussions or effects on different areas of his development: mentalistic, as in the support for and development of theory of mind, and affective, as in the integration and "repair" of relations that are not sufficiently secure.

A complex picture emerges from this work, which we hope will contribute to helping deaf children. It confirms the effectiveness of embracing an integrated conception of development (Marchetti, 1997) that cannot but lead us to consider the contexts in which a child is born and grows up, to be the source, resource and irrefutable potential for the development of deaf children.

REFERENCES

Abu-Akel A. A Neurobiological Mapping of Theory of Mind. Brain Research Reviews 2003; 43: 29-40.

Ainsworth, M.D.S., Blehar, M., Waters, E., Wall, S., *Patterns of attachment*. Hillsdale: Erlbaum, 1974.

Astington, J.W. "What is theoretical about the child's theory of mind: a Vygotskian view of its development". In *Theories of theory of mind*, P. Carruthers, P.K. Smith (Eds.), Cambridge: Cambridge University Press, 1996, It. tran. "Cosa c'é di teorico nella teoria della mente del bambino? Un approccio vygotskiano". In *Teoria della mente e relazioni affettive*, O. Liverta-Sempio, A. Marchetti (Eds.). Torino: UTET, 2001

Baron-Cohen S. The autistic child's theory of mind: a case of specific developmental delay. Journal of Child Psychology and Psychiatry 1989; 30: 285-298.

Baron-Cohen, S. (1995), L'autismo e la lettura della mente. It. Tran. Roma: Astrolabio, 1997.

Baron-Cohen S., Leslie, A.M., Frith, U. Does the autistic child have a "theory of mind"? Cognition 1985; 21: 37-46.

Baron-Cohen, S., Tager-Flusberg, H., Cohen, D.J. (Eds.), Understanding other minds. Perspectives from developmental cognitive neuroscience. Second Edition. Oxford: Oxford University Press, 2000.

Bowlby, J. (1969), *Attaccamento e perdita, vol. 1: L' attaccamento alla madre.* It. Tran. Torino: Boringhieri, 1972.

Bowlby, J. (1973) *Attaccamento e perdita, vol. 2: La separazione dalla madre.* It. Tran. Torino: Boringhieri, 1975.

Bowlby, J. (1980), *Attaccamento e perdita, vol. 3: La perdita della madre.* It. Tran. Torino: Boringhieri, 1983.

Bowlby, J. (1988), *Una base sicura.* It. Tran. Milano: Raffaello Cortina Editore, 1989.

Brown J.R., Donelan-McCall N., Dunn J. Why talk about mental sates? The significance of children's conversations with friends, siblings and mothers. Child Development 1996; 67: 836-849.

Brown R., Hobson R.P., Lee A., Stevenson J. Are there "autistic-like" features in congenitally blind children? Journal of Child Psychology and Psychiatry 1997; 38: 693-703.

Bruene M. Theory of mind and the role of IQ in chronic disorganized schizophrenia. Schizophrenia Research 2003; 60: 57-64.

Bruner, J. *Acts of meaning.* Cambridge: Harvard University Press, 1990.

Bruner J.S., Feldman C. Costruzione narrativa dell'esperienza sociale e teoria della mente: cosa manca agli autistici. Età evolutiva 1993; 45: 84-101.

Camaioni, L., Ercolani, A.P. , *Peabody Picture Vocabulary Test-revised*, Italian version under validation, Roma: Università "la Sapienza", 1998.

Castelli, I., Lecciso, F., Pezzotta, C. *"Il certificato di acquisizione" della teoria della mente: origini e declinazioni dei compiti di falsa credenza in condizioni evolutive tipiche e atipiche.* Numero 1 della Collana dell'Unità di Ricerca sulla Teoria della mente, Milano: ISU, Università Cattolica del Sacro Cuore, 2003.

Chess S., Fernandez P. Do deaf children have a typical personality? Journal of American Academy Child Psychiatry 1980; 19: 654-664.

Corcoran, R. "Theory of mind in other clinical conditions: is a selective 'theory of mind' deficit exclusive to autism". In *Understanding Other Minds. Perspective from Developmental Cognitive Neuroscience,* S. Baron-Cohen, H. Tager-Flusberg, D.J. Cohen (Eds.). New York: Oxford University Press, 2000.

Courtin C., Theory of mind in deaf children: consequences of sign language communication. Enfance 1999; 51, 3: 248-257.

Courtin, C., Melot, A.M. "Development of theories of mind in deaf children". In *Psychological Perspectives on Deafness,* Marschark (Ed.), Malwah, NJ: Erlbaum, 1998.

Custer W.L. A comparison of young children's understanding of contradictory representations in pretence, memory, and belief. Child Development 1996; 67: 678-688.

Davies, M., Stone, T. "Psychological Understanding and Social Skills". In *Individual Differences in Theory of Mind. Implications for Typical and Atypical Development,* B. Repacholi, V. Slaughter (Eds.), New York and Dove: Psychology Press, 2003.

de Villiers, J. "Language and Theory of Mind: what are the developmental relationships?" In *Understanding other Minds. Perspectives from developmental cognitive neuroscience,* S. Baron-Cohen, H. Tager-Flusberg, D.J. Cohen (Eds.). Oxford: Oxford University Press, 2000.

de Villiers, J.G., de Villiers, P.A. "Linguistic determinism and false belief". In *Children's reasoning and the mind,* P. Mitchell, K. Riggs (Eds.). Hove: Psychological Press, 1999.

de Villiers, J.G., de Villiers, P.A. (2000), "Linguistic Determinism and the Understanding of False Beliefs". In *Children's reasoning and the mind,* P. Mitchell, K. Riggs (Eds.). Hove: Psychological Press, 2000.

de Villiers J.G., Pyers J.E. Complements to Cognition: a longitudinal study of the relationship between complex syntax and false-belief understanding. Cognitive Development 2002; 17: 1037-1060.

de Villiers, P., Hosler, B., Miller, K., Whalen, M., Wong, J. Language, Theory of Mind and Reading: a study of oral deaf children. Paper presented at Society for research in child development, Washington, DC, 1997.

Dunn, L.M., Dunn, J. *Peabody Picture Vocabulary Test-revised.* Circle Pines, Minnesota: American Guidance Service, 1981.

Dunn J., Brown J., Slomkowski C., Tesla C., Youngblade L. Young children's understanding of other people's feelings and beliefs: individual differences and their antecedents. Child Development 1991; 62: 1352-1366.

Erting, C.J., Prezioso, C., Hynes O'Grady, M. *The Interactional Context of Deaf mother-infant Communication.* Barkeley: University California Press, 1989.

Fonagy, P., Redfern, S., Charman, T. (1997), "Sviluppo della teoria della mente e ansia da separazione". It. Tran. in *Teoria della mente e relazioni affettive. Contesti familiari e contesti educative*, O. Liverta-Sempio, A. Marchetti (Eds.). Torino: UTET, 2001.

Fonagy P., Target M. Attachment and reflective function: their role in self-organization. Development and Psychopathology 1997; 9: 679- 700.

Fonagy, P., Target, M. *Attaccamento e funzione riflessiva,* It. Tran. Milano: Raffaello Cortina, 2001.

Freedman D.A. Congenital and perinatal sensory deprivation: same studies in early development. American Journal Psychiatry 1971; 127, 2: 1539-1545.

Frith, U. *Autism: explaining the enigma.* Oxford University Press, 1989.

Frith C.D., Corcoran R. Exploring Theory of Mind in People with Schizophrenia. Psychological Medicine 1996; 26: 521-530.

Frith U., Happe' F., Siddons F. Autism and the Theory of Mind in Everyday Life. Social Development 1994; 3: 108-123.

Garfield J.L., Peterson C.C., Perry T. Social Cognition, Language Acquisition and the Development of Theory of Mind. Mind and Language 2001; 16: 495-541.

Gerrans, P., McGeer, V. "Theory of Mind in Autism and Schizophrenia. Synthesis". In *Individual Differences in Theory of Mind. Implications for Typical and Atypical Development,* B. Repacholi, V. Slaughter (Eds.), New York and Dove: Psychology Press, 2003.

Happe' F.G.E., Frith U. Theory of mind and social impairment in children with conduct disorder. British Journal of Development Psychology 1996; 14: 385-398.

Harris, M. *Language experience and early language development.* Hove, U.K.: Erlbaum Associates, 1992.

Harris P.L. From simulation to folk psychology: the case for development. Mind and Language 1992; 7: 120-144.

Hobaon R.P. On acquiring knowledge and the capacity to pretend: response to Leslie (1987). Psychological Review 1990; 97, 1: 114-121.

Hughes C., Dunn J. Understanding mind and emotion: longitudinal associations with mental-state talk between young friends. Developmental Psychology 1998; 34, 5: 1026-1037.

Klagsbrun M., Bowlby J. Responses to separation from parents: a clinical test for young children. British Journal of Projective Psychology and Personality study 1976; 21: 7-26.

Leslie A.M. Pretense and Representation: the origins of "theory of mind". Psychological Review 1987; 94: 412-426.

Leslie, A.M. "The Theory of Mind Impairment in Autism: evidence for a modular mechanism of development?" In *Natural Theories of Mind. Evolution, development and simulation of everyday mindreading.* A. Withen (Ed.). Oxford: Basil Blackwell, 1991.

Leslie, A.M. (1994), "ToMM, ToBY and Agency: core architecture and domain specificity". In *Mapping the Mind. Domain specificity in cognition and culture,* L.A. Hirschfeld, S.A. Gelman (Eds.). New York: Cambridge University Press, 1994.

Leslie A.M., Frith U. Autistic children's understanding of seeing, knowing, and believing. British Journal of Developmental Psychology 1988; 6: 315-324.

Liverta-Sempio, O., Marchetti, A. (Eds.) *Teoria della mente e relazioni affettive.* Torino: UTET, 2001a.

Liverta-Sempio, O., Marchetti, A., Lecciso, F. *Il SAT Famiglia e il SAT Scuola: strumenti di misura dell'ansietà di separazione da genitori e insegnanti.* Milano: ISU, Università Cattolica del Sacro Cuore, 2001a.

Liverta-Sempio, O., Marchetti, A., Lecciso, F. *Compiti di falsa credenza di primo ordine adattati per bambini sordi.* Unità di ricerca sulla teoria della mente – Milano: Università Cattolica del Sacro Cuore, 2002c.

Liverta-Sempio, O., Marchetti, A., Lecciso, F. *Mental language and theory of mind in mother and deaf child.* Milano: Unità di ricerca sulla teoria della mente, in preparation.

Marcelli, D. *Psicopatologia del bambino (5° edizione italiana).* Parigi: Masson, 1989.

Marchetti, A. (Ed.) *Conoscenza, affetti, socialità. Verso concezioni integrate dello sviluppo.* Milano: Raffaello Cortina Editore, 1997.

Marschark, M. *Psychological development of deaf children.* New York, Oxford University Press, 1993.

Mazza M., De Risio A., Surian L., Roncone R., Casacchia M. Selective impairments of theory of mind in people with schizophrenia. Schizophrenia Research 2001; 47, 2-3: 299-308.

Meadow K.P., Greenberg M.T., Erting C. Attachment behavior of deaf children with deaf parents. Journal of Academic of Child Psychiatry 1983; 22, 1: 23-28.

Meadow, K.P., Greenberg, M.T., Erting, C. "Attachment behavior of deaf children of deaf parents". In *Annual progress in child psychiatry and child development,* S. Chess, A. Thomas (Eds.). New York: Brunner/Mazel, 1985.

Meins, E. (1997), *Sicurezza e sviluppo sociale della conoscenza.* It. Tran. Milano: Raffaello Cortina Editore, 1999.

Meins E., Fernyhough C., Russell J, Clark-Carter D. Security of attachment as a predictor of symbolic and mentalising abilities: a longitudinal study. Social Development 1998; 7: 1-24.

Meins E., Fernyhough C., Wainwright R., Clark-Carter D., Das Gupta M., Fradley E., Tuckey M. Pathways to understanding mind: Construct validity and predictive validity of maternal mind-mindedness. Child Development 2003; 74: 1194-1121

Meins E., Fernyhough C., Wainwright R., Das Gupta M., Fradley E., Tuckey M. Maternal Mind-Mindedness and Attachment Security as Predictors of Theory of Mind Understanding. Child Development 2002; 73: 1715-1726.

Perner J., Frith U., Leslie A.M., Leekam S.R. Exploration of the autistic child's theory of mind: knowledge, belief, and communication. Child Development 1989; 60, 3: 689-700.

Perner J., Leekam S.R., Wimmer H. Three-year-olds difficulty with false-belief: the case for a conceptual deficit. British Journal of Developmental Psychology 1987; 5: 125-137.

Peterson, C.C. "The Social Face of Theory of Mind: the development of concepts of emotion, desire, visual perspective, and false belief in deaf and hearing children". In *Individual differences in Theory of Mind. Implications for typical and atypical development,* B. Repacholi, V. Slaughter (Eds.). New York and Hove: Psychology Press, 2003.

Peterson C.C., Siegal M. Deafness, Conversation and Theory of Mind. Journal of Child Psychology and Psychiatry 1995; 36: 459-474.

Peterson C.C., Siegal M. "Psychological, Biological, and Physical Thinking in Normal, Autistic, and Deaf Children". In *The Emergence of Core Domains of Thought,* H.M. Wellman, K. Inagaki (Eds.). San Francisco: Jossey-Bass, 1997.

Peterson C.C., Siegal M. Changing Focus on The Representational Mind: concepts of false photos, false drawings and false beliefs in deaf, autistic and normal children. British Journal of Developmental Psychology 1998; 16: 301-320.

Peterson C.C., Siegal M. Representing Inner Worlds: theory of mind in autistic, deaf and normal hearing children. Psychological Sciences 1999; 10, 2: 126-129.

Peterson C.C., Siegal M. Insight into Theory of Mind from Deafness and Autism. Mind and Language 2000; 15, 1: 123-145.

Peterson C.C., Slaughter V. Opening Windows into the Mind: Mothers' Preferences for Mental State Explanations and Children's Theory of Mind. Cognitive Development 2003; 18: 399-429.

Peterson C.C., Peterson J.L., Webb J. Factors Influencing the Development of a Theory of Mind in Blind Children. British Journal of Developmental Psychology 2000; 431-446.

Pickup R. Frith C. Theory of mind impairments in schizophrenia: Symptomatology, severità and specificità. Psychological Medicine 2001; 31, 2: 207-220.

Pilowsky T., Yirmiya N., Arselle S., Mozes T. Theory of mind abilities of children with schizophrenia, children with autism, and normally developing children, Schizophrenia Research 2000; 42, 2: 45-55.

Reed T., Peterson C.C. A comparative study of autistic subjects' performance at two levels of visual and cognitive perspective-taking. Journal of Autism and Developmental Disorders 1990; 20: 555-567.

Remmel E., Bettger J.G., Weinberg A. The impact of ASL on theory of mind. Paper presented at TIRSL 6: 1998 November; Washington, DC.

Repacholi, B., Slaughter, V. (Eds.) Individual differences on theory of mind. Implications for typical and atypical development. New York: Psychology Press, 2003.

Rieffe C., Meerum Terwogt M. Deaf children's understanding of emotions: desires take precedence. Journal of Child Psychology and Psychiatry 2000; 41, 5: 601-608.

Russell P.A., Hoise J.A., Gray C.D., Scott C., Hunter N., Banks J.S., Macaulay M.C. The Development of Theory of Mind in Deaf Children. Journal of Child Psychology and Psychiatry 1998; 6: 903-910.

Ruffman T., Perner J., Parkin L. How Parenting Style Affects False Belief Understanding. Social Development 1999; 8: 395-411.

Sacks, O. Vedere voci. Un viaggio nel mondo dei sordi. Milano: Adelphi Edizioni, 1989.

Sarfati Y., Hardy-Bayle M.C., Brunet E., Widloecher D. Investigatine theory of mind in schizophrenia: Influence of verbalization in disorganized and non-disorganized patients. Schizophrenia Research 1999; 37, 2: 183-190.

Schlesinger, H., Meadow, K.P. Sound and sign: Childhood deafness and mental health. Barkeley: University California Press, 1972.

Siddons F., Happe' F., Whyte R., Frith U. Theory of mind in everyday life: an interaction-based study with autistic, retarded and disturbed children. Paper presented at European Developmental Psychology Conference, Stirling, Scotland, 1990.

Siegal M., Beattie K. Where to look first for children's understanding of false beliefs. Cognition 1991; 38: 1-12.

Siegal, M., Peterson, C.C. "Children's Theory of Mind and the Conversational Territory of Cognitive Development". In Origins of an understanding of mind, C. Lewis, P. Mitchell (Eds.). Hove: Erlbaum, 1994.

Siegal, M., Peterson, C.C. "Conversazione, sviluppo cognitivo e teoria infantile della mente". In Il pensiero dell'altro. Contesto, conoscenza e teoria della mente. O. Liverta-Sempio, A. Marchetti (Eds.). Milano: Raffaello Cortina, 1995.

Siegal M., Varley R. "Neural Systems Involved in 'Theory of Mind'". Nature Reviews Neuroscience 2002; 3: 463-471.

Siegal M., Varley R., Want S.C. Mind over Grammar: Reasoning in Aphasia and Development. Trends in Cognitive Sciences 2001; 5: 296-301.

Slough, N.M., Goyette, M., Greenberg, M.T. Scoring indices for the Seattle version of the separation anxiety test. Washington: University of Washington, 1988.

Slough N.M., Greenberg M.T. Five-year-olds' representations of separation from parents: responses from the perspective of self and other. New directions for Child Development 1990; 48: 67-84.

Symons D.K., Clark S.E. A longitudinal study of mother-child relationships and theory of mind in the preschool period. Social Development 2000; 9: 3-23.

Tager-Flusberg H. Autistic children's talk about psychological states: deficits in the early acquisition of a theory of mind. Child Development 1992; 63: 161-172.

Tager-Flusberg, H. "What language reveals about the understanding of minds in children with autism". In *Understanding other minds: perspectives from autism*. S. Baron-Cohen, H. Tager-Flusberg, D.J. Cohen (Eds.). Oxford: Oxford University Press, 1993.

Van Ijzendoorn, M.H., Sagi, A., Lambermon, M.W.E. (1992), "Il paradosso del caretaker multiplo". In *Dalla diade alla famiglia*. L. Carli (Ed.). Milano: Raffaello Cortina Editore, 1999.

Vygotsky, L.S., (1934), *Pensiero e Linguaggio*. It. Tran. Bari: Laterza, 1990.

Youngblade L.M., Dunn J. Individual differences in young children's pretend play with mother and sibling: links to relationships and understanding of other people's feelings and beliefs. Child Development 1995; 66: 1472-1492.

Zaitchik's D. When representations conflict with reality. Cognition 1990; 35: 41-68.

Wimmer H., Perner J. Beliefs about beliefs: representation and constraining function of wrong beliefs in young children's understanding of deception. Cognition 1983; 13: 103-128.

Wood, D., Wood, H., Griffiths, A., Howarth, I. *Teaching and Talking with Deaf Children*. Chichester and New York: John Wiley & Sons, 1986.

Woolfe T., Want C., Siegal M. Signposts to Development: theory of mind in deaf children. Child Development 2002; 73, 3: 768-778.

Chapter 8

SOCIAL AND INTRAPERSONAL THEORIES OF MIND
"I Interact Therefore I Am"

Joan Lucariello,[1] Mary Le Donne,[2] Tina Durand,[1] Lisa Yarnell[1]
[1]Boston College; [2]Teachers College - Columbia University

Knowing others is basic to social interaction. Knowing the self is the hallmark of introspection. Very different activities are these. Hence, it is somewhat surprising that most accounts of theory of mind (our understanding of mental and emotional states) view knowing self and knowing other as one and the same cognitive ability. Such is the "integrated" view of theory of mind (ToM). Where differences in self- and other-knowing have been recognized, self-knowing has been assigned ontogenetic primacy and cast as the very means to knowing the other. More recently, ToM has been defined as differentiated. According to the "Functional-Multilinear Socialization (FMS)" model of theory of mind (Lucariello, 2004), the activities of knowing self and knowing other serve very different functions making them independent cognitive activities. Furthermore, if ontogenetic primacy exists, the FMS model frames the direction as other-knowing preceding self-knowing.

This chapter begins with a review of these contrastive theories of ToM. Next, a study in support of the FMS model's view that ToM is differentiated into Social (reasoning about others' mental and emotional states) and Intrapersonal (reasoning about one's own mental and emotional states) kinds is presented. However, given these strikingly different proposals in the literature on the nature of theory of mind, additional information on the relation of language to theory of mind can be instrumental in arbitrating among them. We know that language plays a fundamental role in the development of ToM. Accordingly, in a second study reported here, we tease apart reasoning about self from reasoning about other and examine the relation of language to each. If theory of mind is integrated, language should be comparably related to each of these forms of reasoning. If ToM is differentiated, however, language might be more associated with one form of reasoning than another. Since language is fundamental to ToM development, the form with which it is most associated can be taken to be developmentally primary. Data from this second study also support the proposals of the FMS model of ToM.

A metarepresentational ToM - a milestone in theory of mind (ToM) development - is the focus. Metarepresentation is an advanced understanding of mental states that is based in the ability to maintain multiple, contrastive representations of an object or event. This ability affords our distinguishing mental states from reality by keeping in mind both representations of reality and representations that contrast with that reality. A metarepresentational ToM is evident in behaviours such as false belief (knowledge of another's erroneous belief with respect to reality), distinguishing appearance from reality, and representational change (knowledge of one's own past false belief). See Table 1 for an illustration of these behaviours with respect to the unexpected identity task. A Metarepresentational ToM is attained around 4- to 5-years of age as indicated by success on tasks that measure these metarepresentational behaviours (e.g., Flavell, Flavell & Green, 1983; Astington, Harris & Olson, 1988; Gopnik & Astington, 1988; Perner, 1991).

Table 1. Metarepresentational Theory of Mind Tasks

Tasks	Domain and Metarepresentational Theory of Mind Conditions	
	Social (Other)	Intrapersonal (Own)
BELIEFS		
Task 1:	**Unexpected Identity: Rock-Sponge**	**Unexpected Identity: Rock-Sponge**
	C first sees a sponge painted to look like a rock and then touches it.	C first sees a sponge painted to look like a rock and then touches it.
	False Belief	*Appearance-Reality*
	Q: What will another kid who does not touch the object think it is?	App Q: What does object appear to be?
		Reality Q: What is object really?
		Representational Change
		Q: What did you think the object was before touching it?

table 1 cont.

	Domain and Metarepresentational Theory of Mind Conditions	
Tasks	Social (Other)	Intrapersonal (Own)
Task 2	**Unexpected Contents-Nice Surprise** Mary/Maxi play trick on Sally/Sam, whose favourite snack is M&Ms. M/M puts M&Ms in toothpaste box and put box on S/S's table. S/S opens box and finds M&Ms inside.	**Unexpected Contents-Nice Surprise** Ask C if he/she prefers, for a snack, M&Ms or toothpaste. C says M&Ms and then is handed a wrapped box. C unwraps and sees toothpaste box. C opens box and finds M&Ms inside.
	False Belief Q: What will another kid think is in box before opening it?	*Appearance-Reality* Reality Qs: What does it look like is in box? App Q: What is really in box?
	Representational Change Q: What did S/S think was inside toothpaste box before opening it?	*Representational Change* Q: What did you think was inside toothpaste box before opening it?
EMOTIONS		
Task 2	**Unexpected Contents-nice surprise**	**Unexpected Contents-nice surprise**
	Representational Change (as part of Task 2 also ask RC Emot Q) Q: How did S/S feel about what was inside box before opening it?	*Representational Change* (as part of Task 2 also ask RC Emot Q) Q: What did you feel about what was inside box before opening it?
Task 3	**Appearance-Reality Stories (6)** C presented w/stories with character who "really feels" one way but looks another way on face (e.g., Diana falls and gets hurt, but tries to hide how she feels so that other kids will not laugh at her.)	**Appearance-Reality Stories (6)** C presented with same stories as in "other" condition except C is inserted as the character (e.g., you fall and get hurt, but try to hide how you feel so that the other kids will not laugh at you).
	Appearance-Reality Reality Q: How does Diana really feel? App Q: How does Diana try to look on her face?	*Appearance-Reality* Reality Q: How do you really feel? App Q: How do you try to look on your face?
PERCEPTIONS **Task 4**	**Turtle Viewing** C sees turtle in Position A. E asks C: How do I (E) see turtle, lying on its back or standing on its feet? E and C switch seats Q: Now how do I (E) see turtle...?	**Turtle Viewing** C sees turtle in Position A. Q: How do you/C see turtle lying on its back or standing on its feet? E and C switch seats Q: Now how do you see turtle...?

table 1 cont.

Tasks	Domain and Metarepresentational Theory of Mind Conditions	
	Social (Other)	Intrapersonal (Own)
	Representational Change Test Q: When I first asked you, before trading seats, how did I see turtle…?	*Representational Change* Test Q: When I first asked you, before trading seats, how did you see turtle?
Task 5	**Colour Filters (3 trials)** Object (purple cake) placed behind colour filter (green) so only C sees illusion.	**Colour Filters (3 trials)** Object (purple cake) placed behind colour filter (green) so only C sees illusion.
	Level 2 Perspective-Taking Appearance Q: Does it look green or purple to you? Perspective-Taking Q: Does it look green or purple to me?	*Appearance-Reality* Appearance Q: Does it look green or purple to you? Reality Q: Is it truly green or purple?

8.1   THE "INTEGRATED" VIEW OF ToM

Three current accounts of ToM origins – modular mechanism, theory-theory (TT), sociocultural - advocate an "integrated" ToM. Reasoning about own and others' internal states are equivalent cognitive abilities that derive from the same theory of mind. Hence these reasonings are said to emerge together and at the same ontogenetic point.

The modular basis account of theory of mind – Theory-of-Mind Mechanism/Selection Processing (ToMM/SP) (Leslie & Thaiss, 1992; Leslie & Polizzi, 1998; Scholl & Leslie, 1999; German & Leslie, 2000, 2001; Scholl & Leslie, 2001) proposes that ToM has a specific, innate basis. With respect to specificity, the essential character of ToM is said to be determined by specialized mechanisms deploying specialized representations that do not apply to other cognitive domains and hence can be selectively impaired. With respect to innateness, the essential character of ToM – including concepts of belief, desire, and pretense – is thought to be part of our genetic endowment, which is triggered by appropriate environmental factors. The origin of ToM is thought to be a cognitive module that spontaneously and postperceptually processes behaviours that are attended, and computes the mental states that contribute to them. In doing so, it imparts an innate concept of belief, which is hence available to the child prior to other abstract concepts that are acquired through general theory construction. Supplemental processing – termed selection processing – represents general executive processes that come in when the child is to select the correct content of beliefs that are false. The SP is needed because the ToMM automatically attributes beliefs with contents that are true. This prepotent response needs to be sometimes inhibited, as in the case of false belief. On the ToMM/SP account of ToM origins, the innate concept of belief encompasses beliefs of both self and other. Indeed, one would not posit such a module unless such a distinction was presumed cognitively irrelevant.

The theory-theory (TT) or conceptual change account of ToM (Perner, 1991; Gopnik, 1993; Gopnik & Wellman, 1994; Wellman & Cross, 2001) describes ToM development in terms of an implicit theory that affords generalizations in which beliefs and desires, and so forth are interrelated. Perner's (1991) account discusses children's ToM development as a move from "situation-theorists" at 2-3 years of age to "representational theorists" at 4-5 years of age. Whatever the theories attributed to the child on TT accounts, they do not encompass a significant distinction between the mental states of others and self. Indeed, Wellman, Cross & Watson (2001) state that ToM development is "...of an interrelated body of knowledge, based on core mental-state constructs such as "beliefs" and "desires," that apply to all persons generically, that is, to both self and others" (p. 678).

The sociocultural account too makes no differentiation in ToM across reasoning about self and others' mental states. The contextual variables said to affect development of ToM reasoning would do so comparably for reasoning about own and others' representations. These sociocultural variables include the semantics of language (Vinden, 1996), conceptions of self and personhood (Vinden & Astington, 2000), and social interactions (Dunn, Brown, Slomkowski, Tesla & Youngblade, 1991; Perner, Ruffman & Leekam, 1994; Lewis, Freeman, Kyriakidou, Maridaki-Kassotaki & Berridge, 1996; Hughes & Dunn, 1998; Ruffman, Perner, Naito, Parkin & Clements, 1998).

8.2 DIFFERENTIATED ToM: DEVELOPMENT FROM SELF TO OTHER

A fourth account of ToM – simulation theory (ST) (Harris, 1992) does differentiate between reasoning about self and others' representations. However, it assigns primacy to reasoning about own representations. Children are said to improve their theory of mind understanding through a simulation process. Understanding other minds is based in using one's own experience to simulate that of others. The simulation process beings with children feeding into their own perceptual and or emotional system another person's currently attended visual target and or emotional stance toward the target on-line. It develops to attributing the stance that is being simulated to the other person (e.g., "liking X") then to imagining another person's intentional stance (e.g., pretend another person sees an invisible object or wants an object they themselves do not want). The fourth developmental step is imagining an intentional stance toward counterfactual targets. Hence on ST, persons start out with more accurate and more advanced reasoning about their own mental states than those of the other.

8.3   THE FMS MODEL: DIFFERENTIATED ToM AND DEVELOPMENT FROM OTHER TO SELF

The FMS model takes a functionalist perspective on ToM whereon ToM is viewed in terms of its functions in our lives. A functionalist view is not adopted by any other major theory of mind account.

One key function for ToM is social interaction. Understanding and predicting the mental and emotional states of others, especially when these are inconsistent with reality, is critical in the conduct of nimble social interaction. False belief, which entails reasoning about another's contrastive and erroneous beliefs with respect to reality, is a case in point. Hence the false belief task measures social ToM in terms of social metarepresentation.

The second function for ToM is intrapersonal. Two major intrapersonal uses of metarepresentational ToM include reflection and learning. "Intrapersonal-reflection" is metarepresentational reasoning that entails one's own contrastive mental representations about an object or event where no learning is involved. It is used in distinguishing appearance from reality. When intrapersonal ToM entails learning it can be termed "constructivist." Representational change, and the tasks assessing it, is a case of "intrapersonal-constructivist" metarepresentational reasoning. Representational change entails learning in the form of knowledge replacement. One maintains contrastive representations of one's past, incorrect knowledge of an object or event and one's new, corrected knowledge of such.

With theory of mind understood as differentiated into Social and Intrapersonal forms the question arises as to how development proceeds. Is it synchronous, with both kinds developing roughly simultaneously ontogenetically, albeit on parallel courses? Or is there a basis on which to argue that one form has ontogenetic primacy. Several lines of evidence support the view that the social functions of ToM precede the cognitive functions. With form following function, development of Social ToM would precede that of Intrapersonal ToM.

First, the theory of mind literature itself speaks to the basis of theory of mind in social interactive processes. The metarepresentation evident in false belief develops more readily in children who have social interactions with siblings (Dunn et al., 1991; Perner et al., 1994; Lewis et al., 1996; Ruffman et al., 1998) and with friends, with whom they engage in frequent reference to mental states (Hughes & Dunn, 1998), and with adult kin (Lewis et al., 1996). Success on false belief tasks also depends on conversational experience and awareness (Siegal & Peterson, 1994, 1996, 1999) and social understanding mediated by early conversational experience (Woolfe, Want & Siegal, 2002).

Second, we appear to have a biological predisposition toward social interaction, as proposed by Gelman & Lucariello (2002). This biological predisposition, described as knowledge and functioning in the "sociality" domain, includes our recognition of persons as persons and social interaction guided by principles of agency, mental state understanding, and emotional valence.

Third, the sociocultural theory of Vygotsky posits social origins for cognitive functions. This is evident in his notion of *internalization.* "Every function in the child's cultural development appears twice: first, on the social level, and later, on the individual level; first, between people (*interpsychological*), and then *inside* the child (*intrapsychological*)[...] All the higher functions originate as actual relations between human individuals." (Vygotsky, 1978, p. 57, emphasis in original). Hence, through internalization cognitive functions and processes performed on an external plane between persons come to be performed internally, within the child. ToM could be one such cognitive function.

Finally, Mead (1934) proposes that the self is the product of social interactions. "The self is something which has a development; it is not initially there at birth, but arises in the process of social experience and activity..." (Mead, 1934, p. 135). Moreover, social interaction and others are primary and precede the existence of self. "The process out of which the self arises is a social process which implies interaction of individuals in the group, implies the pre-existence of the group." (Mead, 1934, p. 164).

Accordingly, on the FMS model, social and intrapersonal metarepresentational ToMs are functionally distinct. They do not rest in a single, underlying ToM ability. Hence understandings of own and others' representations are not purported to emerge necessarily together at a single ontogenetic time point.

8.4 LOCAL CULTURE AND INDIVIDUAL DIFFERENCES: EVEN GREATER TILT TOWARD SOCIAL ToM

Some socialization experiences orient the child to the mental and emotional states of others. These experiences would presumably foster development of Social ToM. Other socialization experiences orient the child to his/her own mental states and these would presumably recruit Intrapersonal ToM.

Among the socialization experiences likely fostering Social ToM is an interdependent or collectivist self-concept. Hereon the self is understood fundamentally in terms of one's relations to others (Markus & Kitayama, 1991). Maintaining one's relationships with others and ensuring positive social interactions requires knowing how others are feeling, thinking, and likely to act and should lead to more readily accessible knowledge of the other (Markus & Kitayama, 1991). Indeed, Chinese children, who presumably have an interdependent self-concept, show greater perspective-taking ability than Australian children, with presumably an independent self-concept (Fu-Xi & Keats, 1989). Additionally, 4- and 5-year old Japanese children (who presumably have an interdependent self-concept) perform successfully on the other-belief false belief task, while generally failing an own-belief ("source") task (Ruffman et al., 1998).

Socialization in the "pragmatic-interpersonal" model of language use would also direct children's attention to others and their mental states. This model is evident in uses that organize children's behaviour on a social and emotional plane (e.g., vocatives, social expressions) (Blake, 1994). Also included are pragmatic uses that attempt to regulate others' actions (Halliday, 1975; Nelson, 1981; Blake, 1994). Socioemotional functions such as "interpersonal expressive" (Blake, 1994) or "interpersonal"/"interactive" (Halliday, 1975; Nelson, 1981), which establish, describe, and manage relationships are features of pragmatic-interpersonal language.

Development of Intrapersonal ToM is facilitated by socialization practices that orient individuals to their own mental states. These sociocultural experiences include an independent self-concept and a referential-intrapersonal model of language use.

The independent self-concept is one whereon individuals seek to maintain their independence from others by attending to the self and by discovering and expressing their unique inner attributes (Markus & Kitayama, 1991). The person is a self-contained motivational and cognitive universe (Geertz, 1975). Accordingly, an independent self-concept directs the individual's attention to his or her own mental states (Greenfield & Bruner, 1966; Markus & Kitayama, 1991). Also, an independent self-concept may facilitate complex reasoning with respect to one's own mental states, such as hypothetical and counterfactual reasoning (Markus & Kitayama, 1991). Reciprocally, Delgado-Gaitan (1994) has shown that an interdependent self-concept detracts from the development of "critical thinking" processes in children.

The "intrapersonal-intentionality" model of language socialization also serves to direct children's attention to their own mental states. It is evident in the conversational approach whereon the child is seen as an intentional agent, with mental states, from the outset of life (Snow, 1986). Indeed, characteristics of child-directed speech, such as expansions and requests for clarification, focus on the child's intentional states. Moreover, expression of intentional states is proposed as the basis for word learning and early multi-word utterances (Bloom, 1993). Furthermore, expressions of one's internal states is seen in more advanced language uses, such as the symbolic (as in pretend play) and hypothetical (e.g., "if...) (Halliday, 1975).

Socialization experiences vary with respect to self-concept and language use. Such variation affords individual differences in ToM development. To illustrate, we can examine the typical socialization experiences of low-income children. These experiences would propel development of social metarepresentational reasoning.

Low-income children tend to be socialized into the pragmatic-interpersonal model of language use (e.g., Miller 1982, 1987, 1988). Parents of these children do not rely on the intrapersonal-intentionality language style in interacting with their children. Often adult speech is not directed to very young children nor does it typically include expansions and clarifications of child meaning (Brice Heath, 1983). Moreover, socioemotional functions predominate in maternal speech (Blake, 1994). Not surprisingly, low-income children's uses of language are consistent with their socialization. These uses have been described as "contextualized" (Snow, 1991). Language is used largely to serve interpersonal and emotional functions (Brice Heath, 1983, 1989; Miller, 1986; Blake, 1993, 1994). Uses such as teasing and story telling are commonly used by low-income children (Brice Heath, 1983; Miller, 1986). Moreover, low-income children tend to rely more heavily on socioemotional functions and use more socioemotional semantic-syntactic expressions than do middle-income children (Blake, 1994).

The socialization of low-income children with respect to self-concept would also more likely lead to development of social ToM. An interdependent self-concept is characteristic of minority children, many of whom are low-income (Delgado-Gaitan, 1994; Greenfield, 1994; Goldenberg & Gallimore, 1995).

8.5 CLAIMS OF FMS MODEL OF ToM

The FMS Model of ToM proposes that ToM has distinct functions which serve as the basis for distinct forms. One function for ToM is social interaction. ToM so used consists in reasoning about others' mental and emotional states and is termed Social ToM. ToM is also used for intrapersonal, cognitive functions, such as reflection and learning. These functions entail reasoning about own mental and emotional states. Such reasoning is termed Intrapersonal ToM. Social interactive uses for ToM are thought to be primary in the developmental process leading to the ontogenetic primacy of Social ToM. Moreover, individual differences in

ToM development are predicted due to varying socialization experiences. The socialization experiences of low-income children should lead them to have strength in Social ToM.

8.6   EMPIRICAL SUPPORT FOR THE FMS MODEL
8.6.1   Study 1

The hypothesis that metarepresentational ToM differentiates into Social and Intrapersonal forms was explored first in a study of thirty low-income 5-6-year-old children (see Lucariello, 2004, for a fuller description of this study). Since low-income children are thought to have particular strength in Social ToM (due to their socialization experiences), they represent a good sample to begin study of differentiated ToM.

Procedure. Children were presented with an "unexpected identity" task consisting of the rock-sponge deceptive object methodology (Flavell et al., 1983; Gopnik & Astington, 1988). See Table 1, the first task listed, for a description of this task. Children were tested for their understanding of false belief, which is a Social ToM task. They were also tested for their understanding of the appearance-reality distinction and representational change. Both of these are Intrapersonal ToM tasks. For each of these tasks, each child was assigned a score of "1" if passed and a score of "0" not. Children were scored as having passed the representational change task, if they correctly reported their initial representation of the object as a rock. Similarly, they were scored as having passed the false belief task, if they correctly reported the false belief that another child would think the object was a rock. To pass the appearance-reality question, children had to answer the appearance question correctly (stating that the object looks like a rock) and the reality question correctly (stating that the object really is a sponge).

Results. A mean score for each of the three tasks – false belief, appearance-reality distinction, representational change - was computed by tallying children's scores per task and dividing by the total number of children. These means are presented in Figure 1.

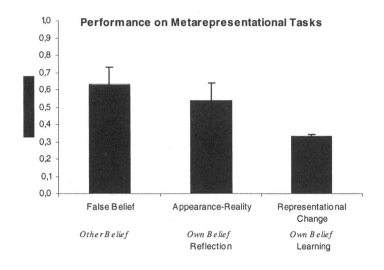

Figure 1. Mean Proportion Correct Responses on the Metarepresentational Tasks (Study 1).

Task means were compared by paired (non-independent) t-tests. Children did best on the false belief task. This was the only of the three tasks on which a clear majority of children were successful. Nearly two-thirds succeeded on this task. Performance was weakest on the representational change task. Only one-third of children succeeded on this task. The mean score on the false belief task (M = .63; SD = .49) was significantly higher than that for representational change (M = .33; SD = .48), $t(23)$ = 2.29, p <.032. No significant difference in mean scores was found between the false belief and appearance-reality tasks.

Finally, mean scores across the two intrapersonal reasoning tasks of appearance-reality and representational change tasks were compared. Better performance was found on the appearance-reality task, $t(23)$ 1.74, p<.05, one-tailed, p < .10, two-tailed. See Figure 1. Use of a one-tailed test is justified because representational change was predicted to be more challenging than appearance-reality. The latter entails only reflection, whereas the former entails learning.

In addition, intertask Pearson correlations on children's theory of mind performance were computed. These data are presented in Table 2. As can be seen, no significant correlations were found across any of the three tasks.

Table 2. Correlations for Metarepresentational ToM Tasks (Study 1)

	1	2	3
1. False Belief	-	.32	.18
2. Appearance-Reality	-	-	.30
3. Representational Change			-

Discussion. The FMS model's view of metarepresentational ToM as differentiated was supported by the findings. Children's performance across own and other belief tasks was not correlated. These data support the idea of a differentiated ToM. Also, supporting the idea of a differentiated ToM was children's uneven task performance. Their greatest success was on the Social ToM task of false belief. Moreover, children performed better on this task than on the intrapersonal (learning) task of representational change.

These findings add to those from other recent studies showing differential task performance across tasks measuring own and other reasoning. Performance across false belief ("other" belief task) and representational change ("own" belief) tasks is not correlated for 3-year-olds nor for 4-year olds (Moore, Barresi & Thompson, 1998). Similarly, while inter-task correlations were found for nearly every task among 8 that measured false belief in preschoolers, a notable exception was the "recall-own-false-belief" task (Cutting & Dunn, 1999). Moreover, an ordering of successful performance has been found, with false belief acquired prior to representational change (Gopnik & Astington, 1988). In addition, while 5-year-olds commonly pass the other-belief reasoning task of false belief, a "source" task proved very difficult for 4 and 5-year old children, with the majority of 5-year-olds failing this task (Ruffman et al., 1998). Finally, while children in the 3-5-year-old age range were able to explain why another might experience mixed emotions about a given situation, they were unable to provide an occasion on which they themselves experienced mixed emotions (Hughes & Dunn, 1998). All these findings, along with the present ones, speak to a distinction between "own" and "other" ToM reasoning.

Clearly, however, further research is needed to buttress the claim of a differentiated ToM. Study of language functioning in relation to a differentiated ToM can help address this issue since language plays a significant role in ToM development.

8.6.2   Study 2: Leaning on Language for Insights into the Nature of ToM

Considerable research shows that language is fundamental to the development of metarepresentational ToM. For example, false belief understanding has been linked to discourse in terms of conversational experience and awareness (Siegal & Peterson 1994, 1996; Siegal 1997;

Peterson & Siegal, 1999; Siegal, Varley & Want, 2001; Woolfe et al., 2002) and perspective-shifting (Lohmann & Tomasello, 2003).

Moreover, general language ability is highly correlated with false belief (Jenkins & Astington, 1996). Such has also been demonstrated through analysis of atypical populations. Level of verbal ability is a crucial factor for those children with autism who pass false belief tasks (Happe', 1995). In addition, children with autism, who typically fail ToM tasks, are delayed in language achievements and show linguistic performance patterns that differ from those of non-autistic children (Tager-Flusberg, 1993).

Furthermore, syntactic understanding appears key to ToM development. Earlier language ability in terms of syntax predicts later theory of mind test performance on false belief and appearance-reality tasks (Astington & Jenkins, 1999). The specific understanding of sentential complements is thought to underlie the development of metarepresentational reasoning (de Villiers & Pyers, 1997; Tager-Flusberg, 1997, 2000; de Villiers, 2000; de Villiers & de Villiers, 2000; Hale & Tager-Flusberg, 2003; Lohmann & Tomasello, 2003). Sentential complements afford the embedding of tensed propositions under a main verb. The embedded clause is an obligatory linguistic argument that can have an independent truth value. The main clause can be true while the embedded clause may be false (e.g., Sally thinks (falsely) that the sponge is a rock). Astington and Jenkins (1999) note that acquisition of object complementation promotes false belief understanding because the syntax of complementation provides the format needed to represent false beliefs. "The syntax and semantics of sentential complements allow for the explicit representation of a falsely embedded proposition. Complements uniquely provide the means for discussing contradictions between mental states and reality" (Hale & Tager-Flusberg, 2003, p. 348).

Mental state terms/reference (e.g., *think, know, believe*) has also been found to facilitate theory of mind development (Olson, 1988). The idea is that in learning the referents of these terms children also learn the relevant concepts. Significant improvements over time in tests of false belief and affective-perspective-taking were associated with quantitative and qualitative changes in children's references to mental states in their conversations with friends (Hughes & Dunn, 1998). Moreover, initial individual differences in the frequency of mental state talk in this social context were significantly associated with ToM performance more than a year later. In addition, mother's use of mental state utterances in describing pictures was correlated with children's later theory of mind understanding (Ruffman, Slade & Crowe, 2002).

Given the major role that language plays in the development of theory of mind, particularly a metarepresentational ToM, study of the functioning of language in relation to a differentiated ToM can be instrumental in addressing the issue of whether ToM is differentiated.

The hypotheses of the FMS model were explored in a second study (Lucariello, Durand, Tatelman & Yarnell, 2004; Lucariello, Durand & Yarnell, in preparation). Two forms of ToM reasoning – Social and Intrapersonal – were distinguished and studied. A measure of child language was administered so that the relation of language to each could be examined. If theory of mind is integrated, language should be comparably related to each of these forms of reasoning. If ToM is differentiated, however, language might be more associated with one form of reasoning than another. Since language is fundamental to ToM development, the form with which it is most associated can be taken to be developmentally primary.

Also addressed in Study 2 is the hypothesis that Social ToM is primary in general for children. Accordingly, both middle-income and low-income children served as participants. Moreover, to more fully explore the nature of a differentiated ToM, such was explored across 3 domains of mental states - beliefs, emotions, and perceptions.

Participants. One-hundred-twenty-two kindergarten children served as participants. Seventy-three were low-income and forty-nine were middle-income. Income status was determined by eligibility to free or reduced lunch.

Procedure. In a first visit with each child, the Test of Early Language Development Third Edition (TELD-3) (Hresko, Reid & Hammill, 1999) was administered. The TELD-3 assesses receptive and expressive language and overall spoken language. It measures syntax and semantics.

In a second visit with each child, ToM tasks were administered. Within income group, children were randomly assigned to either the Social ToM or Intrapersonal ToM condition. Within each condition, children received, in an order that was counterbalanced across children, five metarepresentational reasoning tasks. See Table 1. Across the Social and Intrapersonal conditions, tasks were identical except for whether the child had to reason about own (Intrapersonal condition) or others' (Social Condition) internal states.

A description of the five tasks, and the associated theory of mind behaviours tested, is found in Table 1. In the belief domain, two tasks were administered. The unexpected identity task was the same as used in Study 1. The "unexpected contents-nice surprise" task was modelled after Harris, Johnson, Hutton, Andrews & Cooke (1989) and Cutting & Dunn (1999). These two tasks assessed false belief, appearance-reality, and representational change.

In the emotion domain, the "unexpected contents-nice surprise" task assessed representational change with respect to emotion. In addition, the child was presented with 6 appearance-reality stories to assess understanding of the appearance-reality distinction. This task, and 4 of the 6 story stimuli, were drawn from Harris, Donnelly, Guz & Pitt-Watson (1986), Gross & Harris (1988), and Gardner, Harris, Ohmoto & Hamazaki (1988). Two story stimuli (afraid of the dark; wet cat) were constructed by the experimenters. All stories portray a character who really feels one way but (for good reason) appears (looks on face) another way. Harris and colleagues used stories wherein the character was always another child. For the present Intrapersonal condition, these stories were adapted to make the C the character. In 3 stories (falling and getting hurt, having a stomach ache, and being afraid of the dark), the character was feeling a negative emotion (feeling "sad") and displaying a positive emotion (looking "happy" or "okay"). In the other 3 (funny lady, winning a game, wet cat), the character was feeling a positive emotion (feeling "happy" or "okay") and displaying a negative (looking "sad") emotion.

In the perception domain, representational change was assessed in the turtle task (Gopnik & Slaughter, 1991). A perspective-taking version of this task was constructed by the experimenters for the Social condition. In addition, perspective-taking (Social condition) and understanding appearance-reality (Intrapersonal condition) were assessed in the colour filters task (Flavell, Green & Flavell, 1986).

Results. The TELD-3 Receptive Language and Expressive Language subtest standard scores are added and transformed into the Spoken Language Quotient. Mean Quotient scores were computed for each income group in the two conditions. These are presented in Figure 2. A 2 (income) X 2 (condition) ANOVA on TELD scores revealed only a main effect of SES. Middle-income children (M = 108.20) had higher scores than low-income children (M = 97.04), $F(1, 122) = 27.12, p < .001$.

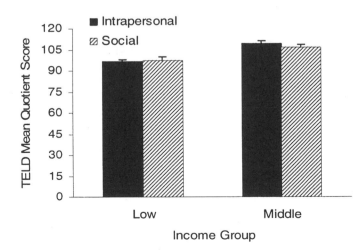

Figure 2. TELD Mean Quotient Scores by Income and Condition (Study 2).

A theory of mind score for each domain - consisting in the mean proportion of correct responding - was computed by tallying for each child the number of tasks responded to correctly over the total number of tasks the child received (Belief Social 0-3; Belief Intrapersonal 0-4; Emotion 0-7; Perception 0-4). Scores were then tallied across children to obtain the mean. These data are presented in Figure 3. A mean total theory of mind score for each condition was computed by tallying for each child their proportion correct responding across the total number of tasks received (Social 15 and Intrapersonal 14) and tallying across children to obtain the mean.

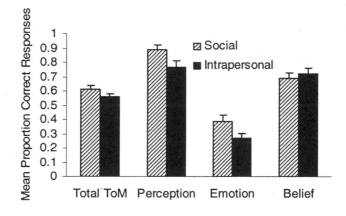

Figure 3. Mean Proportion Correct ToM Scores (Total and Domain) by Condition (Study 2).

A 2 (income) X 2 (condition) X 3 (Domain) MANCOVA (TELD Quotient score as the covariate) was run on ToM Domain Scores. It showed a main effect for condition with Social ToM reasoning better than Intrapersonal (F = 5.17, p < .01). It also showed significant univariate effects in the emotion and perception domains, with better Social ToM (Perception $F(1, 122) = 7.52, p < .01$; Emotion $F(1, 122) = 6.95, p <.01$. A separate ANCOVA was run for Total ToM scores. It also showed a main effect for condition, with Social ToM reasoning better than Intrapersonal (F (1, 122) = 3.72, $p <.056$).

Pearson correlations were run on ToM domain scores and Total ToM scores for the Social and Intrapersonal conditions. See Table 3. With respect to interdomain relatedness, belief and emotion reasoning were significantly correlated in the Social Condition. No interdomain correlations were found for the Intrapersonal condition.

Table 3. Intercorrelations among Tom Scores and TELD Mean Quotient Scores for Social and Intrapersonal Conditions (Study 2)

ToM and Language Measures	1	2	3	4	5
		Social (n=61)			
1. Belief ToM	-	.33**	.20	.67***	.37**
2. Emotion ToM		-	.15	.78***	.43***
3. Perception ToM			-	.49***	.39**
4. Total ToM				-	.50***
5. TELD Mean Quotient				-	-
		Intrapersonal (n=61)			
1. Belief ToM	-	.02	.06	.45***	.09
2. Emotion ToM		-	.05	.44***	.30*
3. Perception ToM			-	.69***	.29*
4. Total ToM				-	.23
5. TELD Mean Quotient				-	-

*p <.05. **p <.01 ***p < .001

Pearson correlations between TELD Mean Quotient scores and ToM Domain scores and Total ToM scores were also run for each condition. These data are also presented in Table 3. Language was much more correlated with Social ToM than with Intrapersonal ToM. In the social condition, language was correlated with all three mental state domains and with total theory of mind. In the Intrapersonal condition, language was correlated only, and more weakly, with the emotion and perception domains.

To explore which specific tasks by condition were correlated with language, Pearson correlations were run for the TELD Mean Quotient scores and each of the ToM tasks in each of the 3 domains by condition. Significant correlations are presented in Table 4. In the Social condition, language was correlated with almost all tasks in both the emotion (5 of 7 tasks) and perception (3 of 4 tasks) domains. In the belief domain, language was correlated only with Social ToM tasks.

Table 4. Significant Correlations of TELD Scores with Theory of Mind Performance by Domain, Task and Condition

Domain and Task	Correlations with TELD Mean Quotient Scores	
	Social Condition	Intrapersonal Condition
Emotion		
Appearance-Reality Stories:		
Fall and Get Hurt	.36**	.31*
Stomach Ache	.27$^+$	.08
Afraid of Dark	.24$^+$	.24
Funny Lady	.33*	.10
Wet Cat	.39*	.11
Belief		
Unexpected Contents: Nice Surprise:		
Representational Change	.38**	.14
False Belief	.26*	-
Perception		
Representational Change: Turtle Viewing	.37$^+$	.04
Level 2 Perspective-Taking (Social)		
Distinguishing Appearance-Reality (Intrapersonal)		
Colour Filter: Cake	.30*	.36**
Colour Filter: Boat	.34**	.28*

** $p < .01$, $p < .05$, $^+$ = trend

Discussion. All the findings indicate that ToM differentiates into Social and Intrapersonal kinds and that Social ToM has developmental primacy. The analyses on ToM domain scores and total ToM scores showed that ToM reasoning was better in the Social ToM condition for both groups of children. This was true for total ToM score and for reasoning in two domains - emotion and perception.

The correlational analyses on ToM domain scores showed that Intrapersonal and Social ToM reasoning operate differently. This is further evidence for their differentiated status. Reasoning about beliefs and emotions was correlated when reasoning about others' internal states (Social ToM condition), but not when reasoning about one's own internal states (Intrapersonal ToM condition). Moreover, the evidence of integration in reasoning among domains of mental states in Social ToM, and the lack of any such integration in Intrapersonal ToM, can be taken as another indicator of the developmental primacy of Social ToM.

Finally, the language data further illuminated the nature of ToM and showed ToM to be differentiated. Language was more highly correlated with Social ToM than with Intrapersonal ToM. Moreover, since language is fundamental to metarepresentational ToM development, its greater link to Social ToM is further evidence that Social ToM is primary in development.

8.7   GENERAL CONCLUSIONS

The data from these two studies support the FMS Model of ToM (Lucariello, 2004). ToM has distinct functions which serve as the basis for distinct forms. One function for ToM is social interaction. ToM so used consists in reasoning about others' mental and emotional states and is termed Social ToM. ToM is also used for intrapersonal, cognitive functions, such as reflection and learning. These functions entail reasoning about own mental and emotional states. Such reasoning is termed Intrapersonal ToM. Social interactive uses for ToM are primary in the developmental process leading to the ontogenetic primacy of Social ToM. Moreover, individual differences in ToM development are predicted due to varying socialization experiences. The socialization experiences of low-income children lead them to have strength in Social ToM.

Development of Intrapersonal ToM reasoning, especially within the emotion domain and toward integration across domains of mental states, requires study. It would seem that knowing other's mental and emotional states could facilitate reasoning about one's own internal states. The mechanisms by which this is accomplished need to be identified.

ACKNOWLEDGMENTS

This research was supported in part by a Collaborative Fellows Grant from Boston College. Portions of this research were presented at the meetings of the Cognitive Development Society Oct '03 and AERA April '04.

REFERENCES

Astington, J.W., Harris, P.L., Olson, D.R. (Eds.) *Developing Theories of Mind*. Cambridge: Cambridge University Press, 1988.

Astington J.W., Jenkins J.M. A longitudinal study of the relation between language and theory-of-mind development. Developmental Psychology 1999; 35: 1311-1320.

Blake I.K. The social-emotional orientation of mother-child communication in African American Families. International Journal of Behavioural Development 1993; 16: 443-463.

Blake, I.K. "Language development and socialization in young African-American children." In *Cross-cultural roots of minority child development*, P.M. Greenfield, R.R. Cocking (Eds.), Hillsdale, NJ: Erlbaum, 1994.

Bloom, L. *The Transition from Infancy to Language: Acquiring the Power of Expression*. Cambridge, MA: Cambridge University Press, 1993.

Brice Heath, S. *Ways with words*. Cambridge, MA: Cambridge University Press, 1983.

Brice Heath S. Oral and literate traditions among Black Americans living in poverty American Psychologist 1989; 44: 367-373.

Cutting A.L., Dunn J. Theory of mind, emotion understanding, language, and family background: Individual differences and interrelations. Child Development 1999; 70: 853-865.

de Villiers, J. "Language and theory of mind: What are the developmental relationships." In *Understanding other minds: Perspectives from developmental cognitive neuroscience* (2nd Ed.), S. Baron-Cohen, H. Tager-Flusberg, D. Cohen (Eds.), Oxford: Oxford University Press, 2000.

de Villiers, J.G., de Villiers, P.A. "Linguistic determinism and the understanding of false beliefs". In *Children's reasoning and the mind*, P. Mitchell, K. Riggs (Eds.), Hove, Sussex: Psychology Press, 2000.

de Villiers, J., Pyers, J. Complementing cognition: The relationship between language and theory of mind. In Proceedings of the 21st Annual Boston University Conference on Language Development. Somerville, MA: Cascadilla Press, 1997.

Delgado-Gaitan, C. "Socializing young children in Mexican-American families: An intergenerational perspective." In *Cross-cultural roots of minority child development*, P.M. Greenfield, R.R. Cocking (Eds.) Hillsdale, NJ: Erlbaum, 1994.

Dunn J., Brown J., Slomkowski C., Tesla C., Youngblade L. Young children's understanding of other people's feelings and beliefs: Individual differences and their antecedents. Child Development 1991; 62: 1352-1366.

Flavell J.H., Flavell E.R., Green F.L. Development of the appearance-reality distinction. Cognitive Psychology 1983; 15: 95-120.

Flavell J.H., Green F.L., Flavell E.R. Development of knowledge about the appearance-reality distinction. Monographs of the Society for research in Child Development 1986; 51, 1: Serial No. 212.

Fu-Xi, F., Keats, D.M. " 'The Master and the Wolf': A study in the development of social perspective taking in Chinese and Australian children." In *Heterogeneity in cross-cultural psychology*, D.M. Keats, D. Munro, L. Mann (Eds.), Amsterdam: Swets, Zeitlinger B.V, 1989.

Geertz C. On the nature of anthropological understanding. American Scientist 1975; 63: 47-53.

Gelman, R., Lucariello, J. "Role of learning in cognitive development." In *Stevens' handbook of experimental psychology: Vol. 3. Learning, motivation, and emotion* (3rd ed.), H. Pashler (Series Ed.), C.R. Gallistel (Vol. Ed.), New York: Wiley, 2002.

German, T., Leslie, A. "Attending to and learning about mental states." In *Children's reasoning and the mind*, P. Mitchell, K. Riggs (Eds.), Hove, U.K.: Psychology Press, 2000.

German T.P., Leslie A.M. Children's inferences from knowing to pretending and believing. British Journal of Developmental Psychology 2001; 19: 59-83.

Goldenberg, C., Gallimore, R. "Immigrant Latino parents' values and beliefs about their children's education: Continuities and discontinuities across cultures and generations." In *Advances in motivation and achievement: Culture, motivation and achievement* (Vol. 9), M. L. Maehr, P.R. Pintrich (Eds.), Connecticut: Jai Press, 1995.

Gopnik A. How we know our minds: The illusions of first person knowledge of intentionality. Behavioural and Brain Sciences 1993; 16: 1-14.

Gopnik A., Astington J.W. Children's understanding of representational change and its relation to the understanding of false belief and the appearance-reality distinction. Child Development 1988; 59: 26-37.

Gopnik A., Slaughter V. Young children's understanding of changes in their mental states. Child Development 1991; 62: 98-110.

Gopnik, A., Wellman, H.M. "The theory theory." In *Domain specificity in cognition and culture*, L. Hirschfeld, S. Gelman (Eds.), New York: Cambridge University Press, 1994.

Greenfield, P.M. "Independence and interdependence as developmental scripts: Implications for theory, research, and practice." In *Cross-cultural roots of minority child development*, P.M. Greenfield, R.R. Cocking (Eds.). Hillsdale, NJ: Erlbaum, 1994.

Greenfield P.M., Bruner J.S. Culture and cognitive growth. International Journal of Psychology 1966; 1: 89-107.

Gardner D., Harris P. L., Ohmoto M., Hamazaki T. Japanese children's understanding of the distinction between real and apparent emotion. International Journal of Behaviour and Development 1988; 11: 203-218.

Gross D., Harris P.L. False beliefs about emotion: Children's understanding of misleading emotional displays. International Journal of Behaviour and Development 1988; 11: 475-488.

Hale C.M., Tager-Flusberg H. The influence of language on theory of mind: A training study. Developmental Science 2003; 6: 346-359.

Halliday, M.A.K., *Learning how to mean: Explorations in the development of language*. London: Edward Arnold, 1975.

Happe' F.G.E. The role of age and verbal ability in the theory of mind task performance of subjects with autism. Child Development 1995; 66: 843-855.

Harris P.L. From simulation to folk psychology: The case for development. Mind and Language 1992; 7: 120-144.

Harris P.L., Donnelly K., Guz G.R., Pitt-Watson R. Children's understanding of the distinction between real and apparent emotion. Child Development 1986; 57: 895-909.

Harris P.L., Johnson C.N., Hutton D., Andrews G., Cooke T. Young children's theory of mind and emotion, Cognition and Emotion 1989; 3: 379-400.

Hresko, W.P., Reid, D.K., Hammill, D., *Test of Early Language Development* (3rd Edition). Austin, Texas: Pro-ed, 1999.

Hughes C., Dunn J. Understanding mind and emotion: Longitudinal associations with mental-state talk between young friends. Developmental Psychology 1998; 34: 1026-1037.

Jenkins J.M., Astington J.W. Cognitive factors and family structure associated with theory of mind development in young children. Developmental Psychology 1996; 32: 70-78.

Leslie A.M., Polizzi P. Inhibitory processing in the false belief task: Two conjectures. Developmental Science 1998; 1: 247-254.

Leslie A.M., Thaiss L. Domain specificity in conceptual development: Neuropsychological evidence from autism. Cognition 1992; 43: 225-251.

Lewis C., Freeman N. H., Kyriakidou C., Maridaki-Kassotaki K., Berridge D.M. Social influences on false belief access: Specific sibling influences or general apprenticeship? Child Development 1996; 67: 2930-2947.

Lohmann H., Tomasello M. The role of language in the development of false belief understanding: A training study. Child Development 2003; 74: 1130-1144.

Lucariello, J. "New insights into the functions, development, and origins of theory of mind: the Functional Multilinear Socialization (FMS) Model. In *The development of the mediated mind: Sociocultural context and cognitive development*, J.M.Lucariello, J.A. Hudson, R. Fivush, P.J. Bauer (Eds.), Mahwah, NJ: Erlbaum, 2004.

Lucariello J., Durand T., Tatelman T., Yarnell L. Low-income children's cognitive capital: Strength in social critical thinking. In Understanding human development to inform educational practice. Paper session conducted at the American Education Research Association, San Diego, 2004 April.

Lucariello, J., Durand, T., Yarnell, L., *Evidence for a differentiated theory of mind in kindergarten children.* Manuscript in preparation.

Markus H.R., Kitayama S. Culture and the self: Implications for cognition, emotion, and motivation. Psychological Review 1991; 98: 224-253.

Mead, G.H., *Mind, self & society.* Chicago: University of Chicago Press, 1934.

Miller, P., *Wendy, Amy, Beth: Learning language in South Baltimore.* Austin: University of Texas Press, 1982.

Miller, P. "Teasing as language socialization and verbal play in a white working-class community." In *Language socialization across cultures. Studies in the social and cultural foundations of language, No. 3,* B.B. Schieffelin, E. Ochs (Eds.), New York: Cambridge University Press, 1986.

Miller P. The socialization of anger and aggression. Merrill-Palmer Quarterly 1987; 33: 1-31.

Miller P. Early talk about the past: The origins of conversational stories of personal experience. Journal of Child Language 1988; 15: 293-315.

Moore C., Barresi J., Thompson C. The cognitive basis of future-oriented prosocial behaviour. Social Development 1998; 7: 198-218.

Nelson K. Individual differences in language development: Implications for development and language. Developmental Psychology 1981; 17: 170-187.

Olson, D.R. "On the origins of beliefs and other intentional states in children." In *Developing theories of mind,* J.W. Astington, P. Harris, D.R. Olson, (Eds.), Cambridge, MA: Cambridge University Press, 1988.

Perner, J., *Understanding the Representational Mind.* Cambridge, MA: MIT Press, 1991.

Perner J., Ruffman T., Leekam S.R. Theory of mind is contagious: You catch it from your sibs. Child Development 1994; 65: 1228-1238.

Peterson C.C., Siegal M. Representing inner worlds: Theory of mind in autistic, deaf, and normal hearing children. Psychological Science 1999; 10: 126-129.

Ruffman T., Perner J., Naito M., Parkin L., Clements W.A. Older (but not younger) siblings facilitate false belief understanding. Developmental Psychology 1998; 34: 161-174.

Ruffman T., Slade L., Crowe E. The relation between children's and mothers' mental state language and theory-of-mind understanding. Child Development 2002; 73: 734-751.

Scholl B.J., Leslie A.M. Modularity, development, and 'theory of mind.' Mind And Language 1999; 14: 131-153.

Scholl B.J., Leslie A.M. Minds, modules, and meta-analysis. Child Development 2001; 72: 696-701.

Siegal, M., *Knowing children: Experiments in conversation and cognition.* Hove, England: Psychology Press/Taylor & Francis, 1997.

Siegal M. Language and thought: The fundamental significance of conversational awareness for cognitive development. Developmental Science 1999; 2: 1-34.

Siegal, M., Peterson, C.C. "Children's theory of mind and the conversational territory of cognitive development." In *Origins of an understanding of mind,* C. Lewis, P. Mitchell (Eds.), Hove, England: Erlbaum, 1994.

Siegal M., Peterson C.C. Breaking the mold: A fresh look at questions about children's understanding of lies and mistakes. Developmental Psychology 1996; 32: 322-334.

Siegal M., Varley R., Want S.C. Mind over grammar: Reasoning in aphasia and development. Trends in Cognitive Sciences 2001; 5: 296-301.

Snow, C.E. "Conversations with children." In *Language acquisition,* P. Fletcher, M. Garman (Eds.), 1986.

Snow C.E. The theoretical basis for relationships between language and literacy in development. Journal of Research in Childhood Education 1991; 6: 5-10.

Vinden P.G. Junin Quechua children's understanding of mind. Child Development 1996; 67: 1707-1716.

Vinden, P.G., Astington, J.W. "Culture and understanding other minds." In *Understanding other minds: Perspectives from developmental cognitive neuroscience*, S. Baron-Cohen, H. Tager-Flusberg, D.J. Cohen (Eds.), Oxford: Oxford University Press, 2000.

Wellman H.M., Cross D. Theory of mind and conceptual change: Reply. Child Development 2001; 72: 702-707.

Wellman H.M., Cross D., Watson J. Meta-analysis of theory-of-mind development: The truth about false belief. Child Development 2001; 72: 655-684.

Woolfe T., Want S.C., Siegal M. Signposts to development: Theory of mind in deaf children. Child Development 2002; 73: 768-77.

Chapter 9

DISCURSIVE PRACTICES AND MENTALIZATION ABILITY IN ADULTS AT WORK

Silvia Gilardi,[1] Andreina Bruno,[1] Cristina Pezzotta.[2]

[1]*Department of Psychology, Catholic University of the Sacred Heart, Milan;* [2]*The Theory of Mind Research Unit, Department of Psychology, Catholic University of the Sacred Heart, Brescia*

9.1   LISTENING TO ADULTS AT WORK

Our contribution intends to consider the relationship between the theory of mind and language in the area of working world.

In our organizational life we constantly meet the other's mind: the adult at work is continuously stimulated to take into consideration the other's thought, be it a colleague, a superior or a client, for example to make decisions, manage a working group, persuade or sell.

The language practices used in organizational contexts represent one of the main tools through which the encounter of minds takes shape: language used to talk about professional practice and to interact with the other organizational actors is the means through which people, on the one hand, make visible (also to themselves) the meanings of their work, on the other hand negotiate and build a sense of organizational action which permits them to work together.

Focusing on the language is therefore a unique vantage point from which to observe the characteristics of the theory of mind in action in different organizational contexts.

Let's consider some examples. We are in a training session with a group of social workers in a drug rehabilitation community run by a no-profit association that manages several such communities. The staff is extremely angry because the top management is not responding to repeated requests for additional personnel and has proposed a reorganization of their shifts that they deem to be unacceptable: the members feel they are misunderstood and unappreciated in their educational function, and the explanations supplied by the top management about the financial woes that the Association is experiencing does nothing to cool their resentment. One of the staff members suggests a solution that all the others agree with: ask the chief in charge to visit the community and actually see the way they work *"with his own eyes"*.

The language used expresses a thought about the characteristics of the other's thought: the assumption shared by the staff is that if the real circumstances are the same, different minds will see the situation in the same way.

Here is another example. It is the transcript of a conversation between a nurse and his supervisor.

The nurse is describing the case of a coma patient and is saying that the patient's son have come to shave him and ask if they can take him home, without taking into account that he is in very serious condition. He blames them for not being sensitive. The supervisor asks: *"do you think the relatives realize the situation?"*. *"How can they not realize it: just look at him"*. *"Do you think that they see what you see?"*. *"They can't possibly not be aware of the situation"*.

These two scenarios describe how theory of mind can be used in different ways and levels in the working organizations, and argue in favour of considering mentalistic ability as a mode of mental functioning, that may be used to a greater or lesser extent, and is sensitive to contextual factors, never wholly stabilized but "in motion" (Astington, 1996; Fonagy, Target, 1996; 1997; Dunn, Hughes, 1998; Liverta-Sempio, Marchetti, 2001).

Stimulated by recent attempts to use the *life-span* approach in the framework of theory of mind studies (Chandler & Lalonde, 1992; Kuhn, 2000; Cigoli & Marta, 2001; Chandler et al. 2003) we think it may be interesting to focus on several aspects concerning the organizational context to understand how people maintain and/or modify interpretative representations of their own mental world and that of others, and how they use them in different stages of the job life cycle and in different organizational contexts.

The aim of this study is to use the linguistic-conversational level to highlight the links between constructs derived from studies on theory of mind and studies on workplace and organizations.

We believe that language is a compelling starting point in a framework in which organizations are viewed as a process of actions and decisions driven by aims, belief and values (Thompson, 1967)[1] that are constantly redefined by the inter-subjective exchanges between actors.

Studies on corporate culture and the narrative approach to organizations emphasize how organizations express themselves through cultural artefacts that relate to the way with which people make sense (Weick, 1995) of their working practices.

With the term culture we refer to the whole of tacit assumptions (Schein, 1999) or of theories in use (Argyris & Schön, 1978), that is the beliefs, rules and values strongly internalised in organizational story, which in a tacit way determine the behaviours and show the way in which the members of the group must feel, think and see reality.

In literature the organizational language is analysed starting from the ascertainment of a main characteristic of individuals, that of *homo fabulans*[2].

Studies and organizational researches widely faced the relationship between organizational culture and language. Besides the perspective by Weick (1995), linked to the organizational process of *sensemaking*, we can consider the studies on the construct of *metaphor* within culture (Morgan, 1997). Such a construct had a peculiar attention in organizational area since metaphor transmits and represents "concentrated" meanings, around which we can converge identifications and interpretative keys peculiar to organizational actors.

Consider also the perspective of *learning organization* and of *organizational learning* (Argyris & Schön, 1978; Senge, 1990; Nonaka & Takeuchi, 1995; Gherardi, 2000), in which organizational language and knowledge are closely connected. They insist on the strategic value of knowledge building and of learning for the organization development and the wellbeing of its members: particularly language has a main role in the processes of learning-in-organizing (Gherardi & Nicolini, 2004) as a means of connection and of reciprocal translation among the different knowledge in action, which permits to build a "discursive community" (Vaux, 1999, quoted in Gherardi & Nicolini, 2002) on which we can found the identity of the organized group.

In the last years the strong growth of the narrative and conversational approach (Zucchermaglio, 1996; Lieblich, Tuval-Mashiach & Zilber, 1998; Van Maanen, 1998) implied a growing centrality of the linguistic dimension both in terms of research, and in terms of organizational intervention.

---

[1] These words refer to a concept of organization meant as "organizing", that is a process rather than a reified entity. We are particularly in debt to Thompson for this concept, to which we put beside the construct of organization as "culture", due to the interest excited in us by such "contamination".

[2] The expression "*homo fabulans*" refers to the concept of "biology of the meaning" suggested by Bruner (1990) meaning the attitude, the "innate" and primitive inclination to organize experience in a narrative form.

Today organizational language is recognized to have a double function: both the heuristic and the generative one.

We point out a double link in the relationship between language and organizational culture: language gives signs on the implicit assumptions of the organization, and at the same time it modifies them.

In this framework, Boje (2001) suggests an interesting differentiation between "narrative" and "antenarrative"[3] with reference to the post-modern context and to complex organizations.

"The crisis of narrative method in modernity is what to do with non-linear, almost living storytelling that is fragmented, polyphonic [...] and collectively produced" (Boje, 2001, p.1).

If organizational stories tell us about organizations in which different practical knowledge and attribution of meaning to work problems even contradictory live together, Gherardi & Nicolini (2002) show in their research how in some organizational contexts the coexistence is exactly permitted by a discursive practice which allows to work together and, at the same time, to preserve the difference of perspective.

With this framework, we consider interesting to cross the studies on discursive practices at work with some spurs coming from the research carried out in the area of theory of mind: inside the distinction between story (or narrative product) and speech (or narrative process) we think that focusing on the mentalistic language permits us to take up the challenge of narration in complex and post modern organizations by recovering the polyphonic qualities of its storytellers.

As regards the working history and organizational life of individuals, analysing the language through which adults recount their working practices seems to be the most popular *medium* for distinguishing the theories of mind commonly used in problem solving and decision making, and for accessing the reflective capabilities of individuals and organizations. We will not refer to complete stories, but to interstitial microstories, not necessarily coherent, rather fragmented: in fact post modern conditions make it difficult (sometimes impossible given the structural conditions) to tell coherent stories.

Our contribution is set out as follows. We will explore the relationship individual-work-organization, using the contribution that the distributed theory of mind can provide in organizational processes.

In order to do it, we identified the organizational focus as the starting point, using in particular the metaphor of "reflective organization".

---

[3] Unlike the "dominant paradigms of (monological) narrative analysis in organizational studies, [...] narrative knowing must include those ways of antenarrative analysis of stories told in organizational communities in which the telling of stories is the currency of knowledge making and knowledge negotiation" (Boje, 2001, p.8).

After defining the framework, we will concentrate on the individual dimension, highlighting, with respect to the organizational processes, the issue of professional identity.

Particularly referring to studies on changes that current work instability is producing on the level of personal and professional identity, we will explore the relationship between the theory of mind and the sense of continuity perceived by individuals.

In the end, we will focus on the area of organizational training, as an organizational process potentially able to support and strengthen the reflective capabilities of the persons within organizations which, in a strategic way, take the value of learning creation and of knowledge managing. On this subject, the theme of language closes our contribution, through the study on how linguistic analysis may represent a training tool for developing mentalistic skills.

9.2 REFLEXIVITY AND WORKING PRACTICE: INDIVIDUAL AND ORGANIZATIONAL EPISTEMOLOGICAL PREMISES

The emphasis on reflexivity in organizational life represents a first possible link between organizational studies and research on the theory of mind: as we will try to point out, the connection is about particular states of mind, of epistemic nature, regarding beliefs on what knowledge is and how knowledge is produced.

Historically studies on theory of mind and those about the development of epistemological beliefs belong to different research traditions, each of them characterized by its own objects of experimental research.

Even if aware of the specificity of the two research areas, the approach of these two trends of study, even if aware of the specificity of the two research areas, reacts to the ascertainment that in the working practice these two aspects are growing deeply intertwined.

In fact, adults at work constantly have to talk to make decisions and solve problems: managing such processes requires to take the other's perspective, think the other's thought, not only facing emotions, wishes, beliefs, but also knowledge which guide every actor's action. Beliefs about data reliability, validity of used sources, and criteria of justification of the truth of our statement come into play. These elements belong to the tradition of studies on metacognition and on the development of epistemological thought.

In other words, the dialogue among minds and attention to one's own mind state and the other's, considered inside working organizations, are enriched and intersect with elements about beliefs, convictions, assumptions, about one's own and the other's way of building knowledge.

Regarding studies on the theory of mind we follow authors like Freeman (2000), Kuhn (2000) and Astington et al. (2002) who suggest to consider the naïve theory of knowledge (folk epistemology) as interlaced to the more general theory of mind (folk psychology): from this point of view, this last area of studies refers to the complexity of mind states and includes both those with a non epistemic nature (wishes, intentions, emotions) and those with an epistemic nature (beliefs, reasoning, inferences) (Groppo & Locatelli, 1996; Mason, 2001; Burr & Hofer, 2002).

Inside organizational literature we can find a reference to both these aspects in the concept of "reflective organization".

From the first contributions by Schön (1983) about the reflective practitioner to the current studies on psychodynamics of organizational life (Quaglino, 2004), the metaphor of reflexivity is suggested as an aspect of crucial functioning for post-modern organization: if the concept of reflexivity is wide and polysemic[4], when referred to organizations it appears to be connected, on the one hand, to the subject of the production of situated placed knowledge, on the other hand to the need to personally satisfy requests which come from both external and internal customers (the company personnel).

So, on the one hand, the studies about organizations share the opinion that the organizations, to keep up with the fast rhythm of changes required by the turbulence of markets and to face complex and unique problems, must equip suitable devices to produce knowledge on processes and on problems and to make it fast available. The organizational actors are pressed to change from passive performers of standard and routine procedures to workers of knowledge, able to face problems for which there is not a predefined solution, and which require innovative solutions.

On the other hand, the admission of the importance of paying attention to subjectiveness both of those to which the service is turned, and of those who supply the service, requires to activate, in organizing, a function of cure meant as a careful and interpretative survey of everybody's needs, of every individual's individuality and diversity.

Let's try to examine closely the theme of mental functioning in organizations.

The reflective capability of adults at work busy in generating new knowledge (to decide how to act, to innovate the way of facing a problem, to settle conflicts) applies on the text represented by the working practices report.

---

[4] See the different use of the term reflexivity in Beck U., Giddens A. & Lash S. (1999).

If we analyse these reports we can explore the mind processes which lead the way of "seeing" the problem.

As suggested by Schön (1983) reflecting on the working practice to produce placed knowledge doesn't mean only what information I used and what strategies I adopted to solve a specific problem, but it means asking "why do I set up the problem exactly this way?"

The question is not expected, since a lot of the problems with which the worker is confronted today are not set, but must be built starting from an indistinct, not focused and often contradictory material.

Moreover, such a construction does not take place alone, but within a process which involves and takes place in the presence of other minds.

So, when facing new, unique and ambiguous problems, not only descriptions of the way in which we performed, but also beliefs, convictions, assumptions concerning "what is the problem" come into action. Therefore, the practice report contains not only the process of *problem solving*, but also the process of *problem setting* which often requires, in organizations, to start a complex process of negotiation among different and even conflicting points of view.

Consider, for example, the doctor, coordinator of a service for minors who speaks about the uselessness of listening to the family members opinions to evaluate the intervention to perform with a new client because *"they are too involved and their impressions suffer from an excessive subjectiveness"*. Based on assumptions about what the reliable data are (only those which come from objective clinical tests and valid psychometric tests), this manager tries to convince his collaborators about the "right" way to define the borders of that client's problem and therefore to justify the meaning of the reception and assessment process that he is suggesting.

We think that a help to analyse the *problem setting* processes involved in the construct of "reflection on working practice" comes from the research on development of epistemological thought.

According to Kitchener & King (quoted in Mason, 2001) a subject's epistemological beliefs influence his way of defining a problem and of cutting out empirical data. Despite the terminological-conceptual differences that we can find in the models proposed by various authors (Fischer, 1980; King & Kitchener, 1994; Kuhn, 2000) it is possible to trace different levels of development of epistemological thought (Mason, 2001; Burr & Hofer, 2002).

A first type, called *objectivist*, involves the conception of absolute and not problematic knowledge, located in the external world; unique data sources are observation or authority, to which we apply, like to oracles, to handle conflictual statements. In this case the responsibility of knowledge is attributed *in toto* to objects of thought, to the disadvantage of thinking subjects.

A second type is called *subjective relativism*: knowledge is considered to be ambiguous and idiosyncratic, strongly influenced by the observer's subjectiveness, a little or not certain at all. On this level it is very difficult to justify a solution as the best alternative because the individual believes that there are no criteria by which to choose among different interpretations.

The third type of epistemological thought, called *rational constructivism*, considers knowledge as a construction process in which we compare evaluations, subjects and judgements, and even if there isn't an absolute point of view, some opinions are more justified than others since there are shared inquiry rules. In this last case a sophisticated theory of mind is used: in fact the importance of the need to consider the view from which we look at reality and the contextual feature of knowledge is recognized.

Even despite the terminological heterogeneity present in treatments of different authors (reflective judgement, critical thought, relativist thought, etc.) everybody agrees on considering that the highest level of development of epistemological beliefs, on which reflective thought is centred, is based on the ability to recognize the existence of a mind who, mediating the relationship with reality, produces a variety of representations. In other words, reflective thought involves the awareness of the essentially constructivist nature of our mind activity.

Recent studies on links between theory of mind and epistemological thought show us that there are strong individual differences in the ability to activate reflective thought.

According to Freeman (2000), it is always possible, both for adolescents and for adults, to fall in a sort of realism in which external reality is used to simplify our own reasoning, where the mediating action of mind in interpreting reality is not taken into account and the role of builder of knowledge doesn't belong to the subject. In this case it is difficult to recognize everybody's attitude towards the content of one's own thinking and to attribute to other people's statements the correct illocutionary force (Searle, 1969), that is to consider the statements contained in a text (written or oral) as expressions of beliefs and of the specific point of view of the author or of the lecturer (Olson & Astington, 1995).

What use of epistemological thought can we observe in organizational language?

As already outlined in the introduction, if we enter a perspective which considers the organization as a sensemaking process, we can assert that every organizational actor draws on ways of thinking, on cognitive models consolidated in time inside his own "community of practice" (Wenger, 1998), starting from the previous experiences, and that are taken for granted. From this point of view, every organizational culture carries its own meaning even about what knowledge is and the places appointed to knowledge. So, in working practices reports we don't find only epistemological beliefs of individual type in action, but shared beliefs on what truth is and what means to use to reach it, beliefs which influence the individual way to practise reflective thought.

A suggestion about it comes from Schein (1985, 1999) who points out how it is possible to differentiate the organizational cultures based on their epistemological premises: in some, it is considered right and true only what comes from the hierarchy; in others, only what comes from a particular area conceived as gifted with education and experience (for example the marketing staff); in others, it is the result of a consensual evaluation since everybody is conceived as carrier of a mind representation of the problem.

These implicit theories on the process through which knowledge is produced influence important aspects of organizational acting: where, for example we take for granted that only the ideas surviving the debate among all actors interested in the problem are true, a lot of space and value will be given to the tools of comparison and dialogue, less to hierarchy.

Other interesting suggestions about variables which influence the use of the theory of mind come from the studies on links between management of knowledge and power. The co-presence of different groups of interest and of different professional groups, each of them carrier of its own vision of reality, is an experience characterizing organizational life.

As pointed out, among others, by Hawes (1991), in some situations the different organizational functions (production, administration, sales and marketing) develop their own linguistic code, representing their own reading of reality as objective and therefore "right", and using it to define and guard the group borders. In the light of the studies on epistemological beliefs such representation reveals the use of a thought of an objectivist type: every organizational function thinks it describes reality and it doesn't recognize nor to itself nor to others the intervention of a mind which interprets in an active way the context in which it acts.

The presence of this theory of mind has a protective function of the interests of every group. Moreover, it influences the communicative processes inside the organization: since for every group *"the "other" is lacking in essential qualities and is at fault any number of ways"* (Hawes, 1991, p. 46), it creates a situation of incommunicability among the different organizational units.

In other contests, on the other hand, the discursive practice creates a link among the different professional communities. We receive an example from the survey by Gherardi & Nicolini (2002), carried out in a medium sized building firm: asking questions related to the safety problem to the site foremen, engineers and main contractors, different ways of "reading" the problem appear, but such a difference can remain and be recognized starting a working practice arranged enough.

What permits these three communities of practice with different ways of thinking and working to stay together?

The answer given by the authors is traced starting form the analysis of language that the entire community built: in fact widespread discursive practices point out that every professional group has in mind the differences between its own practical culture and the others'.

The example is of a site foreman, who checking a beam cut too short since – the bricklayers say -they followed the architect's drawing, states: *"But can't you see that the room is crooked... Don't you know you always have to measure things again? The architect just draws straight lines, he doesn't know what this old building is really like"* (Gherardi & Nicolini, 2002, p. 431).

Through language the difference of ways of "reading" the object of work and of facing the problems is staged; everybody clearly knows the way the other thinks and works, what is his professional culture and is aware of the possible conflicts and contradictions which could derive from it, but it doesn't activate a search of a unique and shared solution. According to the authors, such discursive practice permits to define the identity of every group, recognizing even the differences of power, but at the same time to find contingent conditions to work together and not fight each other. Here we used this research as an exemplification of a temporary organization in which the use of a sophisticated constructivist theory of mind prevails: in such organizations persons recognize the states of mind and use them to give a meaning to their own behaviour and others'.

Briefly, we think we can underline the usefulness of an approach of research which, in a more explicit and systematic way, could explore the naïve theory of mind spread in language and in organizational processes.

Such an exploration can permit to study into depth the metaphor of reflective organization: reflective organization or maybe better reflective organizing can be conceived as a course of actions and decisions in which actors share, in silence, the tacit assumption that mind has a representational character and that representations mediate the interpretation of reality, in an active way. It means, regarding beliefs on knowledge and on its production, getting to a "problematic vision" of knowledge (Carey & Smith, 1993), for which the diversity of opinions is considered to be intrinsic to the process of knowledge itself.

9.3 PROFESSIONAL AUTOBIOGRAPHIES AND THEORY OF MIND: THE SENSE OF PERSONAL CONTINUITY IN THE ADULT AT WORK

We can now proceed in the defined framework of reflective organization, to zoom in and highlight the individual dimension, studying in depth the widely discussed issue of the effects of job flexibility on personal identity[5].

The current job market is characterized largely by instability and rapid change. For companies, market globalisation and the introduction of *Information Communication Technology* are leading to the relentless reorganization of products typology, manufacturing processes and, accordingly, the skills the company requires. For individual workers, this often translates into mobility: people change positions and activities; they change organizations; their links with them tend to become transient and loose.

Dealing with a flexible job market leads to a contradiction: on the one hand great emphasis is placed on workers being enterprising, creative, self-starting, independent; on the other hand there is a perception that flexibility means precariousness, therefore fear, a sense of confusion and loss of control[6]. At the individual level, workers forever dealing with continuously changing tasks, organizations and social networks, experience life in fragments; the risk of uprootedness is never far away because few of the contexts in which to set down roots are solid enough to presage the stability of longer term occupation (Bauman, 2001).

Faced with the risk of fragmentation and confusion, individuals are forced to deal with the problem of keeping heterogeneous and sometimes contradictory parts of themselves together. In this situation, how do adults at work resolve the issue of their "personal continuity"?

In this scenario, where an individual's employment history is characterized by a fickle object-organization and frequent bereavements and losses, Sennett (1999) makes an interesting contribution towards exploring the practices involved in managing the meaning of personal continuity among adults at work.

The methodology centres on language. The author listens to several life stories: based on the assumption that the Ego expresses itself in narrative form, Sennett seeks the narrative form that appears to be most functional for making sense of the individual's experiences of job loss/change, without being overcome by feelings of shame or guilt.

---

[5] The following analysis deepens the main topics discussed in Gilardi, Pezzotta (in press).

[6] See Demazière & Dubar (1997), Bauman (2001), Orsenigo (2002).

One narrative form, detected in the stories of working adults, is believing that a life story is merely an assembly of fragments (Sennett, 1999), a constant starting over, relinquishing memory and acquiring the chameleon-like appearance of a "radar man" (Kaneklin & Gozzoli, in press) who adapts by yielding to all external expectations. However, this strategy cannot guarantee a sense of continuity; indeed, according to Kaneklin and Gozzoli, it comes at a high price, i.e. to save a piece of internal integrity, the only avenue open seems to be that of emotionally withdrawing and putting as little as possible of oneself into relations.

Following Sennet's account, there seems to be another option. When seeking to understand how a group of IT engineers who were downsized by IBM in 1994 tackled the task of making sense of their feelings of failure, he says that the workers find a way not to betray themselves when they cease to place the reasons for being fired on external causes (inept management, outsourcing) and start reflecting on themselves in relation to their professional choices, the criteria with which they interpreted company policy, the beliefs behind certain of their decisions.

They thus begin to become subjects who review and reinterpret the past by placing themselves at the centre of events, however contradictory and painful this exercise may be. The language of the story becomes the language on their thinking ("*I should have realized...*") and the workers begin to attribute to themselves beliefs, suppositions and ideas based on which they made their organizational behavior and career choices. It is a language filled with terms describing the probabilistic nature of the correspondence between mental representation and reality (such as "thinking", "believing", "realizing", etc.) and which, according to Bruner (1996), explain the appearance of a "landscape" of conscience near a "landscape" of action.

In this way they are able to reinterpret their past, recover a sense of correlation between the various pieces and make sense of their retrenchment.

In this new narrative form, the Ego is viewed – says Sennett – as an authorial Ego.

Similarly, Giddens (1991) emphasizes how the narration of identity, reflectively organized, supplies the means for giving coherence to a lifetime of tensions and dilemmas typical of late modern living[7]. In this ambit, we believe the construct of reflective function (Fonagy & Target, 1996; 1997) connected with studies on theory of mind makes useful contributions towards enriching the concept of authorial Ego, and understanding the characteristics of the reflective quality of thought.

---

[7] Giddens considers the self as a reflective project as a general feature of modern social activity in relation to mental organization, therefore not limited to a life crisis, such as the loss of job.

Personal continuity can be found insofar as the workers acknowledge they have a mind that actively mediated the interpretation of their own working reality, and can visibilize this same mind through the use of language.

In recognizing this mind, the workers use the reflective function defined by Fonagy & Target (1997) as the whole of psychological processes which sustain the ability to mentalize, that is the ability to use the mental states to understand one's own and the other's behaviour[8]. Moreover, such a competence implies the capability to recognize that the mental states are representations which can be fallible and can change because they are only based on one out of a wide range of possible perspectives (Fonagy, Target, 1996).

A high level of reflective functioning helps to recognize the self in their personal history, enabling them to feel that they are the protagonists of that story. Through this representation, they can reduce one of the most pervasive feelings in the working environment, i.e. helplessness and hetero-determination, thereby restoring some sense of power and control over their life.

We find particularly relevant turning to the concept of reflective function, since it is full of cross-references to the emotional and intersubjective dimensions[9], which permit to enrich the concept of theory of mind. They also permit to pay attention to the relapses of the use of mentalistic ability on some dimensions of Self which are important for professional life, such as, for example, self-consciousness, autonomy, freedom and sense of responsibility.

Still in the field of studies on theory of mind, another comment on managing the sense of continuity, and dealing with situations of instability comes from more markedly socio-cultural research undertaken by Chandler and Lalonde (Chandler & Lalonde, 1992; Chandler et al., 2003) on suicidal adolescents. The authors refer to the "narrative solutions to the problem of personal persistence" (2003, p. 14), meaning the highly complex interpretative processes with which people can manage the problem of diachronic identity, i.e. the paradox of sameness within change.

A common feature of these strategies is that they all envisage the existence of a *Selfhood as a "centre of narrative gravity"* (2003, p. 14)

---

[8] According to the authors reflective function implies a self-reflective component, about attribution to the self of states of mind, and an interpersonal component, which instead refers to the conferring process the mental states on others (Fonagy & Target, 1996; Amadei, 2003). Moreover, such a competence implies the capability to recognize that the mental states are representations which can be fallible and can change because they are only based on one out of a wide range of possible perspectives (Fonagy & Target, 1996).

[9] In the study of the English authors the expression "reflective function" is used in an interchangeable way with the terms "theory of mind", "mentalization" and "metacognitive monitoring".

capable of connecting the past with the present and anticipating the future. Individuals capable of using narrative type strategies employ a sophisticated, constructivist theory of mind, and demonstrate an ability to recognize mental states and refer to them to find continuity throughout the different stages of their life.

There are other possible ways of ensuring continuity[10], but only those who use narrative strategies can adopt a position of dialogue with change. Change, for them, is not discredited, denied or trivialized: it acts as a graft towards an hermeneutic reinterpretation of their life.

This latter aspect is very interesting if one considers, as suggested earlier, that the hectic pace of change characterizing the present employment scenario presupposes the formation of personalities capable of withstanding a considerable level of uncertainty, and regarding the risk of change as a challenge.

Therefore, the use of the reflective function, to interpret life events and recount them through the use of language, could represent a critical factor in determining an individual's ability to deal with the internal and external evolutionary challenges that the workplace now poses.

What are the conditions for awakening this mentalization process in working adults? In the workplace psychology literature, one condition emphasized by several authors involves including the presence of others in the construction of the story. It is possible to experience this narrative continuity without shame or guilt and reflect on the history of one's mental constructs (what I thought, believed, considered) – argues Sennett – by "*conversing*".

Individuals who belong to a social network that shares vulnerability and mutual dependency[11] can stitch together fragmented lives, lives that endure transitions and loss[12]. The social context, and, we might add, the dialogic-conversational context, is therefore an important variable for

---

[10] The authors in fact indicate the presence of "essentialist positions" (2003, p.12) which define the self as an entity and are based on the idea that there must necessarily exist a core of atemporal identity, some material or transcendental centre immune to change.

[11] The retrenched workers studied by Sennett had in actual fact created an informal mutual support network. Similarly, the creation of informal networks appears to be the approach taken by many professionals in more or less precarious situations; deprived of an organizational container, they self-organize a thinking space for themselves, made up of self-managed meetings, workshops. See, for instance, the workshop organized by a group of female workers described in Nannicini (2002).

[12] Chandler & Lalonde (1992, Chandler et al., 2003) underline the role of culture and the social group both in terms of elements that contribute to the construction of a theory of mind, and in terms of possible resources. According to the authors, in fact, in transit and instability situations, when we are forced to abandon strategies which were once appropriate to ensure personal continuity, the role of the culture of belonging - as an external support which gives the threads to tie together the separate parts of our lives scattered in a diachronic way - becomes crucial (1992, p. 502).

activating this function. Accordingly, relations do not only influence the development of reflective functioning, they also affect the way in which the subject will use his reflective capabilities in the specific situations in which he will take part[13].

To sum up, if a constructivist theory of mind represents an important resource to face the trauma of loss and to support a sense of personal continuity, we can suppose that this ability can be one of the important variables which come into play when dealing with working transition processes and particularly when dealing with unemployment experiences.

We think that an interesting way of research opens also for its applicative aspects: if the use of a constructivistic theory of mind represents an important resource to face the trauma of loss and to support a sense of personal continuity through changes, we can suppose that this dimension can be one of the important variables[14] which come into play when dealing with working transition processes and particularly when dealing with unemployment experiences.

From this point of view, the reflective functioning could be one of the training aims in accompanying to work reintegration, using the group of dialogue as a fundamental tool to learn and reshape one's own cognitive and affective maps.

9.4   PEOPLE   IN   REFLECTIVE   ORGANIZATION: TRAINING AND LANGUAGE

Now it is challenging to study the connection with training as a space to favour the conditions which make a sophisticated use of reflective thought and, in case, its development, possible.

Following our presentation, the training device which comes out of it is centred on the use of language from the conversational point of view.

Various authors (Kramer & Woodruff, 1986; Bendixen, Dunkle & Schraw, 1994; King & Kitchener, 1994), even inside different theoretical models, underline that the developmental level of epistemological thought achieved by every person is linked to the training contexts in which he takes part.

The development of a reflective thought is possible within training courses which help to think over our own and others' beliefs, to recognize

---

[13] Among developmental studies on the theory of mind, the study of Dunn & Hughes (1998) is an interesting analysis of the child's understanding of emotions. In it they point out how the understanding of one's own and the other's emotions changes according to the relationships experienced by the child (with the friends and with the mother).

[14] The capabilities traditionally used in the studies on job hunting are, for example, locus of control, self efficacy, outcome expectations.

their possible fallibility and to take a different perspective. Therefore, an organization can take responsibility for development of reflective professionals, founding counselling and training programmes which have the educational objective to help the development of reflective thought.

Using open-ended problem solving tasks and "ill-structured"[15] problems, encouraging discussion and making criteria of justification of beliefs explicit (with questions like *"what you are saying is a thesis or an hypothesis?"*, *"do you really know it or are you only supposing it?"*) represent examples of instruments through which it is possible to think over one's own and others' beliefs, recognize their possible fallible aspects and assume a different perspective.

Through the aware use of a metacognitive and mentalistic language, mind activity can become an object of consideration and it is possible to make explicit the theory of mind which leads the knowledge processes.

In fact, schemata may predispose one to existing solutions based on assumptions that may be inappropriate, inconsistent, outdated, or oppressive. In these circumstances, the situation requires critical reflection and transformative learning to challenge existing assumptions.

So, in organizational training, the construction of setting in which it is possible to think about language and thought, both through discussion and through work on written text, permits to abandon a conception of knowledge as objective and untouchable to get to, instead, an intersubjective and probabilistic conception and to a limited and relative conception of rationality (see Thompson, 1967)[16].

On the methodological level, the link is with those trends which see training as training-research, that is as a setting which allows the participants to work on themselves and on their own professional practices to build together a knowledge which can be used in one's own context of professional and organizational life. Psychosociological training (Kaneklin & Olivetti Manoukian, 1990; Olivetti Manoukian, Mazzoli & D'Angella, 2003), for example, focuses on the analysis of the working practices and on subjective and cultural meanings produced by organizational actors around these practices, considering them as analysis units fundamental to understand how to produce knowledge within an organizational context. From this perspective, the attention is to arrange training devices in which

---

[15] "Ill-structured" problems can't be solved through pure logic, since they require to take into account alternative positions. They differ from "well structured problems" because they can't be described with a high level of completeness; they can't be solved with a high level of certainty: there is often disagreement on the best solution, even when the problem can be considered solved (King & Kitchener, 1994, quoted in Mason, 2001).

[16] Regarding relapses, in a formative area, we find it important to reaffirm that the theory of mind expresses its explanatory and interpretative-formative power inside a conception of organization as a process, and therefore as an organization seen as organizing rather than an entity divided from actors which are part of it (Weick, 1995, Thompson, 1967).

narration has a central role[17]: in fact through language (oral and written) people can access to their own and others' mind images, connect fragments, rebuild the historical meaning, negotiate over more shared meanings, modify representations and attitude and behavioural results connected to them.

Narration takes on a meaning of training if it forms within settings which, through dimensions of dialogue, (with oneself, with one's own actions, with the others), permit to learn from experience (Bion, 1962) and so to build knowledge on experience itself.

In this approach, reflective capability and language appear to be closely connected.

We find particularly interesting the concept of "formativity" (Kaneklin & Olivetti Manoukian, 1990), that is a double potential capacity: the capacity to think one's own thoughts and to think about internal and external conditions of one's own life and on them, through language, keep a speech. Afterwards, the individual has the capacity to shape his own existence condition: he can anticipate his actions, organize, express and re-formulate them in a project, through the imagination activity of his mind.

The methodologies of training-research (among which is the autobiographic method and the analysis of working practices) underline mental representations through which individuals give meaning to the world: it is exactly on this level that studies on theory of mind represent a useful instrument to comprehend the specific status of one of the mind processes which has influence on the way of using and modifying these representations, that is reflective functioning. The reflective functioning can be obstructed, with the consequence of a limited access to an accurate image of one's own mind experience and one's own and others' mind experience and representational world[18].

The result is, for training committed to producing knowledge on working practices or on professional biography, an invitation to give specific attention to relational, contextual and individual factors which can inhibit or favour reflective functioning and to build setting, which, starting from the comprehension of the reflective functioning present level, can encourage new and sophisticated theory of mind.

According to Olson & Astington (1995), the analysis of linguistic practices used in the organizational context could represent a starting point for the survey of the type of theory of mind in use inside it and to take to a

---

[17] Such a device, which brings into focus the language dimension, is continuous to the approach of analysis of professional practices, through which we tend to make visible, through the lens of action, our own *theories in use*.

[18] Regarding this, both ethological studies by Judy Dunn (Dunn, Brown & Beardsall, 1991) and the research on clinical cases by Fonagy & Target (2000) clearly showed how the socio-emotional characteristics of the context and the person's emotions influence in a significant way the capability and the method of use of the theory of mind.

level of higher awareness the epistemological conceptions which lead organizational action.

Therefore, the arrangement of a "formativity" setting in which language is taken up as an object of reflection can represent an useful means to develop awareness about one's own and others' way of building knowledge. From a Vygotskian's point of view (Vygotskij, 1934), in fact, language carries out, besides a function of representation of the mind processes, also a function of transformation of psychic functions, taking up a generating role for the thought.

In conclusion, we can underline the fertility of the connection among frameworks referring to different disciplinary areas: in fact the theory of mind used in an organization strongly influences its personnel management policy, its strategies of knowledge management, the methods of internal and external communication. Suggestions resulting from these paradigmatic contaminations demand us to promote, in future works, field research on the theory of mind widespread in the working practices and on the contextual factors which take part in the use of this ability in the relationship individual-work-organization.

REFERENCES

Amadei G. La valutazione dei cambiamenti in una cornice evolutiva. A e R - Abilitazione e Riabilitazione 2003; 12, 1: 48-62.

Argyris, C., Schön, D.A. *Organizational Learning: a Theory of Action Perspective*. Addison-Wesley, Reading Mass, 1978.

Astington, J.W. What is theoretical about the child's theory of mind? A vygotskian view of its development. In *Theories of theories of mind,* P. Carruthers, P.K. Smith (Eds.), Cambridge University Press, 1996.

Astington J.W., Pelletier J., Homer B., Theory of mind and epistemological development: the relation between children's second-order false-belief understanding and their ability to reason about evidence. New Ideas In Psychology 2002; 20, 2-3: 131-144.

Bauman, Z. *The Individualized Society*. Cambridge: Polity Press, 2001.

Beck, U., Giddens, A., Lash, S., *Modernizzazione riflessiva*. Trieste: Asterios, 1999.

Bendixen L.D., Dunkle M.E., Schraw G. Epistemological beliefs and reflective judgments. Psychological Reports, 1994; 5, 3: 1595-1600.

Bion, W.R., *Learning from Experience*. William Heinemann, Medical Books, Ldt, 1962.

Boje, D.M., *Narrative Methods for Organizational & Communication Research*. Thousand Oaks, CA: Sage Publications, 2001.

Bruner, J.S., *Acts of meaning*. Harvard University Press, 1990.

Bruner, J.S., *The culture of education*. Harvard University Press, 1996.

Burr J.E., Hofer B.K. Personal epistemology and theory of mind: deciphering young children's beliefs about knowledge and knowing. New Ideas In Psychology 2002; 20, 2-3: 199-224.

Carey S., Smith C. On understanding the nature of scientific knowledge. Educational Psychologist 1993; 8, 3: 235-251.

Chandler, M., Lalonde, C.E. Folk theories of mind and Self: a cross-cultural study of suicide in native and non-native groups. Paper presented at V European Conference on

Developmental Psychology, Siviglia, 1992. In *Il pensiero dell'altro. Contesto, conoscenza e teorie della mente*, O. Liverta-Sempio, A. Marchetti (Eds.), Milano: Raffaello Cortina editore, 1995.

Chandler M., Lalonde C.E, Solor B.W., Hallett D. Personal persistence, identity development and suicide: a study of native and non-native north American adolescents. Monographs of the Society for Research in Child Development 2003; 68, 2: 273.

Cigoli, V., Marta, E. Come la mente tratta la relazione con l'altro? Il caso delle relazioni familiari. In *Teoria della mente e relazioni affettive. Contesti familiari e contesti educativi*. O. Liverta-Sempio, A. Marchetti (Eds.), Torino: UTET, 2001.

Demazière, D., Dubar, C., *Analyser les entretiens biographiques*. Éditions Nathan, 1997.

Dunn J., Brown J., Beardsall L. Family talk about emotions, and children's later understanding of other's emotions. Developmental Psychology 1991; 27: 448-455.

Dunn J., Hughes C. Young children's understanding of emotions within close relationship. Cognition and Emotion 1998; 12: 171-190.

Fischer, K.W. A theory of cognitive development: the control and construction of hierarchies skills. Psychological Review 1980; 87: 477-531.

Fonagy P., Target M. Playing with reality: theory of mind and the normal development of psychic reality. International Journal of Psycho-Analysis 1996; 77: 217-233.

Fonagy P., Target M. Attachment and reflective function: their role in self-organization. Development and Psychopathology 1997; 9: 679-700.

Fonagy P., Target M., Playing with reality: III. The persistence of dual psychic reality in borderline patients. International Journal of Psycho-Analysis 2000; 81: 853-873.

Freeman, N.H., Communication and representation: why mentalistic reasoning is a lifelong endeavour. In *Children's reasoning and the mind*, P. Mitchell, K.J. Riggs, Psychology Press, UK, 2000.

Gherardi S. Where learning is: Metaphors and situated learning in a planning group. Human Relations 2000; 53, 8: 1057-1080.

Gherardi S., Nicolini D. Learning in a Constellation of Interconnected Practices: Canon or Dissonance? Journal of Management Studies 2002; 39, 4: 419-436.

Gherardi S., Nicolini, D., *Apprendimento e conoscenza nelle organizzazioni*. Roma: Carocci, 2004.

Giddens, A., *Modernity and Self-Identity*. Polity Press in association with Blackwell Publishers Ltd, 1991.

Gilardi S., Pezzotta C., Teoria della mente e mondo del lavoro. In *Contesti culturali e teoria della mente: normalità e patologia*. O. Liverta-Sempio, A. Marchetti , F. Lecciso (Eds), Milano: Raffaello Cortina editore (in press).

Groppo, M., Locatelli, M.C.,*Mente e cultura. Tecnologie della comunicazione e processi educative*. Milano: Raffaello Cortina Editore, 1996.

Hawes, L.C. Organising Narratives/Codes/Poetics. Journal of Organizational Change Management 1991; 4, 3: 45-51.

Kaneklin, C., Gozzoli, C., Identità adulta al lavoro e cultura della flessibilità. In *Identità in movimento*, E. Marta, C. Regalia (Eds.), Milano: Carocci editore, in press.

Kaneklin, C., Olivetti Manoukian, F., *Conoscere l'organizzazione*. Roma: La Nuova Italia Scientifica, 1990.

Kuhn, D., Theory of mind, metacognition and reasoning: a life-span perspective. In *Children's reasoning and the mind, P. Mitchell, K.J. Riggs, Psychology Press, UK, 2000.

King, P.A, Kitchener, K.S., *Developing reflective judgement. Understanding and promoting intellectual growth and critical thinking in adolescents and adults*. San Francisco, CA: Jossey Bass, 1994.

Kramer D.A., Woodruff D.S. Relativistic and dialectical thought in three adult age-groups. Human development 1986; 29, 5: 280-290.

Lieblich, A., Tuval-Mashiach, R., Zilber, T., *Narrative Research.* Thousand Oaks, CA: Sage Publications, 1998

Liverta-Sempio, O., Marchetti, A. (Eds.), *Teoria della mente e relazioni affettive. Contesti familiari e contesti educativi.* Torino: UTET, 2001.

Mason, L., *Verità e certezze. Natura e sviluppo delle epistemologie ingenue.* Roma: Carocci Editore, 2001.

Morgan, G., *Images of organizations.* Beverly Hills, CA: Sage Publications, 1997.

Nannicini, A. (Ed.), *Le parole per farlo. Donne al lavoro nel postfordismo.* Roma: Derive Approdi, 2002.

Nonaka, I., Takeuchi, H., *The knowledge Creation Company.* Oxford University Press, 1995.

Olivetti Manoukian, F., Mazzoli G., D'Angella, F., *Cose (mai) viste. Riconoscere il lavoro psicosociale dei Ser.T.* Roma: Carocci Editore, 2003.

Orsenigo A. La costruzione dell'identità lavorativa in un mondo sollecitato dalla flessibilità. Spunti, 2002; 6: 7-26.

Olson D.R., Astington J. Thinking about thinking: learning how to take statements and old beliefs. Educational psychologist 1993; 28, 1: 7-23. It, Tran.: Pensare il pensiero. Imparare ad interpretare le affermazioni e a considerare le credenze. In: O. Liverta-Sempio, A. Marchetti. (Eds.) *Il pensiero dell'altro. Contesto, conoscenza e teorie della mente.* Milano: Raffaello Cortina editore, 1995.

Quaglino, G.P., *La vita organizzativa. Difese, collusioni e ostilità nelle relazioni di lavoro.* Milano: Raffaello Cortina Editore, 2004.

Schein, E.H. *Organizational Culture and Leadership.* Jossey – Bass Inc., Publishers, 1985.

Schein, E.H., *The Corporate Culture Survival Guide.* Jossey – Bass Inc., John Wiley & Sons Inc. Company, 1999.

Schön, D.A., *The Reflective Practitioner.* New York: Basic Books, 1983.

Searle, J.R., *Speech acts: an essay in the philosophy of language.* New York: Cambridge University Press, 1969.

Senge P.M. The leaders new work. Building learning organizations. Sloan Management Review 1990; 32, 1: 7-23.

Sennett, R. *The Corrosion of Character. The personal Consequences of Work in the New Capitalism.* New York-London: W.W. Norton & Company, 1999.

Thompson, J.D., *Organizations in Action.* New York: McGraw-Hill, 1967.

Van Maanen, J., *Qualitative Studies of Organizations.* Thousand Oaks, CA: Sage Publications, 1998.

Vaux J. Social Groups and Discursive Communities: Context and Audience in the Explanatory Practices of the Artificial Intelligence (AI) Community. Paper presented at the Transformation of Knowledge Conference; 1999 January 12-13: University of Surrey.

Vygotskij, L.S., (1934) *Thought and Language.* The M.I.T Press, 1962.

Weick, K., *Sensemaking in Organizations.* Beverly Hills, CA: Sage Publications, 1995.

Wenger, E., *Communities of Practice. Learning Meaning and Identity.* Cambridge, UK: Cambridge University Press, 1998.

Zucchermaglio, C., *Vygotskij in azienda. Apprendimento e comunicazione nei contesti lavorativi.* Roma: La Nuova Italia Scientifica, 1996.

AUTHORS

Antonietti Alessandro — Department of Psychology, Catholic University of the Sacred Heart, Milan
E-mail: alessandro.antonietti@unicatt.it

Gilardi Silvia — Department of Psychology, Catholic University of the Sacred Heart, Milan
E-mail: silviagilardi@yahoo.it

Lillard Angeline — Department of Psychology University of Virginia
E-mail: lillard@virginia.edu

Lucariello Joan M. — Boston College
E-mail: lucariel@bc.edu

Marchetti Antonella — The Theory of Mind Research Unit, Department of Psychology, Catholic University of the Sacred Heart, Milan
E-mail: antonella.marchetti@unicatt.it

Olson David R.: — HDAP, Ontario Institute for Studies in Education (OISE), University of Toronto
E-mail: dolson@oise.utoronto.ca

Pelletier Janette — Institute of Child Study, OISE, University of Toronto, Canada
E-mail: jpelletier@oise.utoronto.ca

Shatz Marylin — Department of Psychology, University of Michigan
E-mail   mshatz@umich.edu

Siegal Michael — Department of Psychology, University of Sheffield
E-mail: M.Siegal@Sheffield.ac.uk

OTHER AUTHORS

Astington Janet Wilde — Institute of Child Study, OISE, University of Toronto
E-mail: jwastington@oise.utoronto.ca

Bruno Andreina   Department of Psychology, Catholic University of
                        the Sacred Heart, Milan
                        E-mail: andreina.bruno@unicatt.it
Durand Tina   Boston College
Dyer Jennifer   California State University, Monterey Bay
Le Donne Mary   Teachers College - Columbia University
Liverta-Sempio Olga   The Theory of Mind Research Unit, Department of
                        Psychology, Catholic University of the Sacred
                        Heart, Milan
                        E-mail: olga.sempio@unicatt.it
Lecciso Flavia   The Theory of Mind Research Unit, Department of
                        Psychology, Catholic University of the Sacred
                        Heart, Brescia
                        E-mail: flecciso@infinito.it
Massaro Davide   The Theory of Mind Research Unit, Department of
                        Psychology, Catholic University of the Sacred
                        Heart, Milan
                        E-mail: davide.massaro@unicatt.it
Pezzotta Cristina   The Theory of Mind Research Unit, Department of
                        Psychology, Catholic University of the Sacred
                        Heart, Brescia
                        E-mail: colicri@yahoo.it
Varley Rosemary   Department of Human Communication Sciences,
                        University of Sheffield, Sheffield S10 2TA, UK
Want Stephen C.   Department of Psychology, University of British
                        Columbia, Vancouver, Canada V6T 1Z4
Yarnell Lisa   Boston College

Subject Index